TURTLING

FOLLOWING MY PASSION

ROBERT KRAUSE

STURNBRIDGE PUBLISHING

Turtling

Following My Passion

Robert Krause

FIRST PRINTING

ISBN: 979-8-9886302-0-3
eBook ISBN: 979-8-9886302-1-0
Hardcover: 979-8-9886302-2-7

Library of Congress Control Number: 2023911714

SP
Sturnbridge Publishing

To the "turtlers" of the world…

You're the ones who have made, and will continue to make, a difference in the conservation of turtles everywhere. From the dedicated scientists, academics, authors, and zoologists, to the reptile veterinarians, breeders, and enthusiasts. And then there's those of you who at one time or another have taken the initiative to move that turtle from the middle of the road to safety. And let us not forget those little children with their smiling faces as they attentively watch that turtle, whether it be far off on a log or right there in the aquarium that Mom and Dad set up. They are the future "turtlers."

As turtlers, we must all support the organizations that promote chelonian education and conservation. I applaud the following who are tirelessly working hard to make a difference:

> Florida Turtle Conservation Trust (FTCT)
> Turtle Conservancy (TC)
> Turtle Room (TR)
> Turtle Survival Alliance (TSA)
> Turtle and Tortoise Propagation Group (TTPG)
> United States Association of Reptile Keepers (USARK)

Let us never forget that each and every one of us is on the same ship on the same journey, performing the tasks needed to reach our goal of saving turtles from extinction.

Keep on turtling!

FOREWORD

BOB KRAUSE IS THE embodiment of passion, integrity, and humility. I had the privilege of having a front row seat to Bob's incredible journey. Bob can find joy in the simplest of things and was more than comfortable in tackling the complex.

Jim Collins describes a Level 5 Leader as "Someone who builds enduring greatness through a paradoxical combination of personal humility plus professional will." This is Bob.

Bob is a life-long learner and a life-long teacher. I met him in my role as a Vistage chair. Vistage, the largest CEO organization in the world, exists solely to help high-integrity leaders make great decisions that benefit their companies, their families, and their communities. Being by Bob's side, I learned that living a life of joy—whether at work (building turtle habitats or hamster cages that rivaled some of the prettiest doll houses "and being rewarded for them"), sitting on his patio with his wife Denise (enjoying the activity of the turtles that lived in the pond on their property), or traveling the world (committed to protecting the species that exist in some of the hardest to reach parts of the globe)—is who Bob Krause is.

The best lives are those built around intentionality. Bob is a person who is clear on who he is, why he has a place on this earth, and how he can make it a better place. Bob's infectious joy and laughter brighten all who meet him. He is committed to all whom he meets, whether they reside on this planet as a mammal or a reptile.

There is a Native American proverb that says, "We did not inherit the earth from our ancestors; we borrow it from our children." Bob embodies this, as many of the seeds that he has planted will benefit generations yet to come.

If you are picking up this book it is either because you share Bob's passion about turtles or you may be looking for a guide on how to live a more purposeful and passionate life.

You could not find a better guide for either of those journeys.

—Bob Berk
Chair, Vistage International
Chairman of the Board, AGHF

INTRODUCTION

THIS IS A BOOK about passion.

I imagine everyone is passionate about something, maybe some more than others. If there's something that motivates you to get out of bed each morning, then I think you're going to appreciate my story. If there's not, then maybe something herein can inspire you to find your passion, your reason to get out of bed each morning. Passion, I have learned, and as you'll read in the pages of this book, can take a person a long ways.

You're probably never too old to find your passion, but in my case, I learned you're never too young. I was four years old when, as a reward for helping her carry our shopping bags one day, my mother bought me a little green turtle from the pet department of a Woolworths discount store. It came complete with a plastic turtle bowl with a palm tree, and accompanied by an orange metal can of Hartz Mountain dried flies labeled as turtle food.

And the love affair began.

My passion for turtles took me on a wild ride that included a hands-on childhood love affair with nature, a mind-boggling entrepreneurial career in the pet industry, travels all over the world, and a retirement (or more accurately a second career) focused on my chelonian conservation initiatives. But for all that I have done and seen, nothing ever gave me, or gives me to this day, more pleasure than time simply spent turtling. And when I look back, I can see that turtling is what drove everything else.

What is turtling? Well, I'm sure every turtle enthusiast has their own idea, but for me, it initially meant the simple act of entering a turtle or tortoise's environment to get as close as possible to them, to photograph, study, or catch them, or sometimes just quietly observe them. Over the years, as I increased my knowledge and my circle of acquaintances, meeting people who had a similar passion, I learned that turtling also meant something else: the sharing of information, stories, and experiences; in other words having a great time talking turtles, and gaining stronger friendships, more knowledge, and wonderful memories.

But you don't have to be a fan of turtles to appreciate passion. It comes in all forms, and once it hits you, the best thing to do—perhaps the only thing—is to follow it. As I can attest, and as I trust the following pages will confirm, you never know where your passion is going to take you.

1

STICKING MY NECK OUT

TWENTY MINUTES BEFORE THE grand opening, there were already people lined up at the door. Dozens of cars were parked on both sides of the street. Members of the Elk Grove Village police department were directing traffic. Right alongside them were our costumed animals waving the people in.

The doors would open at precisely 10 a.m. I'd been at the store since 5:30 making sure all of the animal and bird displays and aquariums full of tropical fish looked perfect, all while keeping the lights off so as to not wake the puppies. All this not to mention that, well, I'd been too excited to sleep. I walked the aisles checking our inventory and psyching myself up for the employee meeting at seven sharp.

At the meeting, my partner Ray and I issued each employee a light blue smock and nametag and reminded them that smoking, still a relatively popular habit in 1971, was allowed only during breaks and only in the back room.

I looked around to see that everyone was dressed appropriately: no jeans and the fellas with button-down shirts and ties.

I knew we had instructed everyone on the basics of properly servicing the customers, while explaining the optimum care and products needed, but I just had to emphasize once again the importance of approaching customers in a helpful way; no pushiness, no hard selling. In addition, the cashiers were trained for every feasible situation regarding cash and credit card transactions, along with the usage of return forms, credit vouchers, and live pet purchase warrantees. We were ready.

Ten o'clock finally came and the doors opened to *Noah's Ark Pet Center*, 9,270 square feet of retail space—what we billed as the world's largest pet store. The business model, though years in the making, was based on a simple plan: to offer the largest selection of pets and their related supplies, and to provide the highest standard of professional advice on the selection and care of the right pet for the customer. The health and well-being of the animals for sale in our store would be our top priorities.

We had four specially designed departments: *puppies and kittens*, with a very large purebred selection all housed in spacious kennels; thousands of *tropical and coldwater fish* in over a hundred display aquariums; *cage and ornamental birds*, including hundreds of parakeets, cockatiels, canaries, finches, parrots, macaws, cockatoos, and toucans, all displayed in spacious aviaries and cages; and *small animals and reptiles*, including hamsters, gerbils, rats and mice, guinea pigs, rabbits, ferrets, chinchillas, and even a few small, exotic animals like a kinkajou, a coati mundi, a couple of tame and handleable monkeys, and a female wallaby with joey. Our reptile department included a large selection of turtles and tortoises, boas and other snakes, iguanas, anoles, chameleons, and exotic lizards, not to mention amphibians, tarantulas, and scorpions.

Each department had a manager who supervised employees assigned to that department exclusively. The entire store was then supported by a full-time veterinarian technician as well as a local vet on call.

None of it was random. For several years, I'd been planning on opening a pet store, almost buying a franchise at one point, and then deciding that I'd be better off starting from scratch. I wanted my pet store to be different. Most of the pet stores back then were small and not merchandised very well. Not wanting to open just another pet shop limited by space or inventory, I wanted to open a complete pet center—an *"emporium,"* with specialized departments where people could come and select a pet from a wide and extensive inventory, as well as receive advice for the pet's care and/or animal husbandry requirements. Everything imaginable under one roof. And once I'd decided that, I spent a few years holding down my full-time job as a computer programmer while taking on part-time jobs at various pet shops, learning the trade from the ground up and the inside out.

It had been a dream, but it had also been laborious. Long nights at the dining room table calculating costs and creating budgets, sketching and re-sketching my dream store's floor plan. Visiting potential suppliers. Trying to put the funding together. But never doubting the vision.

Somewhere during those early planning days, as if to reaffirm my efforts, I stumbled upon a poster in a gift shop on a rare night out on the town with my patient wife, Marie. The poster quoted a saying by James Bryant Conant that had apparently been passed around by the scientists who'd worked on the Manhattan Project during World War II. Above a cartoon character of a turtle, it read:

Behold the turtle. He only makes progress when he sticks his neck out.

That poster was meant for me. I bought it and hung it up in our apartment.

The hard work was a labor of love. And a destiny. I was only four years old the first time I set foot in a pet shop. It was the pet department of the Woolworths five-and-dime store on the northwest side of Chicago, a short bus ride from our family's apartment on Richmond Street. I was mesmerized by all the animals, especially the aquarium full of turtles, and it was that day that my excursions into pet shops began, never imagining that someday I would have my own shop.

And so, on that November morning in 1971, I watched as Noah's Ark Pet Center filled with people—families and children—seeing the same wide-eyed expression on the faces of many of them that I imagine I had on my face in Woolworths at such a young age. I felt good about our store's chances of success but life, and business, give no guarantees. I knew there would be struggles. I knew there would be hard times and sacrifices. I knew there would be moments when I might wonder why I'd left a good, steady job as a computer programmer in an age when computers were just beginning to dominate everyday life.

But I also knew that those moments would be fleeting. My life to that day had pointed in only one direction. My background and my turtle passion left no choice. I gazed around the store at my employees assisting customers. I watched people carrying their purchases to the register. At one point I noticed the people waiting in line at the check-out, some with plastic bags of tropical fish, one with a birdcage, several with supplies, one customer with a baby parakeet in a small cardboard carrier, and an entire family cuddling the newest member of their family in the form of a cocker spaniel puppy. I listened to all of their wonderful comments and observed their children's excitement and hoped they'd all become regular customers. Then and there, despite the fact that I'd stuck my neck out just like the turtle in that poster, I knew I was exactly where I was supposed to be.

2

—.—

FASCINATION

IT TOOK ABOUT A half hour's rowing before I neared my destination. As I slowed and began maneuvering the boat as quietly as I knew how, the warmth of the late-morning sun and the stillness of the water seemed to mesmerize me, or was it the echoed silence that held me in its grasp? More than anything, surely it had to be the anticipation of what was awaiting me.

From a distance, the untrained eye wouldn't be able to decipher what those shiny domed objects were, let alone appreciate their beauty. The half-submerged logs, which were once tall trees dotting the shoreline, were covered with them, and as I inched closer, remaining perfectly still became impossible for all of us.

Soon, the movement on the logs became a fidgeting frenzy as the domed objects became unsure of what was approaching them. Closer still, I could focus in on their beautiful colors and striking features as many of them began diving into the lake. I could even see some of them through the clear water as they swam to safety beneath the surface. There were a few that, for one reason or another, remained on the logs, peering out at the commotion. I learned to sit perfectly still and observe those for quite some time as they resumed their basking.

Midland painted turtles.

It wasn't my first excursion in observing midland painted turtles. I'd been doing it all week and I was becoming something of an expert. I was just twelve years old that summer at Camp Oconto, situated on the bank of the crystal-clear waters of Waubee Lake in Lakewood, Wisconsin. There was no other place on earth I would have rather been.

I noticed that the turtles would always try to attain the highest and most suitable positions, sometimes pushing others into the water while doing so. When a turtle would find that one particular place on the log, it would stretch its hind legs out while at the same time raising and flattening them to capture as much of the sun's warmth as possible. The turtles always seemed to be so content, never bothered even by the occasional dragonfly that might land on their carapaces.

I watched the way they responded to the sun's intensity as a cloud slowly cleared the sky. It was then that they would seek a better basking spot by nudging other members of the group into the water. Sometimes, without warning and for no apparent reason, they would dive into the water and, as swiftly as they vacated the log, they'd return, climbing back up to resume their thermo-regulating positions.

All the other boys at camp were into fishing or swimming or any of the other camp activities. I'd tried fishing many times before, but never had much luck beyond catching the occasional bluegill. Without a mentor to show me the right techniques, I tried to learn on my own but with my twelve-year-old logic, I assumed the bigger fish were in deeper water and smaller fish were in shallower areas. I'd go out in the middle of the lake and end up catching nothing while boring myself to death. I eventually discovered that the bigger fish liked to hang out among the lily pads and hide themselves in and around fallen logs close to shore. This is also when I discovered something else in those same environs, something more inter-esting to me than even the biggest fish: the turtles.

I found catching turtles with my net much more fun than sitting in a boat waiting for a fish to bite. I learned that the sundrenched coves around the lake, with their floating logs and branches, full of lily pads and vegetation, were home to hundreds of midland painted turtles, along with a few snapping turtles. Every morning after breakfast, it became my daily routine to race down to the shoreline where the rowboats were anchored and off to my turtle coves I went.

I enjoyed catching them and bringing them aboard and watching their behavior. I'd listen to the bumping and scratching sounds they'd make scurrying around the bottom of the aluminum rowboat. Before rowing back, I'd release most of them, but one or two of the smallest ones always accompanied me to camp for a couple of days.

If my passion for turtles was stoked at that summer camp, it was initially lit eight years earlier on the day I carefully carried home a little green turtle from the Woolworths' pet department. The third-floor apartment of ours on Richmond Street where I lived with my older brother, Tom, and my parents was where I brought my prized turtle home. It was a small apartment with only one bedroom, a kitchen, a bathroom, and a living room that held our cherished RCA Victor, black-and-white console television, the only source of entertainment for Tom and me on Saturday mornings. We never missed watching the cartoons before Mom and Dad got out of bed.

My father worked for the Canadian Pacific Railroad as a sales freight agent, selling transportation to various industries and serving customers in the Chicago area. His given name was Albert, but everybody called him Bobby, though to this day, I do not know why. Whatever the reason, it explains why I was given an alternative nickname: "Sonny."

Dad was the youngest of eleven children. My grandparents emigrated from Germany and settled on the northwest side of Chicago. My paternal grandfather, Carl, passed away in 1941, five years before I was born, and my grandmother lived in a brick two-flat not far from our apartment.

My mother, named Mary (but always called Marie by her family), was of Italian descent and the oldest of four children. My maternal grandparents emigrated from Italy, met in Baltimore, and moved to Chicago. They also owned a brick two-flat not far from us. Mom worked as an accountant at the Hills-McCanna Company, a manufacturer of valves. Sometimes on weekends, she'd take Tom and me to the office. We'd take the Montrose Avenue bus to Western Avenue and transfer to a southbound streetcar. The main floor of Hills-McCanna was a large open office with numerous desks. While she worked, she'd have us sit at one of the unoccupied desks, allowing us to pass the time by playing with a key-driven mechanical calculator called a comptometer.

Tom and I were close. He always looked after me and made sure I was safe. He was the wild one, always getting into mischief, while I was the quiet one. We were raised as Christians in the Lutheran religion and I was told that when my brother was born, there was a rift in the family as to how their first child would be raised. My mother's side wanted Tom to be Catholic, putting a lot of pressure on Mom because Dad wanted to give Tom a Lutheran upbringing. Without approval, Tom was whisked away and baptized Catholic. When my father found out, Tom was then baptized a second time in the Lutheran church. This pushing and tugging between the families contributed to some of the challenges we would face as we got older.

On Sundays, Tom and I always dressed properly with a tie, a sports coat, and a fedora hat. Early in the morning, we'd attend bible school for an hour in the church basement, then join all the parishioners for the ten o'clock church service. For a kid, it was a long two-and-a-half-hour ordeal, but I'm sure some things must have sunk in. Later, I would become an altar boy and it was around this time that I began making a conscious point of living by certain principles, always trying to do the right thing. I prayed for forgiveness when I didn't, and always thanked God for the wonderful things in my life.

It helped, too, that I was surrounded by hardworking role models. My parents and grandparents were nose-to-the-grindstone, always diligent, and always saving for the future. My grandparents on both sides were able to take their life savings in their middle-age years and buy homes that offered upstairs apartments they could rent out. My mother and father took a similar path, worked hard, and saved for a brighter future of owning their own home as well.

This happened to be a time before the age of shopping malls and strip centers. Instead, each neighborhood in the city had its own grocery store, bakery, butcher shop, hardware store, and various other small, mom-and-pop establishments, all within walking distance. But there were also much more extensive shopping destinations in the city, usually where three major streets would intersect. These were referred to as *Six Corners*. Our Six Corners was where Milwaukee Avenue, Irving Park Road, and Cicero Avenue came together. It was here, a short bus ride away, where you could find much larger stores, like Sears Roebuck, Kee Department Store, Hillman's Groceries, Walgreens, and my personal favorite, Woolworths with its pet department.

Woolworths carried anything and everything, from clothes to toiletries, and toys to household goods. It was our tradition to stop at their lunch counter and have something to eat or maybe just enjoy a chocolate phosphate. While sitting there, I could hear the parakeets chattering as if they were calling me to hurry on over to the pet department. It was a large department that included many different types of animals, sometimes even squirrel monkeys. They had hamsters and white mice as well as bee bee parrots, parakeets, java rice birds, and canaries. They also had guppies and a gigantic, square, metal-framed aquarium filled with goldfish, mystery snails, and eastern spotted newts.

And then there was a separate aquarium where numerous, little green turtles always stacked themselves high on one another's backs. The first time I saw them, I was immediately enamored. They all had what appeared to be smiles on their faces as they gazed at me. A little red patch behind their eyes gave this type of turtle its common name—the red-eared turtle.

Every week while shopping with Mom, I visited that turtle aquarium, dreaming about taking one of those little guys home. Then came that special Saturday when Mom rewarded me for helping carry the shopping bags by buying me one of the turtles. The clerk told Mom how easy they were to take care of while showing us the two different sizes of plastic turtle bowls, each complete with an island and a palm tree. After I pointed to the turtle I wanted, the clerk placed him into a white, cardboard container, same as the Chinese carry-out containers of today. We chose a turtle bowl, picked up a small orange metal can of Hartz Mountain turtle food, and off we went, me smiling the whole way home.

The turtle's place of residence became the kitchen windowsill where he could look out over the factory roof next door and enjoy some sunshine. My daily routine found me taking him out of his bowl and letting him crawl around on the floor, as I lay face-to-face with him, watching his every move.

I don't remember exactly what happened to him, but the poor little guy only lived a few months, ending up as that classical disposable pet. I'm sure Mom gave him a respectable burial, cleaned up the turtle bowl, and put it up on a shelf somewhere.

Today, I know many turtle enthusiasts whose interest in turtles began in the exact same way if not in a similar manner. The sad thing is that all of us now realize that those poor little lifeforms were each sentenced to a slow demise, eating meaningless diets of dried flies while being confined to those small plastic turtle bowls in unfiltered water. Nevertheless, that brief experience left such an impression on me that it stirred an insatiable fascination that continues to this day.

3

THE NATURAL WORLD

IN 1951, WHEN I was five, my parents decided that I should attend kindergarten at Alexander Graham Bell Elementary School, which happened to be in the same neighborhood as my Grandma Krause's home. It was also decided that I would live with her during the week.

Gram lived with Dad's sister Frieda on the first floor, while Dad's other sister Ulma lived upstairs with her husband, my uncle Ed. On weekends, I went back home. But during the week, I stayed with Gram where I had my own bedroom and enjoyed a backyard to play in, and with its own apple tree, to boot, luxuries we didn't have at our apartment.

Kindergarten was wonderful, though being called "Bob" instead of "Sonny" took some time getting used to. One day we were all asked to bring in empty cans, bottles, and cartons so we could build a pretend grocery store. I was only five, but somehow the concept of putting together a store resonated with me even then.

Gram didn't speak much English and actually taught me a bit of her native German. She read the Bible every day in addition to reading to me from her large edition of *Grimm's Fairy Tales*. With the help of the pictures, I learned to understand most of what she was saying, and I came to look forward to those special moments between the two of us. And speaking of special moments, Gram always had something cooking in the kitchen. My favorites were her buttered noodles, roast pork, potato pancakes, and her sky-high apple pies.

Being an industrious woman, she always worked hard, not only in and around the house, but in creating a means of supplemental income by collecting other people's throwaways around the neighborhood, back before recycling was even a term. I learned early on that scrap metal, newspapers, and used cardboard boxes had value. As it happened, Uncle Boykin, one of my father's brothers, was a scrap hauler who rode his horse and wagon down the alleys of the north side of Chicago picking up scrap metal and cardboard. I would hear the clickity-clack of his horse's hooves as he neared our backyard gate, his route taking him through our alley every Tuesday, the day before the city picked up the trash.

Gram would be ready for him. In the basement, I would help her break down the corrugated boxes she'd collected, sometimes soaking them in water first as her German ingenuity had taught her that doing so made them easier to break apart and fold flat, after which we'd tie them into flat bundles for my uncle. I loved when he came around with his old white horse who was so well behaved, chewing his cud as we loaded the wagon. One day, Uncle Boykin pulled up in a big truck, a sign of progress that nevertheless made me sad. I never knew what happened to his horse.

I admired Gram's perseverance and never once thought it odd to see her pulling her Radio Flyer wagon down the alleys picking up what she could. I even helped her bring home an old, discarded car hood one day. Gram walked with a limp and shuffled her feet but never complained. A few years later I overheard one of the neighbors refer to Gram as "that old junk lady." Through tears, I defended her, arguing how hardworking and smart she was to be able to make a living from other people's discarded items.

I got to know my other grandparents well also. On Sundays, back home with Mom, Dad, and Tom, we'd often go over to Grandma and Grandpa

Cascios's house. They, too, lived in the downstairs of their house, with the upstairs serving as the home for my cousins Connie, Donna, and Patsy. The house would come alive on those Sundays. My grandma, my mom, and my aunts would be in the kitchen making homemade rolls, pasta, soup, and salads. The pasta gravy, as Italians referred to their sauce, had to simmer all afternoon. Meanwhile the men would hang out in the garage or basement smoking or shucking oysters.

The dinner ritual was always the same—soup, salad, and then either mostaccioli, manicotti, or lasagna. That was all we needed, though on special occasions, there might be a roast beef or ham. If it was over the holidays, homemade cannolis were the tradition. My grandparents, it was pointed out to me on more than one occasion, lived through the depression. As a result, my grandma kept a cache of canned goods and dried pastas, beans, and rice stored under the stairs leading down to the basement. It looked like an old-fashioned Italian delicatessen, but my grandparents were determined to never go hungry again.

After dinner everyone would sit around the big dining room table and laugh while telling stories or playing cards. In the summers, we kids would play out in front of the house. Then when it got dark, the fireflies would light up the neighborhood and we'd enjoy catching them and watching how they'd glow as they'd turn on and then turn off. When one of the neighborhood kids smashed one on the sidewalk, just to see the streaks of light on the pavement, it made me heartsick to see one of God's creatures have its life ended in such a way.

Sometimes, if Tom or I needed a haircut, my grandpa would bring out a kitchen stool to cut our hair. It was his profession. He worked for his lifelong friend, a man by the name of Thomas Troy who owned a barbershop in the Bankers Building in downtown Chicago. Mr. Troy had no one else and when he sold his business and retired, my grandparents welcomed him into their home and took care of him in his later years. He became a virtual member of our family, and everyone referred to him as Uncle Tom. During Christmas gatherings, he would reach into his jacket pocket and present silver dollars to me, my brother, and our cousins. I'd always keep mine in a safe place along with the old Indian Head and 1943 steel pennies that I collected. A dollar was a lot of money in those days.

As it turned out, my Aunt Ulma passed away in 1952 and Uncle Ed moved out of the upstairs apartment in Grandma Krause's house. The three-bedroom flat became my family's new home. Mom, Dad, and Tom moved in, and I joined them; our family was together again. Tom and I shared our Aunt Ulma's old steel-frame bed in our very own bedroom. Mom and Dad had their own room too and the much smaller center bedroom became our TV room.

I enjoyed the school years, was a decent student, and had lots of friends. But I enjoyed the summers even more. We always took family trips—a train trip one year and road trips other years, either out west to the national parks or to Florida. But my favorites were the summer trips we took to a farm in Crivitz, Wisconsin.

The farm was owned by the Krolls, an immigrant Polish family. On a hunting trip with friends, Dad had met one of the Kroll's sons, Zeph, who, invited us to visit the farm one summer, and that vacation turned into an annual tradition. The farm was a one-day drive, 275 miles from our home, and then an additional twenty-plus miles out of Crivitz, up a long, steep, winding, dirt road, through the Nicolet National Forest, filled with pine and hardwood trees. There were only three outposts on the road—one mostly abandoned hunting cabin, a farmhouse occupied by two old-timers, and finally the Kroll's farm. The forest was so dense, the sun was only visible in a few small areas on the entire road. Sometimes, if it was raining, we wouldn't even be aware of it until the sky finally became visible as we reached the last incline opening up to the farm.

The farm was originally cleared years earlier by the Kroll family with nothing more than draft horses, a couple of wagons, a plow, and crude tools—axes and long handled saws. The Krolls were true homesteaders and for the most part self-sustaining. They kept dairy cows for milk and cheese and raised chickens for meat and eggs. They always had two or three pigs that were butchered each fall. They had ducks and they had a turkey that made a habit of following me around. They owned two draft horses, too, although these were eventually replaced by a tractor. They grew and harvested corn, potatoes, onions, beets, cabbage, cucumbers, and tomatoes. The farm even had an apple orchard. And the family hunted grouse, pheasant, rabbit, squirrel, and deer. The property had a crystal-clear brook running through it that was home to beautiful rainbow trout. There were several small lakes in the area that provided crappie, bluegill, and bass.

Early one morning, my father and I went fishing on one of those lakes. It was quiet and serene, and the only sounds were the creaking of the oars, the gentle lapping of the water, and the call of an invisible loon echoing in the distant mist. Dad taught me the proper way to row a boat, a skill I would appreciate even more later in life. At the time, I was just a small boy grateful to be spending such precious moments with his dad.

The farm included two large barns, several outbuildings, sheds, coops, and a two-room farmhouse. Mrs. Kroll did the cooking, a master at making any meal taste delicious no matter the ingredients. But I never quite got used to drinking the cow's warm, unpasteurized milk out of Mrs. Kroll's old pickling jars. Their home had electricity, but no running water. Up the hill a bit, there was an old-fashioned open well, where we retrieved water every morning with a bucket on a rope. Around back and down a path was a little closet of a shed that I learned was called an outhouse. This was my first experience with a Sears catalog serving a dual purpose.

Neither Mr. nor Mrs. Kroll could speak English but were always somehow able to communicate in their native Polish tongue, along with a lot of pointing, smiling, and laughing. Over the summers, I learned how to catch rainbow trout in the fast-moving, cold waters of a brook located at the far end of the property. And I mastered the art of hunting squirrels and rabbits with a 22-caliber rifle and a twelve-gauge shotgun, the results of which were delicious, iron-skillet-prepared meals that today could never be replicated.

Me, four years old, on Kroll's Farm.

This is the environment where the Krolls raised their five children who were close in age to my mother and father. This is also where I discovered everything that was involved with farm life. And I loved it—from milking a cow to slopping the pigs, and from collecting eggs and picking cucumbers to jumping out of the barn loft into piles of hay. The smell of the horse and cow manure as well as the sweet smell of the hay loft stays with me still.

Of course, by then my interest in nature was firmly established. I took note of the wildlife all around the farm, including the many leopard frogs and garter snakes. Anticipation was half the fun. Days before our trips, I would busy myself getting together all my empty mayonnaise jars, my butterfly net, and an old pillowcase or two.

One year, my grandparents accompanied us. On our second day at the farm, Dad, Grandpa, Tom, and I went to a remote lake with Zeph. The five of us rowed out into the lake past what looked like giant telephone poles haphazardly protruding a couple of feet out of the water. To my absolute delight, the poles were covered with all sizes of snapping turtles. I had never seen anything like it, and I watched wide-eyed as most of these various-sized, prehistoric-looking turtles dropped into the water upon our approach. Through the clear water, I could see them rapidly swimming below the surface while a few, for one reason or another, stuck to the wooden poles without moving. I knew right then and there that I was just going to have to have a snapping turtle someday.

When we arrived at the shoreline and got out of the boat, giant bullfrogs began jumping out from under a blanket of dried leaves and into the water. I dove on top of one and caught him. I ended up keeping him in a minnow bucket until the day we were to leave for Chicago. Our 1955 Pontiac was full with the six of us and we had no room for the minnow bucket. I wanted badly to take that bullfrog home and convinced everyone that he'd be okay in a ventilated jar on the back windshield. We began our journey back home with the bullfrog resting within inches of my grandma's head. Even though we periodically stopped and checked on the frog, he only made it halfway—unfortunate for him and me, but a relief for my grandma.

As the years passed, the Kroll family split up. The children married and moved to the city. Mr. Kroll passed away. Zeph and Mrs. Kroll tried to keep up with the farm but couldn't do it. They bought a little house in town and moved. The farm fell into disrepair and was eventually abandoned altogether.

Years later, I returned to the town as a young adult and found Zeph and Mrs. Kroll's house. Mrs. Kroll answered my knock at their door. She didn't recognize me all grown up but smiled politely and talked to me in Polish. Then Zeph came to the door, and I told him who I was—Bobby's son from Chicago. He was very cordial and agreed to take me out to the farm. By then, everything looked different. I could see that the farm was slowly falling apart and melting into the earth, and I found myself wanting to cry.

Years after that experience, I tried to recapture some of the old memories by camping out in Crivitz. I made a stop at an antique store and got to talking to the couple who owned the place and they agreed to let me camp on their back acreage alongside a remote one-acre pond. I had my snorkeling equipment with me and decided to explore.

I was gliding through the clear water observing the beautiful aquatic plants, floating vegetation, and bluegills when suddenly I saw it—a striking midland painted turtle just swimming along. I followed it slowly until I was close enough to reach out and grasp it. It flailed its legs in an attempt to free itself and I soon released it, watching it as it shot through the seaweed until it descended out of sight. Within the hour, I repeated the experience six or seven times.

I'd never snorkeled with turtles before. Somehow, blending into their environment made me feel content, even complete. The whole experience brought to mind the wonder of those long-ago childhood days and I was glad I'd made the trip.

Referring to people of his and my age, turtle biologist Tim Walsh once said, *"Our childhood was the time of the last generation of outdoor children."* Oh, how true that is. Today we live in an age of cell phones, texting, social media, and computer gaming. And although the strides in technology in the decades since my childhood have been both stunning and wonderful in their own ways, I find myself grateful for the opportunity I had as a kid to spend time on Kroll's Farm, a place with nothing to entertain me but the beauty, grandeur, and simplicity of the natural world.

4

— · —

VALUES

If, LIKE ME, YOU were a kid with an eye for nature, you could find it in places other than the obvious environs of Kroll's Farm. You had to look a little harder for it, but even in a city like Chicago, it was there.

Ours was a well-established neighborhood, a thirty-minute walk down Addison Street directly west from Wrigley Field, but there were still a few empty lots here and there. They were typically overgrown with weeds, grasses, and a few trees and we called them prairies. You had to be careful when you explored one of these prairies because they were commonly used as dumping grounds for boards, concrete, and other building remnants left over from the construction of adjacent buildings. I found the lots to be prime locations for catching butterflies and other insects, garter snakes, and leopard frogs. They were all plentiful, especially on damp and rainy days. Underneath the building materials is where you'd find the garter snakes. Chasing the butterflies would often take me over fences, through gangways, and into many neighbors' backyards and gardens.

Caterpillars and insect larvae were common, everything from giant Cecropia and Polyphemus moth larvae on the apple trees, to tomato hornworm larvae on the tomato plants. These always came home with me and continued their lives either inside one-gallon jars or in one of my two specially designed enclosed areas between the screen and the windows of our back porch. I supplied branches and leaves, replacing them daily with fresh ones until the caterpillars spun their cocoons.

Throughout the warmer days of 1957 and 1958, my friend Jimmy Swatalla and I would always look forward to our Shiller Woods Forest Preserve excursions. Taking the Addison Street bus west from Western Avenue all the way to the end of the line on Cumberland Avenue would get us to the back entrance of this nature preserve. With its open fields, marshes, and forests, Shiller Woods was where we learned what the Midwest environment had to offer in the form of nature. To the bus driver's perpetual amusement, we'd always board the bus fully equipped with our butterfly nets and duffel bags (filled with jars, pillowcases, sandwiches, and toilet paper). We'd dig into our pockets for the required fare (a dime), and then take our seats, ready for our expedition.

On our initial outing, in mid-April of that first year, after the last of the winter snow had melted, we waded through freezing cold, ankle-deep water into a wooded area of the preserve to follow the ear-splitting, high-frequency calls of what we thought were thousands of crickets. But as we crept closer to the sound's source, it went suddenly silent, only to begin again a short distance behind us where we had just walked. We learned patience. By remaining still, we could wait them out. Soon enough, we heard a solo *peep*. A minute later, another. And then another and another until we realized we were right in the middle of hundreds of little spring chorus frogs, the males *peeeeping* away with tiny, ballooned necks in their attempts to attract mates. Jimmy and I couldn't stop smiling.

The excursions always included chasing tiger swallowtails, fritillaries, and red-spotted purples, as well as searching under boards and rotted logs for beetles, toads, and whatever else we could discover. Many times, we would disagree on ownership. There would be ongoing debates as to whether a particular critter belonged to the one who saw it first or the one who ultimately captured it. Sometimes the matter was settled by the well-respected kid law of "Dibbies." If you were the first to yell out "Dibbies!" then the specimen belonged to you. The problem was, this could be counteracted if the other person astutely declared "Changies!" Changies trumped Dibbies. Eventually, with the wisdom of young Solomons, Jimmy and I came to agree that the proper way to proclaim ownership was to holler, "Dibbies, no Changies!" That would settle the matter forever.

This rule generally worked well, especially when both of us were on the run after a black swallowtail butterfly. But sometimes not so well. One day, while rolling over a rotting tree stump, we encountered a rare specimen. A real catch—a banded red, black, and yellow neonate snake. An eastern milk snake, we would later learn. Jimmy was the one who uncovered it while I looked on, but in the excitement, he forgot to yell, "Dibbies no Changies!" As he grabbed the snake, I hollered the magic, legally binding words and could immediately see the disappointment on Jimmy's face. My very good friend was almost in tears as we bagged the snake and I couldn't help but feel a twinge of guilt. Nevertheless, the rule was the rule and fair was fair.

When we returned home, I set the snake up in a small, unused aquarium in a naturalistic setting. I was proud of how I'd arranged the dried leaves and branches. I put a small bowl of water in the aquarium and set it down alongside the garage next to my other set-ups of turtles and garter snakes. Then, two days later, as if it were meant to be, my milk snake somehow escaped. To make matters worse, Jimmy was the one who found its flattened, dried remains by the curb in front of my house. I never felt right about the whole incident and believe to this day that the final outcome was my punishment for not giving the snake to Jimmy in the first place.

It wasn't the only lesson in my young life from the animal world. Walking down the alley to a friend's house one day, I noticed a pigeon searching for tidbits of food and grit. Almost absent-mindedly, I picked up a stone and hurled it at him. To my surprise, and horror, the stone hit the pigeon squarely in the head, killing him instantly. I stood open-mouthed, scarcely believing I had just done something so terrible. I picked up the pigeon's lifeless body and found myself starting to cry. Then I returned home with the worst feeling in my stomach and buried the poor pigeon in the backyard next to the garage. Killing that bird for no reason was something that would stick with me my whole life.

While I was learning lessons from nature, I was also busy learning lessons on the value of a dollar. My parents instilled in Tom and me a work ethic early. We were each paid $1.50 as our weekly allowance for keeping our room neat, taking the garbage out to the cement trash box, and alternating chores of clearing the table, and drying and putting away the dishes after dinner.

Needing more cash flow, however, we both found extra sources of income. Tom found a job and it came to him in a rather embarrassing way. Peddlers would frequently drive down our alley selling their wares and services—ice cream, fresh fruits, and vegetables, as well as knife sharpening and various home repair services. Each street vendor had his own way of announcing his presence, from hollering or whistling, to singing out a jingle or ringing a bell. Tom had a habit of helping himself from the fruit and vegetable truck whenever he saw the owner leave to deliver produce to a neighbor's second floor apartment. That ended one day when the vendor caught him red-handed. But rather than scolding him, the vendor offered Tom a job, to ride with him on Saturdays and assist him in his route. Tom had to keep the produce neatly stacked and displayed, and he had to keep an eye on the truck as the owner delivered the produce to his customers. The problem of protecting the produce was often times solved by throwing rotten tomatoes at the young, would-be thieves that Tom would come across. At the end of the day, his boss would drop him off by our back gate with a few dollars and a bonus gift box of assorted fruits and vegetables for Mom.

Me, I made extra money by collecting pop bottles. I'd come home for lunch every day and, afterward, instead of returning directly to school, I'd walk down the alley to Western Avenue where all of the Lane Tech High School boys would sit on the pavement along the storefronts and building walls in the alley eating their lunches. Every one of them had a bottle of pop and when they finished, they'd leave the empty bottle on the pavement. If they saw me coming, they'd roll the bottles down the pavement, enjoying the sight of me chasing them.

The bottles were worth two cents each at the grocery store, and I made thirty to fifty cents every afternoon by cashing them in. Eventually, I brought my wagon with me and collected a lot more bottles. I'd hide the wagon in a pile of old tires behind a gas station until I could return after school. This method turned out to be lucrative even though I risked losing my wagon and inventory if the stash was ever discovered. Happily, that never happened.

I was twelve when I got my first real job—delivering newspapers. Tom came home one day and told me that one of his friends had a neighborhood paper route for *The Booster* but was soon giving it up. The route was extensive, and Tom's idea was that we split it. The route required two deliveries per week, Wednesdays and Sundays, along with returning door-to-door on Thursdays and Fridays to collect payment. At the same time, we handed out numbered coupons for a weekly drawing, with the winning customer receiving fifty dollars. It was a pretty good system and became a good source of tips. On some weeks, we would double our regular income.

After collecting payment from all the customers, Tom and I had to go to *The Booster* office on Saturday mornings, get in line with all the other carriers, and turn in our unused coupons, along with the payments. Then we received half of what we turned in. After the second week, Mom helped us open bank accounts, which became the beginning of my lifelong banking experiences. I opened my first account at Central Savings & Loan on Belmont Avenue, depositing at least half my income every Saturday. Mom taught me how to keep the cash I retained neat and organized, even showing me how to iron the crumpled bills.

But my main interest continued to be the natural world of critters. Although it wasn't as exotic, perhaps, as the Shiller Woods Forest Preserve, there was a much closer wildlife sanctuary, of sorts, in the way of an old, abandoned golf course. Bordering Waveland Avenue on the north and Addison Street on the south, the Waveland Golf Course ceased to exist in the early 1950s. Except for stores on Western Avenue and two blocks of residential housing to the west, the property was mostly barren and extended west from Western Avenue all the way to the Chicago River. Ultimately, this area would become a business district that today consists of several corporate offices including WGN Studios and Bodine Electric. But during the summers of 1957 through 1959, it became a wildlife discovery zone for me and Jimmy.

The golf course was our utopia. Before reaching the main open areas of the course, we had to tunnel our way through seven-foot-tall, over-grown fibrous weeds and wild sunflowers, as if we were forging through a towering jungle, all the while carrying our butterfly nets and supplies. On the other side of the maze, it was beautiful—rolling fields of overgrown grass that were once fairways. The grass was so long it rolled over into clumps, interspersed with wildflowers, weeds, plants, and ground cover. There were several clusters of elm, maple, and poplar trees. What used to be sand traps and embankments became gathering points of scattered pieces of old building material—boards, sheets of plywood, slabs of concrete, tin siding, and roofing materials. These were some of my very first experiences in learning that these micro habitats were actually homes for numerous forms of wildlife including insects, worms, crayfish, frogs, garter snakes, field mice, and rabbits. I can still feel the excitement as I would encounter several snakes and critters all together under pieces of roofing material. Then at the far end of the course that bordered the Chicago River, we'd discover painted and map turtles basking along the shoreline among the tree branches and half-submerged logs.

More than anything, the course was an ideal destination for butterfly collecting and it was common to see tiger swallowtails, black swallowtails, monarchs, buckeyes, red admirals, red-spotted purples, fritillaries, clouded sulphurs, and cabbage butterflies. I became proficient in collecting butterflies and other insects, learning how to net them without hurting their wings while they were either resting on a plant or flying. By making a soft but swift swoop, along with a few side-to-side sweeps, you could fold the net on them with no damage done. Then, you'd place the net on the ground and work your way toward your catch with a relaxing jar, typically an empty mayonnaise jar with a one-inch cotton base moistened with carbon tetrachloride and securely covered with a piece of thin cardboard.

Jimmy's older brother, Raymond, is the one who taught us. He patiently showed us how to make a butterfly net out of a broom stick, a coat hanger, and a package of cheesecloth from the hardware store. We bought the carbon tetrachloride at the grocery store where it was sold as a rug cleaner. It was in Jimmy and Raymond's basement where I watched and learned how to mount butterflies. I admired Raymond because he had such an interest in so many different types of animals. Along with his pigeons—kept in a loft that he and Jimmy built above their garage—he had a great horned owl in a makeshift aviary they'd constructed in a narrow area between their garage and their neighbor's garage.

Whenever I would return home from my excursions, I'd work on spreading and pinning my catches on balsa wood boards I'd purchased at the hobby store. I learned to be patient and precise in the process, holding my breath for long periods of time as I spread the wings into position. (Tom came up behind me one time and blew on the table, scattering my work everywhere. Naturally, a fight ensued.) Once pinned, the catches would sit for a week until I permanently mounted them into Riker specimen mounts, which I bought not far away at Central Scientific Company. In time, I built up a collection of hundreds of butterflies and insects, many of which I have to this day.

There were times I took some of my school friends with me to the abandoned golf course, just to have them experience the fun of being in such a wilderness. By then, I'd reached an age where friends of the opposite sex were becoming more important. I always seemed to have girlfriends but the one who was really special was Laurel Jashob. She came with me one day and obliged to hold a shopping bag as we filled it with garter snakes. Today, close to seventy years later, she's still a close friend, even though I doubt she'd want to hold a bag of snakes for me.

Then there were times I'd go to the course by myself and wander aimlessly. Often, I'd put my butterfly net and gear down and lay in the tall grass and stare at the sky and the clouds floating by. After a while, I'd close my eyes and still be able to see those mysterious tiny particles moving beneath my eyelids as I felt the warm sun beating down upon me. These were wonderful times. For a young boy enamored by nature, how could things possibly get any better?

5

—·—

COLLECTING

BESIDES GOING TURTLING ON my many excursions, I began to frequent pet shops to augment my collection. There was the Gilded Cage Pet Shop and the North Center Pet Shop. I rode my bike regularly to the North Center Pet Shop to buy mealworms and while there I would always cruise through the whole store on the lookout for something new. I'd check out the aquariums of tropical fish and the small animals housed in the cages at the back of the store. Periodically they'd have unusual reptiles, like the rough green snakes I once discovered in a glass display case.

Then, one day, there it was: a Florida box turtle they had just gotten in. I couldn't believe the beautiful colors and patterns on its carapace. It was active and healthy, not even retracting its head into its shell when I picked it up. I had to have it. I'd only brought enough money for mealworms, but the owner of the store recognized me as one of her regular customers and was kind enough to hold the turtle for me while I rode back home for more cash. That box turtle became my prized possession for a long time. I would take it out of its tub and let it explore the backyard almost every day. It came to know me, and it ate earthworms from my hand.

But my very favorite pet store back then was the famous Animal Kingdom, a good thirty-minute bike ride down Milwaukee Avenue. In addition to being a large, departmentalized store, it was home to the television animals. The owner was the celebrated Bernie Hoffman who was always turning up on ABC's Super Circus show, hosted by Mary Hartline. Bernie would appear in a ringmaster outfit accompanied each time by a different animal, like his chimpanzee Bingo, his pet tiger, or his tame turkey vulture. Animal Kingdom was also home to Chelveston, the comical white Pekin duck that made daily appearances on WGN's Ray Rayner morning show.

My visits to these pet stores resulted in additions to my collection that included a three-toed box turtle and many more aquatic turtles, along with various snakes, anoles, and a Texas horned lizard. But my collection grew by way of gifts too, like the baby alligator my school friend, Ann Carlson, picked up on her vacation to Florida with her family. Johnny and Dicky Mitchell, my good friends who lived in the apartment building down the street, once gave me two baby spiny softshell turtles they'd brought back from their summer cottage in Culver, Indiana. They'd found them hiding in the sand beneath the shallow water of the beach. I had only ever seen softshell turtles in pictures, and I couldn't believe I now had two real, live ones. A month or so later, Bobby Detlaff gave me, of all things, a hatchling snapping turtle he'd brought back from a family trip to Wisconsin. From the day I saw those snapping turtles piled on top of the half-submerged wooden poles at the remote lake near Kroll's Farm, I'd had a dream of owning a snapping turtle. Now that dream had come true. Then one day, I was in the backyard feeding my turtles when my Uncle Sam stopped by on his way home from playing golf. He was carrying a cardboard box and said he had a surprise for me. Inside the box was a midland painted turtle that he had picked up as it was crossing the fairway. He knew it would make a nice gift for his crazy, turtle-loving nephew.

As my collection grew, I needed more aquariums. These were always on my wish lists for birthdays and Christmases. When anyone wondered what to get Sonny, the answer was invariably an aquarium. One Christmas, I received my largest aquarium, a complete thirty-gallon setup that kicked off my tropical fish collection. I soon had angelfish, which were rare back then, and the whole family loved watching them in our TV room.

For my butterfly collection, I also collected caterpillars, cocoons and chrysalises, beetles, and other interesting insects. This was a time before the overuse of DDT and other pesticides that adversely affected the environment and depleted the insect populations. I never seemed to have enough mayonnaise or pickle jars in which to keep my catches. I loved watching the caterpillars hatch out of their cocoons and chrysalises. Seeing them emerge and slowly unfold and shape their wings as they began fluttering about was a biology class all its own.

My family, meanwhile, was endlessly patient with my collections. One morning, Tom woke up itching all over with long red welts on his back. In his sleep he had knocked over a jar I'd kept of tomato horn worm caterpillars, which had subsequently crawled all over him. It's a miracle that he tolerated some of his younger brother's ways.

I do have to admit that Tom managed to help out at times. Throughout the summer months I was always bringing garter snakes home and learning about their habits and care. But I wasn't happy with the aquariums I was keeping them in. The bricks I put on the wire mesh covers weren't always effective in eliminating escapes. Tom offered me an old, miniature pinball machine he'd received one year for Christmas. The pinball machine had outlived its usefulness as a game, but it ended up making a fine garter snake cage. I took the legs off and modified the top part by inserting a piece of wire mesh to act as a door and slid it up against the original glass top. I put this new cage out back and set it up with some gravel and a couple of chunks of sod.

The repurposed pinball machine became home to six adult Great Plains garter snakes, and they did well. I fed them night crawlers by hand, which they enjoyed and, in fact, became accustomed to. One day, I watched in amazement as one of the snakes gave birth. Small gelatin-like capsules slid out, one right after another and soon baby snakes were crawling everywhere. It was the first time I'd ever observed the live birth of snakes.

My turtles and my garter snakes were always responsive and gentle, allowing me to handle and handfeed them. I overwintered them by bringing the wash tubs I'd kept the turtles in, as well as the snake cages, into the basement under the windows where they could receive some sunlight. At times, the basement could still be chilly, and the turtles and snakes wouldn't eat much, so I worried about them. But eventually I learned that they were going into their annual dormant period.

One year I decided to try hibernating my box turtles and garter snakes by carefully burying them in one of the wash tubs that I filled with damp leaves and soil mixed together. I placed the tub in an unheated area under the porch along the stairway leading into the basement. I had never heard of this being done before and I was very worried throughout that winter. Every week, I would examine the soil, making sure it felt right, but refusing to dig out the turtles and snakes no matter how tempted I was. When spring finally arrived, even though the weather was still somewhat cold, I couldn't hold out any longer and dug the turtles and snakes out of their hibernaculum. I was thrilled to see that they were perfectly healthy. Over the months, however, the garter snakes had apparently forgotten who I was. Once they warmed up, they started to curl up and strike at me each time I came close.

In the summers, I used to take my turtles out of the wash tubs and allow them to crawl through the grass. I would lay down with my head down low, get up close to them, and watch their every move. One day, I took out five turtles and closely watched them as always. They were enjoying the sun and sat in place with their heads peering out in all directions. As

I lay in the cool grass, I became mesmerized by them, which, eventually, led to a drowsy feeling. I'm not sure how long I slept, maybe only a few minutes, but it had been long enough for the turtles to take off. When I awoke, I couldn't believe what I had done. The turtles were gone. I jumped up and searched for them everywhere, even climbing over the fence into our neighbor's yard. I ended up recovering only three of them, losing two of them forever. Needless to say, I never allowed that to happen again.

All this time, I sought out as much information as I could about turtles, reptiles, amphibians, butterflies, moths, and other insects. I must have read every book that our school library carried about these creatures. One day, they received a brand-new book entitled *Collecting Cocoons* by Lois J. Hussey. This became one of my favorite insect books, and I kept renewing it until the librarian told me I couldn't renew it anymore. She'd order one for me if I was willing to pay for it, which I did, and I eventually bought several more books on reptiles, turtles, butterflies, and insects. This was the beginning of my own library.

Before long, I was taking trips to the Chicago Public Library on Lincoln Avenue where I discovered a treasure trove of nature books. Once, on a school trip to the Chicago Field Museum, while all of my schoolmates were busy buying souvenirs and trinkets, I found a book I'd never seen before: *Reptiles and Amphibians*, a Golden Nature Guide. I slept with that book the entire first week I owned it. Mom and Dad were pleased because now they realized they could give me books for Christmas and my birthday instead of aquariums. One Christmas morning, I unwrapped the giant hardcover book *Snakes of the World*, by Raymond Ditmars. I still have it today.

In addition to collecting insects, turtles, and other reptiles, I began accumulating books about them as well. What I didn't see at the time was that I was also collecting knowledge and experience that would play a huge part in my future.

6

— • —

CAMP OCONTO

KROLL'S FARM, THE "PRAIRIES" of my Chicago neighborhood, Shiller Woods Forest Preserve, the abandoned Waveland Golf Course, the trips to the pet shops, and all the book learning I had done—it all seemed to lead to one very special place, an environment where my passion could really explode: Camp Oconto, a small Christian summer camp in Lakewood, Wisconsin.

The camp offered supervised and structured programs that included fishing, swimming, boating, archery, riflery, and overnight hikes in the wilderness. It was two weeks living in ten-person canvas tents. I went for two summers during my twelfth and thirteenth years, the first summer accompanied by Tom, one of his friends, and one of mine; and the next summer with my friends Terry Hlavac and Bobby Detlaff.

During the days, the lakes and shorelines of Camp Oconto offered painted turtles, snapping turtles, bullfrogs, leopard frogs, and garter snakes. The evenings presented gray tree frogs, American toads, and tiger salamanders. And then there were the supervised excursions to open fields and abandoned farms which brought me into another world of reptiles. I encountered bull snakes, smooth green snakes, garter snakes, red-bellied snakes, and ring-neck snakes. The shaded forests were home to chipmunks by day, and raccoons, porcupines, skunks, flying squirrels, black bear, and white-tailed deer by night. In addition, countless butterflies, moths, and beetles allowed me to add several new specimens to my insect collection. My first Luna moth, unusual fritillaries, and swallowtail butterflies; along with burrowing, carrion, caterpillar hunter, and spectacular, fast-moving tiger beetles became real to me, all of which I had previously been introduced to only as described and pictured in books.

But I also learned the meaning of "turtling" at Camp Oconto, although I would later come to learn that there are other meanings as well. For me, turtling was rowing along the shoreline to find and observe turtles, which is what I would do while most of my friends were fishing. And it was there, at Camp Oconto, where I first encountered the midland painted turtle, in my estimation, the most beautiful freshwater turtle in the world.

It's readily apparent how the midland painted turtle got its name. It isn't just from the coloration and patterns of the reddish-orange lines between its olive-green plates on its upper shell (carapace), or the orange and red patterns over the beige background of its lower shell (plastron); its extremities are colorful as well. The head, neck, and legs are covered with stripes and blotches of yellow, orange, and red. These turtles are gentle and harmless treasures of nature, only capable of protecting themselves by either camouflage or a swift plunge into the water.

Camp Oconto is where I also learned the advanced intricacies of rowing a boat. Rowboat turtling can be complex and challenging and is best accomplished with two people, one maneuvering the boat while the other remains up front with a net at the ready. In my case, it became a very special art, being the only one in the boat. Silence and patience were the first two key ingredients for being able to observe turtles up close. The same can be said of all of nature, the goal of observation being able to blend in as seamlessly as possible.

Rowing rapidly, of course, is not the way to make this happen. I learned to row slowly and silently. I eventually mastered the critical art of cutting the water with the oars while slightly twisting them in order to create thrust on each pull, all the while minimizing the splashing noises. I also developed a technique of turning and stopping with as little commotion and water disturbance as possible.

As I approached my quarry, and at a precise time, I would give the oars one last silent thrust, keeping them submerged in a relaxed position while silently gliding. I'd crouch down and quietly crawl to the bow of the boat, long net in hand, staying as low as possible. This method allowed the rowboat to stealthily approach the half-submerged logs where the turtles were basking. When I was at my net's distance from the log, many of the turtles would start to dive into the water, and it was then that I was usually successful in netting one or two.

I developed another method, too. One could wait seemingly forever for the submerged turtles to surface, but I discovered that if I pounded on the floor of the boat and rocked it back and forth, I'd create both noise and vibration that some of the turtles couldn't resist. More than once, I'd see a curious little guy surface and gaze around.

There were many times during my excursions where I would just sit motionless in the boat and enjoy everything around me. Nature seemed to come alive, from the dragonflies on the protruding aquatic vegetation, to the snails on the lower surface of the lily pads. The only background sounds were the distant echoing bellows of the male bullfrogs in the marsh, or an occasional shriek from a red-tailed hawk as it glided skyward. Back then I didn't understand why those flocks of tiger swallowtail butterflies were fluttering back and forth on the damp substrate of the shoreline. I learned years later that they were ingesting minerals.

By looking closely, I could see all the water beetles swimming in haphazard patterns on the water's surface, while in the distance, I might observe a kingfisher swooping from an overhanging tree branch to catch a small fish. Over time, the fallen trees from the shoreline of those sheltered coves transitioned into beautifully arranged turtle-basking logs, as well as underwater fortresses that served as ambush sites for largemouth bass. All of this became part of my education on biodiversity well before I had ever heard the term. I also learned about "herping" before that term was even coined. Herping is derived from the word herpetology—the study of reptiles and amphibians—and refers to the action of entering the natural habitats of different species for the purposes of observation, photography, or collecting. That certainly was me.

Most of my knowledge of critters had come, of course, by observation of the different species I'd kept as pets, as well as from the books I had read. But studying them in their natural environment was an education all its own. I can still hear the startling shriek of a leopard frog as I watched, motionless with my net, as a large garter snake engulfed him before my very eyes. My first impulse was to save the poor little guy, but I knew it was just part of nature. Years later, wading along shorelines and marshes, I would sometimes hear that same distinct sound and remember that first encounter at Camp Oconto.

I had a near-death experience myself one time along the shoreline. I got out of my rowboat and began walking along one of the lake's marshy bogs looking for hatchling painted turtles. I didn't go more than a few steps before I realized the entire ground was moving. Before I had a chance to turn around, I instantly plunged to my waist in what seemed to be black quicksand. I would have gone farther down if I hadn't slapped my net down to stop my descent. It happened so fast I couldn't even panic. By the time I realized how serious the situation could have turned, I was able to climb out of that smelly muck on my belly and crawl back to the boat. Today, whenever I'm out in the field and I encounter a marshy, floating substrate with the same consistency, I'm comforted by the fact that a strong walking stick always accompanies me.

I began to learn that herping experiences sometimes occur when you least expect them. One rainy evening, we lined up in front of the trading post where we all had accounts set up to purchase snacks and supplies, and as everyone pushed and shoved to get under the eave of the structure, I noticed the reflection of an enormous tiger salamander slithering toward a watery pothole on the dirt road. I immediately got out of line and ran over, not believing what I was seeing. There were too many salamanders to count, and they were everywhere, moving in all directions across the road. Naturally, a few of them had to accompany me back to Chicago.

But of all the camp activities, the overnighters were some of my favorites. This is where the counselors would take a bus load of us to remote locations. We'd camp out, cook on a campfire, and sleep under the stars. Whenever we were asked who was interested in an overnighter, my hand was one of the first to shoot up in the air. In addition to the fun of camping out in the wilderness, these excursions gave me extra opportunities for herping.

Once, we took an overnighter to Hermit's Cave. This was the name given to the remnants of a large fruit cellar in the side of a hill that had at one time been part of a long-abandoned, log cabin homesite from the late 1800s. There, we encountered several ring-neck snakes that had made the old wooden support beams of the cellar their home and were piled on top of each other in the rafters. I was thrilled, of course, but concerned that the rest of the boys might want to harm them. I announced that the snakes were mildly venomous, and everyone ran out of the place except me and Terry Hlavac.

Nights around the campfires were especially memorable. After collecting wood and starting our fire, we'd cover the surrounding ground with fern branches to cushion our sleeping bags. Then after exploring the area, we were ready to turn in. But of course, no one wanted to go to sleep and instead we took turns making up scary stories. You'd have to rotate yourself constantly because the side of your body closest to the fire would get too warm while the other side would be freezing cold. My first experience seeing the northern lights was at Hermit's Cave. The Aurora Borealis lit up the evening sky as if it were the middle of the afternoon. Millions upon millions of stars blanketed the sky as if they were splashed on with a paintbrush, alive with constant streaks of shooting stars from all directions.

One of my favorite day excursions took us to the middle of a secluded abandoned farm. We were on a search for a clear, bubbling spring our camp guide knew was in the area. Everyone except me and a couple of my close friends were interested in filling their canteens. We were more interested in exploring the broken-down remains of the farmhouse to find snakes. Under the scattered pieces of tin roofing material, we discovered that the area was alive with smooth green snakes and red-bellied snakes. My heart pounded with excitement as we turned over the boards and tin roof strips. I picked up and examined a few of the snakes as the rest either sat motionless or slithered off into the tall thick grass.

The last day of camp was always a sad day. The new friends we all made would soon go their own ways. My last year at camp, I took one new friend home with me—an adult raccoon I'd live-trapped two nights before. I was sure I could tame him and make him into a pet and, reluctantly, the camp counselors let me take him home. It was fun watching the parents' reactions when the bus driver unloaded the luggage from the rooftop of the bus, and he handed down my trap with the snarling raccoon peering out. I kept him in the garage and began designing a cage but after the second day, at the insistence of Mom and Dad, I let him go in the forest preserves.

Camp Oconto sure taught me much about the life and habits of many animals, especially reptiles and amphibians. But for all the different critters I observed, spent time with, and learned about, nothing ever displaced my beloved painted turtles as my favorite critters of all.

7

— • —

MOVING ON

BEING YOUNG AND INQUISITIVE, I was fascinated by a small, special room in the basement of my maternal grandparents' house. It was a private room set up for studying, sort of a laboratory that my Uncle Sam had assembled while attending medical school—shelves of jars filled with various specimens and collectibles. The little laboratory stuck with me, and I always dreamed of having something similar in our basement, a little hobby room. Mine would have aquariums and cages and display cases of all manner of critters.

The problem with our basement was that there wasn't much room. For one thing, the basement is where the coal bins were. All the homes in our neighborhood had coal furnaces, and each fall my father would order our winter's supply. Soon a large dump truck would arrive and drop an entire truckload of coal on the street next to the curb in front of our house. Later, a Black man with a shovel and a wheel barrel would magically appear and spend the entire day walking back and forth down our gangway with wheelbarrows full of coal, dumping them through the two ground level windows into the coal bins. Everyone in the neighborhood had these deliveries made about the same time and for weeks, the street and sidewalks would be covered with black coal dust.

Not having an alternative, I brought my reptiles and amphibians into the basement during the winter months, but providing sufficient light and warmth, plus decent ventilation, was always something of a challenge. Then, of course, there were the frequent snake escapes, which typically ended with the escapee being discovered by someone other than me. One of my prized possessions, my gray tree frog from Kroll's Farm, escaped regularly from a terrarium, but he always went to the same spot—my father's workbench, right on top of the cool metal surface of the vice. My father by then was used to all sorts of creatures lurking about and went ahead and used the vice one time to cut a piece of metal while the frog remained steadfastly in place. Neither one seemed to mind the other's presence.

When I was eleven, I was in heaven. We made the big switch from coal to oil. No more coal dust everywhere. No more having to stoke the furnace. Most importantly for me, no need for the coal bins and, thus, extra space that Dad promised me if I would help clean and paint the walls and floor. Additionally, all the old, large, round, tunnel-shaped heating ducts that had been suspended from the basement ceiling were replaced with modern, streamlined, flat and shiny metal raceways. The basement seemed to double in size. Dad installed shelves and provided some folding tables. My new hobby room quickly took shape.

I now had sufficient space for my turtles—painted, map, snapping, soft-shell, mud, and my box turtles (eastern, three-toed, and Florida). My snakes were now neatly lined up in their aquarium/terrariums (garter and smooth green) along with my two Texas horned toads, American chameleons (anoles), my baby American alligator, and my amphibians—the leopard, bull, and gray tree frogs, and my American toads, tiger salamanders, and eastern spotted newts. I displayed my mounted butterflies, moths, and beetles, and maintained my live cocoons in various jars. This became the room I was so proud of. *My* laboratory.

Besides the reptiles I collected or purchased at pet shops, I soon started buying reptiles through mail order. I sent away for additions to my collection from mail order animal dealers that advertised in *Field & Stream* and *Boys Life* magazines. Mom would always be the one to drive me to the Railway Express office to pick up the boxes marked "Live Reptiles." The man there got to know me rather well and telephoned me immediately whenever my shipments came in.

In 1958, I turned twelve and Mom had a birthday party for me. I requested that, if possible, everyone bring a live pet as a present and in addition to acquiring a few more turtles and anoles, I scored a few white mice. My collection just kept expanding.

Of course, there was the matter of feeding everything. I provided my reptiles with a varied assortment of live foods, mainly insects, mealworms, and earthworms. Throughout the summer I'd catch various flying and climbing insects by sweeping my butterfly net through tall grasses, plants, and shrubs. Mealworms were available year-round from the pet stores at a penny apiece. But I soon learned how to raise hundreds of them by setting up a breeding colony in a tub filled with bran, crumpled newspapers, and raw potatoes cut in half.

Earthworms were by far the best protein source for my turtles, and they became the exclusive diet for my garter snakes, too, since I refused to feed frogs to them. After rainfall, I would go out collecting worms but still never had enough. Fortunately, Bobby Detlaff's father used to be an avid fisherman in his earlier years before getting into the hardware business. He had a device that was essentially an electric rod with a wooden handle. By plugging the rod in and pushing it into the ground, you'd produce a mild electrical shock within a roughly thirty-inch radius. If there were any worms in the vicinity, they'd come slithering to the surface. This became my method of harvesting earthworms, at least for a while. I must have depleted the backyard, though, because over time, the numbers of worms slithering to the surface began to decrease dramatically.

Plan B became the Giant Earthworm Company, in El Paso, Texas. I'd seen their ad in a gardening magazine. The Giant Earthworm Company sold in bulk, and I would order all that I needed. Once, I received a letter back from them with a refund. They apologized to "Mr. Krause" and explained that they couldn't fill my order because they had sold out of their giant earthworms for the year. Mom got a chuckle out of the whole thing and hung on to the letter for years.

Alas, the room I'd spent hours in wouldn't last forever.

My mother and father worked hard during my grade school years and eventually saved enough to put a significant down payment on a brand-new house that was being built. The house was due to be completed in the spring of 1960, just before my graduation. It was in a new area of Chicago called Sauganash and moving there meant I wouldn't be attending one of the two high schools that all of my friends would be attending.

My parents tried to convince me that I'd love the move because it was as if we were moving to the country. Our new home bordered a forest preserve with the north branch of the Chicago River passing through it. I was also promised a large portion of the lower level of the house for my reptiles, more space than my basement hobby room. It all sounded great, but of course it was hard thinking about leaving my friends.

Although Mom and Dad were excited about our future new home, it wasn't necessarily an easy time for them. At seventeen, my brother, Tom was getting himself into trouble. A product of the restless times, he wore jeans, black boots, a white t-shirt with a pack of Lucky Strikes rolled up in the sleeve, and, in cooler weather, a black leather jacket. He had tattoos in a time when tattoos were an anti-authority symbol. Tom was the prototypical 1950s, James Dean-type rebel. Naturally, I idolized him, although my parents had a slightly different take on Tom. While Mom tolerated his behavior and made excuses for it, Dad was outwardly unhappy about it. Tom didn't do well in school. He enrolled in Lane Tech, a vocational-technical school to learn a trade but dropped out in his second year. Dad wouldn't allow him to stay home doing nothing and insisted he get a job so he worked at a hamburger joint for a few months before quitting. The tension became bad around the house and Tom ran away a couple of times. I cried when my mother found him sleeping under a neighbor's porch one night.

Eventually, Dad encouraged Tom to enlist in the service. And so, before the new house was complete, Tom joined the Army. But then he went AWOL during basic training with his best friend with whom he'd enlisted. The two were caught in a stolen car in Tennessee and were required to serve six months in a camp for wayward boys in southern Illinois. We all went to visit Tom and even though I was so happy to see him, it was terrible for me to see what my brother was going through.

Mom and Dad moved into our new home while I, once again, stayed with my grandmother for the three months before graduation. I felt the loss thinking of Tom not making it for my graduation, but, to my surprise, they allowed him to attend the ceremony and celebration. Of course he had to return immediately afterward. When Tom finally did come home for good, he still had a difficult time finding himself. He'd come back to a new house in a strange neighborhood. He was turning eighteen now and trying to be independent. He took a few different jobs, but nothing was working out. A year later, however, my mother would open a nightclub/restaurant. Tom would finally find some direction. And as for me, I had new territories to explore.

8

—•—

WORKING MAN

THAT NIGHTCLUB/RESTAURANT MOM OPENED up was actually an existing establishment called Helsings. She left the Hills-McCanna Company in 1960 when we moved to Sauganash and began working for an attorney nearby who had an accounting and law practice firm. But a year later, the attorney passed away. Mom took over the clientele, forming MK Accounting Services. Helsings was one of the clients and the place was doing poorly. When it went into receivership, Mom and Dad decided to buy the assets, bringing in Uncle Sam as an investor.

In its day, Helsings had been a showplace with an elaborate lounge complete with a long and winding leather bar. It had booths and tables, even a balcony, with seating for over a hundred guests. The entire nightclub was centered around a piano bar in front of a full-size stage for entertainment. In addition to a formal dining room, there was a popular coffee shop called Aunt Susie's Kitchen, which was open twenty-four hours a day. Mom and Dad changed the name of the restaurant to The Shores Restaurant, while keeping Aunt Susie's Kitchen as a separate entity. They cleaned it all up, rehired many of the original employees, and, within six weeks, opened the doors. The heavily advertised grand opening not only brought back all the regulars, but new patrons, including curious and sometimes eccentric customers.

This is where Tom found his way. I worked there whenever I could, either as a busboy or organizing the stockrooms or even flipping hamburgers on the grill, while Tom worked full time as a bartender. In just a few weeks he mastered the job perfectly, devising his own ways of learning how to make mixed drinks. That skill, combined with his outgoing, friendly personality made him popular with the customers. He was only eighteen years old, but everyone thought he was a lot older. Tom was rightfully proud of his new occupation.

Unfortunately, the business struggled. A combination of my parents not having the right management in place, and the restaurant's location in a rapidly aging and changing neighborhood would lead to its downfall. I saw the writing on the wall one painful night as I witnessed my accordion teacher, Mr. Totten, getting booed on the stage. My mother had hired him in a last-ditch effort to replace the piano player they could no longer afford. A big family disappointment, the Shores went bankrupt within a year.

By that time, I was well settled into our new home. After graduating from elementary school and leaving all my friends behind in our old neighborhood, I rejoined my family in our new house on Kerbs Avenue. I was new to the neighborhood, with no friends around, so I spent that first summer focusing on my turtles and snakes and building my reptile room in the sub-basement. If I wasn't taking care of my reptiles, I was busy adding to my collection by exploring the LaBaugh Woods Forest Preserve. Our street dead-ended at the forest's edge.

Our section of Kerbs Avenue was a new development that had previously been a landscape nursery. Still standing was an enormous, abandoned greenhouse across the street. Looking for remnants of plant material and other items I could use in my reptile room, I explored the structure and discovered wooden crates of unused glass panes. With the new construction of homes on the street, they were destined to be trashed. I knew the panes, in particular the largest ones, 30-inch by 16-inch, could become the front panels of new snake cages. There was plenty of scrap plywood lying around the construction sites, so I had the raw materials I needed, and I designed a perfect cage. In a month's time, I built six of them. Along with several aquariums and two new galvanized tubs I bought at the hardware store, the snake cages became the main fixtures of my reptile room.

Age 15, with my first kingsnake.

Meanwhile, I found a discarded steel tub that had been used to hand mix cement. This became my pontoon boat to float up and down the river through the woods that summer. It was old, beat-up, and extremely heavy for one person to lug around, but once in the water, and with the help of a long pole, it became a functional means of maneuvering up and down the slow-moving river.

This section of the river, called the North Branch, was totally different from the main branch of the Chicago River that I was accustomed to from exploring the abandoned golf course. The width was only thirty to forty feet, the current was slow and lazy, and there was a noticeable lack of litter. I floated along the North Branch through the forest preserve from the Cicero Avenue bridge all the way east to Foster Avenue where a natural dam terminated my regular excursions. I learned every bend in the river and discovered exactly where I could observe painted and map turtles basking on fallen trees and logs.

There were also several areas in the river where the water flowed into the shoreline, creating a quagmire of substrate that wasn't navigable by foot or by boat. The surface was always covered with leopard frogs hopping in all directions as I would approach. One day, sitting in my tub watching the frogs, I noticed something in the muck slowly moving alongside me. It was completely covered with gook the consistency of oatmeal and I could barely make it out, but as it raised its head and opened its eyes, I could see the outline of a gigantic snapping turtle pushing itself forward. It had to be twice the size of the first ones I saw years earlier in Crivitz, Wisconsin. Then I noticed a second one. Not knowing what I would even do with them, I quickly tried to snag the first, but it wouldn't fit into my net and, worse, the tub almost capsized in the attempt. Alas, I was forced to abandon the catch as they both slowly submerged into the quagmire.

In another spot, there was a fallen tree, half-submerged, which made for some choice turtle-basking spots. At a curve in the tree branch, I thought I identified a large map turtle sunning itself. It was much too large to be my favorite, the midland painted turtle. With my long pole, I slowly pushed myself closer and as I approached, I was excited to see that I was wrong about it being a map turtle. I could tell by its long yellow neck that it was a Blanding's turtle. I had never seen a Blanding's turtle outside of books.

This was not its natural environment and became yet another head-shaking moment for me. Before I could react, the turtle dove into the water without resurfacing, even after a ten-minute wait. On later excursions, I observed this same Blanding's turtle many times on the same log, but I could never get any closer. Why it was there instead of the Blanding's preferred environment of open wetlands remained a mystery.

Then there were times I'd land my tub on a firm piece of embankment and explore the area along the shoreline looking for turtle hatchlings. Again, leopard frogs were everywhere, jumping like popcorn as I made my way through the tall grasses on the shorelines. At the end of each exploration, I took extreme measures to hide my concrete mixing tub. Being too bulky to take back home every day, I'd drag it out of the river near the end of our street and conceal it with piles of leaves and branches. This worked for a few weeks until I was tired of going through the effort. By then, I was thinking that the area itself was a sufficient hiding place, but the disappointing day came when I discovered the tub was gone. I must have searched for it up and down the river for weeks but never found it.

One of my other favorite areas of exploration was in the forest preserve along the railroad tracks of Bryn Mawr Avenue, which bordered the old section of a cemetery. Scattered boards and pieces of flat tin were homes to Dekay's snakes as well as numerous Great Plains garter snakes. All of this was within walking distance of our home.

As my new reptile room was taking shape, I took on chores and jobs around the house to earn money to support my hobby. I cleaned and organized the garage and tried to keep things in order. Once, Dad had me weeding the entire front area of our house. When, shortly afterward, sod was ordered and installed, I realized Dad had been placating me. He tried to convince me that my work had made a difference, but I knew different.

A better opportunity for work soon came along. I was shopping with Mom at Six Corners, and she noticed a help wanted sign in the window of Ono's Gift Shop. Ono's was a large store full of knickknacks, paintings and artwork, statues, carvings, dishes, figurines, ashtrays, glassware, lamps—all the stuff you might see now in garage sales and flea markets. It was owned by a small, quiet-spoken Japanese woman and her American husband.

Mom and I went in to inquire and she did most of the talking. The couple were beginning a complete store renovation by painting all the walls, adding new glass showcases, rearranging all the existing display tables, as well as re-merchandising. In spite of me being underage, the woman hired me on the spot and I started working the very next day. I was thrilled to have my first real job and, at eighty cents an hour, how could I go wrong?

I was to work on weekends only, but in the beginning, I worked many more hours. The owners made me responsible for cleaning and organizing the entire backroom. I worked hard, and within two weeks, it was like a completely different storeroom. I remember my first payroll check was over a hundred dollars for the more than two long weeks I worked. I was in disbelief and learned that day how satisfying it is to earn good wages for hard work. A lesson in capitalism at its best.

The following week, the husband had me accompany him in his step van to their warehouse. Mr. Ono, as I referred to him (although in retrospect I imagine Ono's Gift Shop was named after his Japanese wife), was a tall, gruff fellow. At the warehouse, as he was picking up merchandise, he asked me if I could replicate for the warehouse what I did in the storeroom. Of course, I agreed. On the way back to the store, sitting on the floor of the van holding on for dear life as Mr. Ono swerved through traffic, he told me that he was very pleased with what I had done and gave me a ten-cent raise. I was so proud of advancing my career, now making ninety cents an hour!

Eventually, however, I came to see that my job was becoming something of a hardship for Mom, having to drive me to and from work when I couldn't take the Cicero Avenue bus. I hoped that somehow, we could remedy the situation, but it didn't look promising because I was only fifteen years old and couldn't legally drive. Mom found a solution one day while checking out of the neighborhood IGA grocery store. The store was our neighborhood's go-to place for groceries, fresh meat, and produce. The cashier mentioned the store was in need of a stock boy and was paying $1.10 an hour. It was within walking distance and although I was reluctant to leave my job at Ono's, it made more sense to take the job at IGA. I began by sweeping the floors, cleaning out the restrooms, and stocking the shelves with canned goods. This soon became the job I would have through my high school years, working part time during the week and all day on Saturdays.

But there were many times when I would find myself, as before, with a transportation problem. Von Steuben High was several miles from home and required two bus trips on CTA public transportation to either get home or to the IGA for work. I hitchhiked sometimes, too, but that was never the most dependable way to get anywhere. I decided I needed my own form of transportation, and now that I was earning real money, I felt I could justify it. I had always wanted a motorcycle and Dad showed me a picture in the Sears Roebuck catalog of an Allstate motor scooter. It wasn't exactly what I'd had in mind, but being fifteen years old without a driver's license, I knew I couldn't be picky. Dad got me a discount on it because of his close business relationship with a colleague of his at Sears and soon, I had a brand-new scooter.

I kept working at the IGA, getting an education in retail that I had no idea would become so important to me. Three brothers owned and operated the store and the lessons I would learn from them would end up being priceless.

9

THE WORLD OF RETAIL

THE BROTHERS RANGED IN age from twenty-nine to thirty-seven and they worked well together, each with his own responsibilities. Wally, the oldest, was the butcher—a quiet sort of guy who always smiled as he worked behind the refrigerated glass showcases in the meat department. In those days, there were no prepackaged meats; all the meat was prepared to order. Wally and Ben, their full-time butcher, always gave excellent, personalized service, taking care of the special meat cuttings demanded by customers, and always handling the sometimes-unreasonable requests with a smile. Ben, the old timer in his late fifties, was the jokester with stories galore. I can still see him, cutting and preparing the meat cuts on his gigantic wooden chopping block, an ever-present, saliva-coated, lit Pall Mall cigarette dangling from the side of his mouth.

Eddie was the second brother and the produce manager. He also managed the employees who unloaded trucks, stocked the shelves, and delivered groceries. Eddy had a full-time young fellow working for him whose name was Bill. He was a dependable guy in his early twenties and drove over twenty-five miles each way to work. As hardworking and dedicated as Bill was, he indirectly taught me the importance of an education.

The youngest brother was Tony, who was in charge of the ordering, accounting, finances, banking, and coupon cutting. Tony was the business head of the brothers, always sharply dressed in a white shirt with the sleeves rolled up halfway. Tony walked quickly and you could hear him coming down the aisle from the sound of the cleats on the heels of his dress shoes. Whenever I climbed the stairs up to Tony's makeshift office on the balcony over the cases of pop bottles, either bringing him a cup of coffee or being summoned for some other reason, he took the time to talk to me about my interests. I told him about my turtles and my love of animals, and he talked to me about business in general. If he wasn't figuring out another coupon deal, he was looking at other business opportunities. He talked enthusiastically to me one time about a franchise opportunity. He explained to me what a franchise was and how easily this system allowed people to start a business. He showed me an ad for a McDonalds Hamburger franchise for $30,000. This was in the early sixties when that was a lot of money and McDonalds was still in its infancy.

Marge, in her fifties, short, and with thick glasses, was the full-time cashier and was an amazing, hardworking woman. She performed her duties impeccably and was the face of the store to many customers. How she remembered people's names always impressed me, and being a time before computerized scanning, her memory of prices as she rang them up at the register, especially the unmarked items, was amazing. She ran the entire store front while also managing and coordinating the dairy, snack, and pop vendors. Marge showed me what "multi-tasking" was before I'd ever heard the word. Taking a liking to me, she took the time to teach me a lot and always encouraged me to go out of my way in serving the customers, to be polite and respectful.

The brothers' partnership worked extremely well. I learned the importance of dividing up areas of responsibility, taking pride in your work, and staying the course. I never witnessed any disagreements or arguments. At the time I didn't realize how rare that was.

One day, while on a break, we were sitting on our pop-bottle crates talking. After going out the back door to check on my motor scooter, which I kept chained to a telephone pole, I noticed Eddie acting peculiar. He was in his usual position where he could keep an eye on the customers in the store through an angled wall mirror. The day wasn't very busy and two of our best customers, Mr. and Mrs. Anderson, were in shopping. As they were standing in front of the meat counter waiting for their number to be called, Eddie observed Mr. Anderson sliding a package of Oscar Meyer lunchmeat into his suit pocket. I couldn't believe it. Since Eddy caught him red-handed, I was sure we'd confront Mr. Anderson and get our package of lunchmeat back. But that's not what happened.

Eddie immediately informed Tony who was upstairs doing paperwork and they jumped into action. Eddie casually walked around the butcher counter and whispered to Ben and Wally what Mr. Anderson had done. Tony went up front to the registers, informed Marge, and opened up the second register line. Eddie remained in the produce department. The stage was set. I was told to go back to work and act like nothing happened.

After Mr. and Mrs. Anderson were finished shopping and checked out, I loaded their station wagon with several bags of groceries. After they left, I learned how the problem was solved. The brothers didn't want to lose a good customer by confronting and embarrassing the Andersons. They felt that Mr. Anderson couldn't have put more than two dollars' worth of lunchmeat in his pocket. Ben and Eddy made sure their scales in the butcher and produce departments would weigh the Anderson's purchases a little heavier. Marge made herself busy with other customers and Tony ended up being able to check out the Andersons, adding a number here and there to their total.

What it all amounted to was that the brothers lost no money (the Andersons, saved the embarrassment of being confronted, may have even paid a little more than they otherwise would have) and the store was able to keep a very good customer, even though Mr. Anderson would have to be watched carefully in the future. The lesson I learned was one of resourcefulness and integrity. There are more ways than one to accomplish a task, and I discovered that sometimes you have to make decisions that don't seem to make sense, at least initially. The brothers always had their eyes on the big picture.

When I turned sixteen, my responsibilities grew a little. One of the first things I did after my birthday was get my driver's license. Now I could deliver groceries. Of course the truth came out that I'd only been fifteen when the store hired me, but Marge told me confidentially that everyone knew I was only fifteen anyway.

I loved delivering groceries. The IGA used Wally's 1959 yellow and white Chevrolet station wagon, and on busy Saturdays, I would drive that car to as many as six different stops on each trip from the store. Typically, I'd receive fifty to seventy-five cents in tips on each delivery. I learned that being accommodating in placing the boxes wherever the customer wanted them, and being polite and courteous, paid dividends. But with one customer, being accommodating had its limits. An older female customer persisted in flirting with me. She was a real-life "Mrs. Robinson" and I dreaded having to go to her house. I'd place the groceries on the kitchen counter, thank her with a smile, and exit as fast as possible.

One Saturday, I painfully experienced another lesson while out delivering. I happened to see two of my school girlfriends walking down Kercheval Avenue and in trying to impress them, I scooted up and sat high in the driver's seat with my elbow out the window as I hollered and waved, not at all watching the road. Before I knew it, I rear ended a parked car. Groceries went flying everywhere in the back of the station wagon. I panicked. I got out of the car, picked up a taillight and some car trim, set them on the back of the damaged car, and took off. My foot on the gas pedal wouldn't stop shaking as I finished my delivery route. After I came to my senses, I headed back to the store, trying to figure out what I was going to say and dreading the inevitable consequences. When I walked in the front door, I noticed Marge had a disturbed look on her face. "What happened?" she asked. "What did you do?"

It turned out that the owner of the parked car had seen what had happened from his front window but couldn't get dressed fast enough to catch me. By the time he came out, I had driven away. Of course, it didn't take much for him to figure out it was the IGA station wagon, especially when he saw me, in my white apron, get out and pick up the pieces. By the time I made it back to the store, he was already there talking to Tony in the back room. Tony assured him that the store would pay the damages and take the costs out of my paychecks until paid in full. I was embarrassed and felt terrible that I'd left the scene of an accident. Tony made light of it and handled it with empathy. I was relieved and thankful that the outcome wasn't any worse and happy that I was able to pay for the damages over the next few months.

As involved as I was with my work at the grocery store, I hadn't lost touch with my true passion. I was still expanding my collection of reptiles and learning all I could about them. My hobby did create a problem for my parents, however. We lost a cleaning lady when a harmless ring-necked snake escaped one day and found a place to rest on the lower level of our living room bookshelf. The cleaning lady let out a shriek when she discovered the snake was not, as she had thought, a toy, but rather a real, live snake. That was the last day we saw the cleaning lady.

In 1963, my junior year of high school, the brothers sold the store. The new owners were experienced grocery store owners, and this would be their second location. They immediately started remodeling and upgrading the store. Within six months, the store looked completely different. It was more modern, the old wooden floors were repaired and tiled, new lighting was installed throughout, new fixtures were put in, including an entire aisle of self-serve refrigerator and freezer units. It was like a brand-new store, and even though we all missed Wally, Eddie, and Tony, I observed a new and modern way of retailing.

Soon after, the prices started inching upward and the culture in the store seemed to change. Yes, the new owners had made many improvements, but the place lost its family feel. A few of the employees and even some customers made it known that they weren't happy. Nevertheless, the store was now turning into "big business", and I realized that that was progress. I decided to stay on until just before graduation when I gave my notice.

All in all, with lessons in how there are many different ways to run a business, the IGA helped prepare me for a future that was still years away. I was still in high school, after all, a young man enjoying his youth while making memories that would last a lifetime.

10

LESSONS LEARNED

WHILE I WAS IN high school, my paternal grandmother died, passing away in her sleep. Her death was unexpected. Gram was still active and, in fact, had been in the process of painting the ceiling of her basement the day before her death. It was hard to fathom. My grandmother, who had meant so much to me, was now gone forever. I thought back to her reading *Grimm's Fairy Tales* to me. I thought about helping her break down the corrugated boxes and getting loads of cardboard and scrap metal ready for Uncle Boykin. I remembered the sight of her pulling her Radio Flyer wagon down the street collecting discarded pieces of scrap, and defending her from the kids who knew her only as "the old junk lady." Gram had taught me much.

Soon, there would be another woman in my life. In August of 1961, my friend Ron Ambos introduced me to Marie Alfonso, a girl who had just moved into the neighborhood and would be attending Von Steuben High School with us in September. Ron wanted to be her boyfriend, but, as fortune would have it, things didn't work out for him. Marie and I became the best of friends and started dating. Ron wasn't especially happy about the turn of events, but he accepted it, moved on to another girlfriend, and we all remained friends. I was fifteen years old, and Marie soon became my high school sweetheart. We were inseparable, spending most of our free time together. Marie tolerated my turtle and reptile obsession and even accompanied me on some of my field excursions.

Entering my second year of high school, my obsession continued. I became the aide to Eugene Ray, my biology teacher. Being that he was an avid entomologist, and butterflies, moths, and beetles were a great love of mine, we hit it off from the start. I brought in my Riker specimen mounts to have him critique and drool over, especially the moths I'd hatched from cocoons. Mr. Ray soon developed a lot of confidence in me and more than once he turned the class over to me, excusing himself and leaving the room. (I was allowed in on the secret that whenever he left, it was to satisfy his nicotine addiction in the teacher's lounge.)

Then, during our second semester, Mr. Ray put me in charge of the entire lab in the back of the classroom. He told me to liven it up and make it look interesting. I was excited about the project but as I started uncovering all the filthy, slant-fronted, metal-framed, glass terrariums and display cases amidst the piles of junk, it became clear to me that this was going to be a much bigger assignment than I had thought. The lab counters, tables, and shelves, had been neglected for years.

After inventorying everything, I began cleaning and organizing the terrariums and aquariums, fixing the antiquated piston aquarium pumps, and throwing out anything broken or useless. When the lab started to look like something, I brought in several of my turtles and snakes, along with a few salamanders, frogs, and toads, and I had fellow students donate house plants. We added a tank full of guppies and some crayfish and spiders, along with several jars containing beetle larvae, chrysalises, and cocoons. I cleaned out and organized all of Mr. Ray's storage cabinets and was amazed at the jars of biological specimens that had been left forgotten. There was even a human skull. I donated all my school free time, including study classes, to concentrate on the lab. It took me over two weeks to make it presentable. The results showed and Mr. Ray was well pleased, even though he questioned the large quantity of turtles.

Mr. Ray and I had a unique bond. He could be forgetful and more than once asked me to leave class and drive my motor scooter to a certain butcher shop. He would have me pick up something for his wife to prepare for dinner, having forgotten to go to the shop himself. And at the end of the school year, he let me have that human skull. Years later, when I would leave home for the Army, I would store the skull up in the garage attic. When I came home it was gone and I never did learn what happened to it.

That motor scooter, by the way, served me well and I even used it to take Marie out on dates, one time even into downtown Chicago to see a movie. At the time, we didn't fully realize the dangers of riding down the expressway, especially with Marie riding side saddle in her skirt. But the scooter soon made way for another means of transportation: my first car. The year was 1963 and I was now seventeen. My grandfather always traded his cars in every six or seven years and his 1956 Pontiac with low mileage was in line to be traded in for a new model. I bought it from him for $600, the exact amount the dealer was going to give him credit for.

Having a car opened up many new possibilities. I was now able to explore different areas and neighborhoods which, among other things, exposed me to several new pet stores. I was always on the lookout for them. Instead of hanging out with friends doing nothing, I spent my time finding these stores and if I was out with friends going somewhere, it was not uncommon for me to pull into a pet shop I hadn't noticed before.

Somewhere along the line, I came to understand how economical Volkswagens could be. I handed the Pontiac over to my brother and bought myself a brand-new beetle for $1,750, putting $1,000 down while making monthly payments of $45 on the balance. Late one Saturday night in my senior year, I was out in my new Beetle with my friend Bill Mazurek. We'd just left the Pie Pan Restaurant, our neighborhood hangout, for a joyride and we came upon a Cadillac with Vogue whitewall tires parked in an open garage. I'd always wanted a set of Vogues for my Pontiac. With limited space in my Volkswagen, we drove home and jumped into the Pontiac, which my brother had been using earlier in the evening. We returned to where the Cadillac was, parked down the street, and walked to the garage.

Soon, against all reason, we were jacking up the Cadillac to swipe the tires. To this day, I cannot understand how or why I could make such a stupid decision. As we were in the process of spinning the lug nuts, another car pulled up and the driver saw what we were doing. We bolted for my car and sped off. A close call, I thought, but we'd gotten away. I dropped Bill off, went home, where everyone was asleep, parked the Pontiac, and went to bed.

Not long afterward, the doorbell rang, and I heard Mom going downstairs. When she opened the door, she was greeted by two plainclothes detectives who explained that my Pontiac was at the scene of a crime. It turns out the person who had seen us trying to take the Cadillac tires had jotted down my license plate number. Naturally, Mom and Dad woke up Tom assuming he had once again been up to no good.

As Tom was adamantly denying any involvement and the cops were preparing to take him to the police station, I poked my head out of my room and came clean. *"It wasn't Tom, it was me,"* I called out. The next thing I knew, I was in the squad car where I spilled the beans and told the cops who my partner in crime had been. Then we drove to Bill's house, picked him up, and headed for the police station. Now, as it happened, Bill's father was a police captain and was on duty that night. He talked to us and then arranged a meeting with the owner of the Cadillac. When Bill and I met with him, we apologized profusely. I took full responsibility and agreed to any financial restitution. It was a lesson learned and a huge relief to know that no criminal charges were going to be filed.

In the meantime, Tom seemed to be finding himself, and, in becoming more independent, especially in his career as a mixologist, decided he wanted a place of his own. He had just turned twenty that year and found himself a small, third-floor apartment. As I helped Tom load his stuff into the trunk of his car, I felt totally lost contemplating life without the brother that had always been there for me.

Tom would do well. A year later, he secured a bartending position at one of Chicagoland's premier nightclubs, Mr. Kelly's on Rush Street. He took care of some rather well-heeled clients and rubbed shoulders with famous stand-up comedians and entertainers. Tom enjoyed the lifestyle.

Soon, he would marry. He and his high school sweetheart, Barbara, would have a son before ultimately getting divorced. Tom would then marry Pauline and have three more children. Years later he would work as a bartender at DiLeo's Restaurant on Elston Avenue, try his luck as a part-time undercover store detective for Goldblatts department store, and, finally at age thirty-one, get himself a sweet position as a bartender for the famous Johnny Held's Brown Bear German Restaurant on Ashland Avenue.

Meanwhile, I had my own path to discover. The only problem was that I didn't have a clue as to where that path was, or, once found, where on earth it would lead.

11

DIRECTION

IN MY LAST YEAR of high school, after leaving my job at the grocery store, I began working evenings and weekends at the Standard gas station where one of my best friends, Ray Dreifuss, worked. These were the days when attendants pumped gas for customers, as well as performed other services like checking their oil or cleaning their windshields.

I was nearing the point in my life where I had to start making some serious decisions but, for the most part, I was on my own with this. My parents were from the old school where you worked hard to eke out a good life and, as a result, they didn't encourage me to pursue education beyond high school. I felt that going to college was the right thing for me, but what would come beyond that? What would I study? What would I do? Finally, I decided to enroll in Wright Junior College to test the waters and get my bearings.

But I hated it. I had no direction and no idea as to what direction to take. I dropped out during the second semester and went to work full time at the gas station.

I was now eighteen years old and lost. One day, still looking for clues as to which way to go, I thought my prayers had been answered. I was at Bill Mazurek's house, and I noticed several documents and papers scattered all over the kitchen table. Turns out that Bill's mother, Margo, was involved in a start-up oil well business in southern Illinois with several other investors. They were about to close on another deal and were finalizing the recruitment of a few more potential shareholders. I was intrigued. I asked Margo if I could get involved and she gave me some information to take home to review. I read the material closely, learned the risks involved, and then talked to Dad and Mom about taking the chance. Both discouraged me, but I forged ahead, taking $650 out of my savings account, and buying two 1/64th shares in the Taylorville, Illinois Scholles Oil Well project.

The drilling began later that year and in April of 1965, we struck oil. My head was swimming with dreams of becoming rich. Part owner of an oil well. At eighteen! I drove to Taylorville one weekend with Marie, and Tom and Tom's wife to actually see and even touch my oil well. We took turns taking photos of us opening and closing the relief valve as it sprayed oil all over our hands.

Reality set in upon receipt of my first check: $103.31 for the initial production from May through September of that year. Every monthly check for the next eighteen months was between $14 and $3.55, dwindling a little more each time until the well was finally shut down. I never recovered my initial investment, but I learned a lot from the experience; namely that nothing comes risk-free.

At the gas station, I kept chugging along, but I started thinking about getting some type of sales position. My father was in sales, and it appeared to have served him well. I had heard success stories from those who had worked for the Fuller Brush Company and, while still working at the gas station, I attended a Fuller Brush-sponsored class, learning the policies and techniques of Fuller Brush door-to-door selling.

Everyone in those days was familiar with the Fuller Brush Man. As the name implies, the company got its start selling brushes of all sorts, but then blossomed into a kitchen gadget supplier. The door-to-door business model wouldn't work today as Fuller's customers in that era were stay-at-home housewives. All of the sales were made by salesmen like me, dressed in white shirts, wearing ties, and carrying our deep, square briefcases full of samples and literature, plus several vegetable and pastry brushes we used as giveaways.

Still working at the gas station, I began what I was hoping to be my new career. I drew out a map and established my own sales route in the territory they gave me. In the class, I'd been taught to always knock on the back door and announce your presence with that familiar phrase, *"Fuller Brush Man!"*

Being that there were many apartment buildings in my territory, I felt that there was a wealth of potential sales all within close proximity. I'd been taught a unique and clever selling technique. Once I announced that familiar phrase, I told the customer I was only stopping by to drop off a free sample as I waved both a vegetable and pastry brush. When the prospective customer reached through the half-open screen door for the one she wanted, I would say, *"Hold on a minute—let me get you a fresh, clean one."* This gave me time to open my briefcase and rummage through all of the samples, all the while talking about the special items.

Even though I was pretty good at closing sales, the job ran its course. I quickly learned that door-to-door selling of Fuller brushes was never designed to be a long-term career for most people. The days were long and tiring, and one can only take so many doors being closed in one's face. Meanwhile, my father was nudging me toward finding a serious career. It was now 1965 and I'd been out of high school long enough to have at least established a direction. Dad kept talking about computers. It was the next big field, he said. The wave of the future. There were trade schools that specialized in data processing and computer programming. Maybe that's a direction to go, he suggested.

Without any serious alternatives, and while still working as many hours as possible at the gas station, I enrolled in a six-month Cobol programming course at Computer Business Institute on Wabash Avenue in downtown Chicago. I did well in class and enjoyed learning all about the growing new field of computers. The school had a placement service and upon graduation they arranged an interview for me with the manager of the United States Steel Corporation's data processing center on Lasalle Street. The manager was impressed with how well I did in my classes, but it was only after glancing at my hands that he determined that I had the kind of work ethic the job required. After that, I was hired on the spot. Though it had served me well, never more would I hold a job like the one I'd had at the gas station where my place in life was defined by my dirty fingernails. Again, I ran out and bought two new white shirts and a couple of ties. I had a direction in life now. I was a computer professional.

All this time, an interesting development had been taking place within our family. While I had been trying to find a direction in my life, my parents had been trying to have another child. After a few mishaps, my mother became pregnant and on January 9, 1966, my sister, Mari-Lynn, was born to everyone's delight. I had always been the youngest of the family until that moment. Almost twenty years later, I was the youngest no more.

Everything was going well in the early months of 1966. But then came another interesting development, this one not so delightful. I came home from work one day to find a letter: *Greetings from the US Government.* I was about to be spun in another direction and my future was going to have to wait. As it turned out, I'd been drafted into the United States Army, and during an especially turbulent time in American history—a period of time that included a war in a far-off place called Vietnam.

12

ARMY MAN

MY BOSS AT US Steel made every attempt possible to assist me in applying for a draft exemption, even sending a letter to the draft board explaining US Steel's involvement in the war effort and my important position in the company. All attempts were in vain.

In 1966, the Vietnam War was in full swing. Thousands of eighteen to twenty-year-old men were being drafted and sent there. I had already lost two close friends, and everyone was deathly afraid of the monthly draft calls. Many of my friends were talking about moving to Canada or dodging the draft in other ways. As tenuous as I felt my grip now was on my future, I couldn't see myself as a draft-dodger. Marie and I had talked about getting married someday and even became engaged, but wedding plans would have to wait. A few short weeks after my draft notice, I found myself saying goodbye to her and my family and boarding a train to Fort Leonard Wood in Missouri.

I handled basic training all right—the marching, the running, the buzz cuts, the yes sirs, the no sirs, the waiting, the standing at attention, the polishing, the cleaning, the making your bunk the right way, the KP, and all the physical and weapon training that went along with it. But then came the anticipation and anxiety of what came after. Orders started to be announced during morning roll calls. Numbers were assigned. Low num-

71

bers meant you were most definitely going to AIT—Advanced Infantry Training, and then off to Vietnam. Higher numbers indicated that you were, perhaps, going to be driving a truck or taking some other supporting role. Even higher numbers meant you might be one of the lucky ones assigned to an office job.

Slowly but surely, during roll call each morning, everyone's orders were announced. Everyone's but mine. Then one morning, the corporal got in my face and yelled, *"Krause, what does your father do?!"*

"He's a freight agent for the Canadian Pacific Railroad, Sir!"

The corporal walked away, leaving me perplexed. After thinking about his question, I realized it could have meant only one thing. He had received my orders and knew I had a high number. He must have thought that someone of influence had pulled some strings somewhere, hence, the question about my father. Obviously, he didn't care for that and, as a result, decided that he wasn't going to give me my orders until the very last day, letting me sweat it out the whole time.

The next day, one of my friends suggested I could find out what my orders were in the administration office. I went there immediately where the PFC clerk in charge took my military ID number and looked my orders up. It took him only seconds, but it seemed like minutes. Finally, he said, *"74E20."*

"What's that mean?" I asked.

"Computer programmer/operator," he replied. "You're being assigned to the US Army Office of the Joint Chiefs of Staff in the Pentagon, Washington DC." It was an out-of-body feeling I experienced at that moment, a lightness that came over me that I had never felt in my whole life. And yet, the feeling was tempered when I stopped to think of so many of the guys assigned to AIT, eventually to be sent to the jungles and rice paddies of Vietnam.

When I finally received my official orders, it again hit me why my corporal acted the way he did. I not only had the best orders anyone could have hoped for, but I was allowed to go home on an unheard-of, two-week leave before reporting to Washington, DC.

Commencement was at the end of September and just two days before the ceremony, to get the last punch, our sergeant ordered one last buzz cut for everyone. Marie and my parents attended the commencement and together we all happily drove back home to Chicago. I had to pinch myself repeatedly to make sure I wasn't dreaming. I thanked God many times over for the hand I'd been dealt. My "MOS" number "74E20" was etched into my brain, a number I have never forgotten. I came back home with Marie and my family when just two months earlier, my future was ominous and uncertain.

In fact, Marie and I now decided to get married. She would join me in DC, and we could rent an apartment. The only problem was, I was not yet twenty-one. I needed parental approval and Dad refused, thinking me too young to be married. The wedding would have to wait. We made plans to get married the following July after my twenty-first birthday, and I took off for DC with the Volkswagen loaded up with all my stuff, grateful that I hadn't been able to sell the car before I'd reported to basic training.

My destination was Fort Myer Army base in Arlington, Virginia, close to my new place of work: the Pentagon. At Fort Myer, I shared a room in the barracks with two other guys. At the Pentagon, I worked in the "War Room," sharing the same offices that many of the US Army's top brass frequented, including General William Westmoreland himself, commander of US forces in Vietnam.

I worked the midnight to 8 a.m. shift, processing daily reports for TARCOM, The Army Command Center. TARCOM monitored all military movements throughout the world, wherever there were hot spots. An extension of the Joint Chiefs of Staff, this included Army, Marine, Navy, Air Force, and Coast Guard. Our department received information from every conceivable area of disturbance. Most of the information at this time, of course, was coming to us from Vietnam and other points in Southeast Asia.

I had a temporary security clearance which allowed entrance into most areas until my final Top Secret security clearance came through. They investigated me thoroughly and it dawned on me how fortunate it was that I hadn't had that foolish Vogue tire incident put on my record.

After my shifts, I would take my time returning to the barracks, waiting until the morning rush had subsided as I strolled the waterways around the Jefferson Memorial looking for turtles basking on the embankments. I learned how to fish for carp there, too. I befriended an old gentleman who I saw every morning in his regular spot, his own personal living space where he had his fishing gear, buckets, and all his paraphernalia. He showed me how to make dough balls that he used for bait and sometimes he shared his smoked carp lunch with me.

When my TS security clearance was finalized, they sent me to St. Paul, Minnesota to attend a six-week UNIVAC defense system computer training class. Then it was back to the Pentagon where I started working the day shift. Around this time, I discovered that it was acceptable to seek outside, part-time employment and I took a job at IBMI, a computer service bureau close by. I also found myself a nice one-bedroom apartment on Quebec Street in Arlington, Virginia. Moving off post was inspirational. I bought an aquarium set-up, a used bedroom set, a used dinette set, and living room chairs. Marie would eventually join me there and we decided to buy a brand-new, orange pull-out sofa bed in anticipation of out-of-town guests.

Of course, I hadn't lost my interest in turtles or reptiles. If I wasn't on duty in the Pentagon or working at IBMI, I would often drive out to rural areas exploring. I came across a town by the name of Herndon, Virginia, which back then was pretty small, and it was there that I discovered a lot of unpaved side roads that meandered through the countryside. One day while seeking old, abandoned farms and other ideal herping sites, I encountered a beautiful eastern box turtle sunning himself on the shoulder of one of the red dirt roads. I soon discovered a second one and then a third. The area turned out to be an ideal habitat for the box turtles. I learned that the best times to find them were on warm sunny afternoons, right after a rainfall. I came to recognize the same ones in the same areas. No two were alike but they all had beautiful orange and yellow patterns over an earth-colored background. Once I discovered one with a badly cracked carapace and in seeing this poor soul in the same area over and over again, I came to understand how resilient turtles are. Many times, I would see him seeking nature's healing expertise by remaining almost completely covered in the same exact spot alongside the roadside ditch. Box turtles were common at the time and not a conservation concern. I would sometimes sell them to a pet shop in Falls Church for two dollars each, once trading five of them for another aquarium.

In late June, I traveled back to Chicago for the small wedding that Marie and I had planned at Sauganash Community Church. Marie's entire family was there. Mom and Tom were both there, as well my grandparents. All our friends from Sauganash and several from the old neighborhood attended, too. The only one not in attendance that day was Dad. I was in disbelief that not only did my father refuse to be involved in my wedding, but he also refused to even attend. I chalked it up, as I always had in the past, to the fact that he was just a stubborn German. Years later, I would reflect on this incident as I came to learn more about my father. But at the time, all I could do for retribution was ensure that the wedding procession, horns blaring, drove by my parents' house after the ceremony where my father was neatly tucked inside.

Marie and I honeymooned in the Bahamas. It was wonderful except for two things that stand out in my mind to this day. The first was the sheer number of mange-ridden feral dogs wandering the streets. The second was watching all the fishermen coming into the docks with boatloads of sea turtles flipped over on their backs. Back then, harvesting sea turtles was an accepted practice but to actually witness them being butchered while their heads and legs were flailing back and forth made me sick. I'm glad I'll never see that again.

We returned to DC and Marie was happy to see our new apartment. Right away, she found a job in a real estate office in Fairfax, Virginia. I couldn't wait to get back to my red dirt roads. I took Marie with me once but, as much as she appreciated my insatiable pastime, she didn't quite share the passion. I would often bring one or two of the choicest box turtles home with me, enjoying their behavior for a few days, then take them back and release them on the same dirt roads I found them. One beautifully marked male box turtle had a very outgoing personality and followed us everywhere in the apartment. We named him Oscar and kept him as our pet.

Meanwhile, Marie and I made friends (of the human variety), hosted get-togethers, entertained guests, and took weekend trips to Ocean City, Maryland. These were good times. I excelled in my position in the Pentagon and in October of '67, I achieved the rank of Specialist E5 (Sargent), taking only fifteen months of service to do it. I was proud of myself, and with my salary from both jobs and Marie's income, we were able to continue saving for our unknown future. That future was slated to begin in July of 1968 when my service with the US Army would come to an end.

The year 1968 was an active one for me, and for the country, with two especially solemn days that I would never forget. On April 4, Martin Luther King Jr. was assassinated. President Lyndon Baines Johnson addressed the Joint Chiefs of Staff in an effort to instill calm but the tension in the War Room was palpable. There were riots in cities across the country and these became additional "hot spots" which we began to monitor for several weeks—hot spots in our own country. The additional brass we had to answer to made our jobs even more difficult and the pressure placed on everyone was obvious. Then on June 6, Bobby Kennedy was assassinated. I attended the funeral in Arlington Park National Cemetery, wondering at the shaky state of our nation.

A month later, I received my honorable discharge. Marie had gone back to Chicago ahead of me to find an apartment and return to the job she'd had before. Now it was time for me to leave. I said goodbye to all my friends at the Pentagon and the apartment on Quebec Street, loaded my clothes and Oscar into the new Oldsmobile Cutlass I'd traded the Beetle in on, and headed home.

The Vietnam War era was one of the most difficult times in our nation's history. I was grateful that I was able to learn so much during this period of my life and even more so that I was able to do so without the personal suffering that so many of my fellow soldiers endured overseas. My two years in the Army gave me independence and a life structure that I would continue to build on.

13

—·—

THE BEGINNINGS

BACK IN CHICAGO, MARIE had found us a clean, well-kept apartment on the second floor of a brick two-flat on the northwest side of the city. We settled in and I started looking for a job, quickly finding a well-paying position as a computer programmer/operator for Greyhound Computer Corporation, a subsidiary of the Greyhound Armor Dial Corporation.

Initially, we enjoyed our apartment, but soon began to realize that moving there was a mistake. The landlord and his family lived on the first floor, and they noticed every move we made. We had no privacy whatsoever. We couldn't play music because it was always too loud. We had no parties and few get-togethers. We found ourselves living on pins and needles, even whispering to each other at times.

As soon as our one-year lease was up in 1969, we moved into another second-floor apartment, this one facing a large park consisting of several mature hardwood trees. This is where, for the first time, I witnessed a monarch butterfly migration stopover. I was awestruck. The tree branches weren't even recognizable. They were loaded with thousands upon thousands of monarch butterflies, all clinging to each other. Many were fluttering to find a roost while most were resting and slowly moving their wings. It was an exhilarating sight to behold.

My job at Greyhound required me to start working evenings to get as much computer time as possible for the jobs I was assigned. One evening, I was running a very long COBOL program on one of their IBM 360 computers. I usually had a book on reptiles or turtles on hand during these time spans, my favorite being Dr. Peter Pritchard's *"Living Turtles of The World,"* which I had read cover to cover several times. But on this particular evening, I picked up a *Wall Street Journal* and started scanning the classifieds.

One ad caught my eye: franchisees were being sought for a retail pet center chain by the name of Docktor Pet Centers. Intrigued, I contacted them for information and learned that with an investment of approximately $50,000, I could own a turnkey operation that would include all fixtures, aquariums, cages, racks, cash registers, and a reasonable inventory of products and pets. They'd also provide training and manuals.

Shortly afterwards, I spoke to Ray Dreifuss, whom I had kept in touch with. Ray had just received his CPA degree and didn't like the job he'd taken at a large accounting firm. He wanted more. With his past experience at the Standard gas station where we'd both worked, he was planning to someday buy and run a service station of his own. Ray liked my enthusiasm about the pet business opportunity, and he knew well of my experience with reptiles, tropical fish, and other animals. He'd been with me many times when I'd swerve into the parking lot of a pet store just to pop in and have a look.

I reminded Ray that the retail pet industry was full of mom-and-pop stores run by people who seemed to lack the expertise to operate really successful businesses. These were folks who might have had that passion for a specific animal and decided to try to make a business out of it. Essentially, they just moved their aquariums and cages from their basements or garages to storefronts down the street. They'd hang up signs and, poof, they were pet shop operators. Most drove their businesses by the sale of their live animals rather than the supplies and as a result, many didn't survive very long. The smarter ones learned that the tropical fish, parakeets, cockatiels, reptiles, and small animals were what brought the people through the door, but the added sales of aquariums, cages, food, and supplies were what were necessary to stay in business.

It didn't dawn on me back then, but in time I would come to realize that because of my experiences (my newspaper route, my job at the gift store, the grocery store, my investment in an oil well, my work at the service station, my selling of Fuller Brushes), I'd become a bona fide entrepreneur. Or maybe I was born an entrepreneur and that's what had led to those particular experiences. Either way, I'm sure that at the time I didn't know what the word truly meant. But I knew, and Ray agreed, that together we could succeed in the pet shop marketplace. Ray would take care of the accounting and I would be the animal husbandry expert. We'd learn the rest.

Ray and I flew to Pennsylvania to meet with the franchise director and were very impressed with the organization's professionalism and expertise, something foreign to many in the retail pet industry. The Docktor concept was totally new in that the store designs were highly professional, with customized display fixtures for both the product and the pets. With the pets kept in separate, glass-enclosed show rooms, the odors were kept to a minimum. The business model included a store size of approximately 2,800 square feet located in either a strip shopping center or a regional mall, both of which would be dependent on one or more anchor stores.

Docktor Pet Centers trained their prospective franchisees in many facets of retail operation, but I found myself feeling uncomfortable about their selling techniques. They emphasized the importance of training the store employees to "sell, sell, sell." They performed a role-play demonstration for us with a customer entering the store with a question about their dog's excessive shedding. After asking a few questions the employee recommended coat conditioners and shampoos while going over to the brush display and ripping open a blister-packaged slicker brush, demonstrating its usage. The idea was that, rather than having a slicker brush always available for demonstration purposes, the customer, seeing that the packaging had been destroyed for his or her benefit, would now feel obligated to buy it. This seemed dishonest to me.

The company was formed by two brothers, Milton and Norman Docktor. We later learned quite a bit about them. It turned out that they were instrumental in upgrading the image of the pet shop from the untidy, poorly merchandised mom-and-pop store, to the clean, professionally run establishment that offered quality pets and professional advice. But as their franchise business grew, the brothers disagreed about the direction of the business. Norman wanted to focus exclusively on the big-ticket items: puppies and their related supplies and accessories. Milton believed in the full line concept, offering everything from tropical fish, birds, and reptiles to small animals including puppies and kittens. In the end, the brothers went their separate ways, Milton continuing with the Docktor concept and Norman taking the purebred puppy route by starting a new franchise business called Puppy Palace.

Docktor had been opening franchises on the east coast and was beginning to penetrate the Midwest. They had just opened their first franchise store in the Chicago area, in Niles, a northern suburb, and they were keen to add additional franchise locations in the Chicago market. Ray and I were given the royal treatment. They pushed us a little to make a commitment, but we made it clear that we were not in a position to sign anything. We were on a fact-finding mission, looking to take as much information back home with us as we could before deciding. After filling our briefcases with colorful brochures, literature, notebooks, and a blank contract, we left, advising them that we'd get back to them with either more questions or a decision.

Back home, all the literature and documentation were spread out over my dining room table for a week. I weighed the pros and cons of getting involved in a franchise. Certainly, it simplified the process. But eventually, I came to realize that what Ray and I would be buying was, essentially, nothing more than a job, subject to the requirements and procedures of Docktor Pet Centers. And not a nine-to-five job either. I knew the shop would be open seventy hours per week minimum, plus the hours before and after for cleaning, doing the banking and bookwork, ordering, contacting vendors, and everything else inherent in running a store. Of course, we'd need to be open when people were shopping, and that meant evenings and weekends. All this and then pay a 7 percent royalty to Docktor forever.

I also realized that I wanted to do things differently. I embraced their modern, clean, professional approach, but I wanted to offer so much more than what could be offered within the limits of a 2,800-square-foot store. I had a vision that couldn't be squeezed into such a small space. I made up my mind: if I was going to sacrifice my personal life with this big a commitment, I was going to do it on my own terms.

I called Ray and told him that I wasn't going to sign the franchise contract but that I still wanted to get into the pet industry and do it better than anybody else was doing it at the time. I explained my ideas and we agreed that we would still become partners, but in a completely new concept.

I kept my job at Greyhound while working on my strategy of opening a monumentally sized, state-of-the art department store for pets. Late at night, running long jobs on the computer, I jotted down idea upon idea and drew sketches of my dream pet store on keypunch cards that I began putting in an idea file. I drew fifteen different layouts, eventually coming up with a store with four major departments: puppy, bird, fish, and reptile/small animal. Slowly but surely, it started to come together. I was determined to open a professionally designed and operated retail pet center the likes of which had never been seen before.

The store would be enormous in size and occupy ten to fifteen thousand square feet of well-lit, highly ventilated retail space. Each department would be operated by one of four experienced managers who would focus on the care and sales of their individual department including all of the related supplies. Now my dining room table was filled with files, notes, designs, newspaper articles, and advertisements all relating to my new concept. I had a three-ring binder bursting with details that would soon become a makeshift business plan. I was obsessed. I couldn't do anything but talk, dream, and research the pet business.

Of course, there was the matter of financing. By then, I'd become good friends at Greyhound with a fellow employee by the name of Orlando Martinez, a very determined young man who I admired greatly. He had emigrated from Cuba two years earlier and also aspired to someday start a business. Among the several ideas he had, the one he would finally pursue would be the importing of casual footwear from South America. We shared many ideas on starting a business and he explained to me something very important: how to seek financing by putting a presentation together and approaching a loan officer of a bank. And I had a big edge. Since I was in the service, I was eligible to receive a Small Business Administration (SBA) secured loan.

My mind was made up; I couldn't wait to get into the pet business and open up my pet shop. I already had the tag line. I'd scribbled it down on one of those keypunch cards: *"The World's Largest Pet Center."*

14

— · —

LEARNING, EXPLORING, PREPARING

IN THE 1960S, RESOURCES on how to get into a specific business weren't available like they are today. If you didn't work your way up in the respective industry and learn it over time through experience, you had few sources of information to draw upon. Today, there are courses, college and otherwise, that provide the basics, as well as advanced teachings in just about every field of business. Information is readily available online through a Google search or by consulting Wikipedia. Not only is knowledge available, you can become overloaded with it in a hurry.

Absent these modern conveniences, how was a guy like me to get started in the pet shop business? Well, I used what I had. Back then, the *Yellow Pages* business directory was a decent resource. I found several companies and wrote to them requesting information about their products or services. One thing I learned was that every major market in the United States had one, if not more, pet product wholesalers servicing pet stores with merchandise from various manufacturers. Most of these wholesalers specialized, some concentrating on products for tropical fish, some primarily dog and cat accessories, others focusing on bulk foods and bedding.

I found the names of several wholesalers in the Chicago market and began accumulating as much information as I could about their products. Ultimately, I set up appointments to visit three of them, seeing what services they provided and how they might fit in with my ideas for a store. Auburndale Goldfish Company was the first. Located in the heart of Chicago, they had an extensive live fish department and specialized exclusively in aquatic accessories. The owner, James Snyder, was an old-time goldfish enthusiast who had turned his passion into a successful business. Mr. Snyder introduced me to his son, Jim Jr., and we hit it off immediately. He was around my age, and he took me into his office where we discussed the pet business and my plans to open an unprecedented type of store. I'm not sure if he believed in my vision but it really didn't matter; I couldn't take my eyes off of the ornate, antique Jewel aquarium sitting behind him.

The second wholesaler was Suwannee Water Gardens. Suwannee was also an aquatic specialist carrying tropical fish and goldfish. They were focused on a niche that included pond products, aquatic plants, and live birds. I was surprised to see an immense nest of escaped quaker parrots on the telephone pole in the alley behind their store, a clear indication of either improper bird handling or an unfortunate massive escape during the uncrating of a shipment. Either way, it was probably the only excitement the unfortunate neighborhood residents had known. Suwannee happened to be in a deteriorating neighborhood just west of downtown on the edge of what we called skid row, where the streets were full of individuals who had succumbed to either alcohol, drugs, or mental illness. The business was being run out of a building that should have been torn down years earlier, a contributing factor to its slow deterioration being the constant moisture and humidity created by the ponds of fish, along with the gigantic tropical trees in the front windows that had overgrown their intended containers and were now growing through the creaky, old wooden floors and on into the basement. I had no interest in going down the rickety wooden stairs, but they were proud of their filtration system and insisted on showing me its operation. We descended the narrow stairway and the water dripping from above and the tree roots clinging to the walls made me feel like I was entering a damp, dark cave. It was pretty cool to see an actual jungle growing inside a building in the heart of downtown Chicago, but I left knowing that Suwannee was in the process of going out of business; they just didn't know it yet.

Pioneer Pet Supply was a totally different experience. They were minutes away from O'Hare Airport, which gave them a convenient business location. At the time, Pioneer Pet was the number one wholesaler in the Midwest, offering an extensive array of pet products and accessories. They had a professional sales department, a large warehouse full of merchandise for every pet imaginable, and a tropical fish room. Their fleet of delivery trucks in the parking lot was a sign that they were ramped up for business. My appointment was with a couple of different salespeople, one of whom was the son of Giff Gardner, the president of the company. I was impressed with their presentation and left with a three-ring-binder catalog along with brochures from different manufacturers. I knew for sure that I'd be doing business with Pioneer.

Another valuable source of information was Kroch's & Brentano's, the largest bookstore in downtown Chicago. Before going home after working all night at Greyhound Computer, I would often visit this store and purchase books about everything from opening a business to books on dogs, birds, tropical fish, and every other pet. It was there that I discovered that the SBA had free booklets available on starting a business including one on *Opening a Pet Store*. What a letdown it turned out to be, somewhat informative but so basic and outdated that it was actually humorous.

When Marie returned home from work each day I would be just waking up. I would spend the entire evening, after dinner and before I left for work at 10:30 p.m., at the dining room table studying the various aspects of the pet business. I continually reviewed all the information I had been gathering. I set up files for store fixture companies, office supplies, printing companies, cash register and pricing machine suppliers, air filter and security companies, outdoor signage companies, kennel fabricators, and numerous aquarium and pet product manufacturers and wholesalers. I cut out every pet store advertisement I saw in the newspapers to keep me current on the market. I continued to build my contact list of animal, reptile, bird, and tropical fish suppliers, making new contacts with local puppy breeders as well as live animal and bird suppliers in Florida and California. I would never have thought that opening a business would have become such a long and arduous process.

As my insatiable quest for learning continued, I heard of a new pet shop that had opened in the far Northshore suburb of Evanston: Reptile Ranch, an exclusive reptile store, something never heard of before and most definitely ahead of its time. I couldn't wait to check it out. The owner was an importer/enthusiast by the name of Micky Jacobson. Micky previously worked at two other pet stores running their reptile departments and had finally broken out on his own. The store was unbelievable. It had an extensive assortment of reptiles, amphibians, and assorted arachnids. It appeared that he had the ability to acquire almost anything, from the common to the rare. He inventoried countless species of snakes, iguanas, and lizards, along with turtles and tortoises from around the world. I had never seen so many gopher, leopard, and star tortoises in one place. Micky had hatchling aquatic turtles of all kinds, including a very rare bog turtle. He had retrofitted a fish rack to accommodate aquariums, cages, and various containers. Everywhere you turned there were tubs and enclosures filled with everything imaginable—more and more reptiles, amphibians, tarantulas, and scorpions. Seeing an overcrowded tub of frogs, I felt like I was in an Asian grocery store in Chicago's Chinatown.

But I'll tell you, I was in heaven. The store was amazing. Not to mention what an interesting guy Micky was. He was extremely knowledgeable about every kind of reptile, and it was obvious he had a passion for them. But the sad thing was that even I, with no personal experience operating a store, could see that he lacked the expertise to operate a retail pet store successfully. The place was a mess. With the volume of critters he had, it was impossible to take care of them properly, let alone decorate any of the enclosures so that you could demonstrate proper husbandry to the customers. And seeing that there were very few products for sale made it obvious that he was only concerned with the selling of the animals. I later learned that he ended up closing the store and moving to Tucson, Arizona where he pursued his passion by importing and wholesaling reptiles to dealers nationwide.

As time moved on, I felt the need to start acquiring several other types of pets, not only to enjoy, but to learn the hands-on specifics of their care. In the small apartment we were living in, I already had Oscar, my eastern box turtle from Herndon, Virginia, along with Beu and Franklin, two doxies Marie and I had adopted. Over the years I'd always maintained aquariums of tropical fish, but I wanted the experience of raising piranhas. I bought a 100-gallon aquarium set-up from C & A Aquarium Company in Bensenville, Illinois, a company I had found in the *Yellow Pages*. I bought several small, red-bellied piranhas and watched as they grew enormous in size. They were hearty fish, even surviving an explosive leak in the aquarium that soaked our downstairs neighbor's dining room.

While I already had an extensive reptile background, I needed to learn as much as I could about caged birds. I studied every book I could find on raising parakeets, finches, parrots, and other birds. I'd kept parakeets in the past but had never owned a large parrot. I answered an ad in the local paper and purchased a talking "bronco" double yellow-head Amazon parrot with cage. A bronco is an adult parrot that has never been tamed, and if you're not careful, they'll bite the hell out of you. "Crackers" had a great vocabulary, repeating "Hello," "How are you," "I love you," and his name. Plus, he could cry like a baby or laugh out loud. Very loud. Through a lot of devoted time, bloody fingers, and scratched arms on my part, Crackers eventually became wonderfully affectionate and would ultimately go on to become one of our bird department's mascots, talking up a storm with the customers who would get to know him over the years.

Canaries were popular but I knew very little about them. I learned a lot in *Canary Breeding Tips and Tricks*, by Herman Osman, by far the best book available on them. I also learned that if you were serious about canaries, you had to go to Vahle's Bird Store on Damen Avenue. Vahle's, a second-generation, German-immigrant-owned bird store focused on one thing and one thing only: canaries. It was a relatively small shop, off the beaten track in a neighborhood setting. They imported and bred numerous types of canaries, offering American singers, German rollers, Dutch frills, crested, and border canaries.

When I visited for the first time, I was speechless. The sound of all the birds singing was something not only to hear, but to witness. The store had an old European presence with a tall, tin-tile ceiling suspended over oak-framed glass showcases that rested in a grand circle upon oak hardwood floors. There were countless decorative brass cages, some hanging, some on stands. There were bins of fresh bulk seed mixes. The male canaries were housed in row after row of small, individual, wire-fronted, wooden, box cages that the store displayed across the walls from one side to the other and all the way up to the ceiling. There were people sitting in chairs throughout the store enjoying the spectacle of all the singing canaries. Many watched in amazement while others focused on just which one they thought they might take home with them that day.

Besides the various colors, shapes, and sizes of canaries, I learned they were also selectively bred into three basic song types. The "choppers" were opened mouth, loud singing birds; the "rollers" were closed mouth, quiet singing birds; and the "warblers" were a sort of combination of both. There was no hard selling, just friendly, professional service along with coffee or tea. Once you found the bird you wanted, they brought the cage down from the wall and placed it on one of the glass countertops next to a chair where you could sit and further examine the bird while more intently listening to its singing. I eventually purchased a yellow American warbler along with a brass birdcage and some fresh canary seed mix and treat conditioner. Our apartment came to life from then on, a small pet shop in itself.

I suppose I could have just taken the plunge right then and there and opened my own shop, but I knew it wasn't enough just to have experience taking care of different types of pets. All the things I learned, both small and large, while working in the grocery business and at the service station, kept ringing in my head. They kept reminding me that owning and running a retail business was a lot more than stocking shelves and wiping windshields. The pet business was no different. I needed to learn firsthand not only what to do, but what *not* to do. With my preliminary research complete, the time had come to actually go to work in the pet industry.

Ray was more than willing to do the same. He ended up quitting his fulltime job and immediately went to work for the Docktor Pet Center franchisee in Niles but after a few months, he spotted an ad in the paper for a new purebred puppy mega-retailer by the name of Puppy Corral and he went to work for them. Puppy Corral was a new concept store specializing in purebred puppy sales and their related supplies. Ray was a born salesman, classy and sharp, and he learned as much as possible about puppies and their care, handling, and marketing. During his short tenure of working for Puppy Corral, he became one of their top salesmen, sometimes selling ten or more purebred puppies in a single weekend.

I, on the other hand, continued my employment on the midnight shift at Greyhound Computer Corporation but, at the same time, worked as many hours as I could for various pet stores, learning as much as possible. My first official job in the pet industry was working for the most famous retail bird store in the Midwest, Erling Kjelland's Sedgewick Studio. Erling was a famous canary judge and world-renowned in the avicultural scene. After a very informal interview, he hired me immediately and insisted I start that same day. It turned out that he had just lost an employee and the aviaries and birdcages needed tending to.

I would leave my work at Greyhound and drive to the near Northside Chicago location and be at Sedgewick Studio by 9:30 in the morning and work every day until 3 p.m. It was worth it. Erling was a passionate bird enthusiast, and I grew to love and respect the man. He taught me much about all of the popular cage birds as well as so many different types of rare and exotic finches, soft bills, and parrots. His inventory put many zoos to shame. Besides the commonly kept birds, he had a large assortment of exotic parrots, finches and softbills, even exotic owls and miniature kestrels. It was mind-boggling. Where else could one learn so much, so fast about the care and handling of so many different pet birds? I would have worked there without pay if I had to.

Erling lived in a quirky apartment in the back of the store filled with antiques, stained glass windows, plants, tropical trees, and vines galore. All throughout were birdcages full of little exotic birds. All this along with his two loving pugs, Buffy and Midnight. Erling was always entertaining well-known bird breeders and enthusiasts, sitting with them drinking tea and talking birds. It was there that I met several bird breeders who shared their knowledge and expertise with me.

It was also at Sedgewick Studio where I met the most charming, artistic, and entertaining person I had ever known: Dave McKelvy. Dave was Erling's full-time general manager. He was a person who could talk about any subject and had an opinion to go with it. He knew seemingly everything about animals and their husbandry requirements. Over the years, Dave had worked at various zoos and bird breeding operations and eventually came to Erling, managing the store while living in the upstairs apartment with his wife, Linda, and their young daughter. I always wondered why Dave, so intelligent and worldly, was living in a little apartment above a small local bird store, barely getting by. It wouldn't be until a couple of years later, when I hired him, that I would find out.

Meanwhile, after learning about so many different species of birds, their diets, housing, care, and sourcing, I felt that I had reached a point where it was time to move on. I left Sedgewick Studio on very good terms and kept in contact with everyone I met there. Erling was sad to see me leave but I had made him aware of my quest early on.

After Sedgewick, I went to work at my favorite pet store as a boy, Bernie Hoffman's Animal Kingdom on Milwaukee Avenue. I already had quite a bit of animal husbandry experience with reptiles and small animals, but I lacked the commercial experience. I knew that by working for a full line pet store like Animal Kingdom, I could learn a lot about selling techniques and customer service procedures. Animal Kingdom was one of the first departmentalized pet shops in the United States and in addition to being a large format store, it was the city of Chicago's nucleus of animal shows, parades, chamber of commerce promotions, and events including petting zoos, private banquets, parties, and television appearances. Bernie Hoffman's regular appearances on WGN's Captain Kangaroo, Super Circus, and the Ray Rayner Show were an ongoing source of marketing for the store. Bernie's sons, Bob and Bill, basically ran the store and were always bouncing back and forth throughout the different areas of the place, managing the various aspects of their large, unique pet shop.

The store was like a jungle. A tiger, a chimpanzee, monkeys, a llama, a vulture, a wallaby—you name it, they had it. And all were for sale except their resident exhibition and show animals, their mascots. You never knew what unusual animal you might encounter on any given day. Once, I was summoned to help Bernie unload his station wagon and met the cutest little baby chimpanzee he had just picked up at the airport.

Bill and Bob eventually focused a lot of their efforts on the show animals while Bob's wife Sandy worked in a managerial position with Bill's wife Debbie and their longtime dedicated employee, Steve Maciontek, who started as a teenager and years later became the store manager. Debbie took a liking to me because she respected my experience with tropical fish and especially reptiles, and immediately put me in charge of all reptiles. The first task I took upon myself was the cleaning and redecorating of all the reptile enclosures. Everyone was pleased with the results.

Other marketing initiatives that Animal Kingdom capitalized on were school tours where busloads of children would march into the store with their chaperones to see all the animals. Sometimes I would give the tours and I vividly recall the first one. I'd been working with a very large eastern indigo snake that was one of the main attractions in the reptile department. The snake was enormous, stretching out over six feet. It was an impressive shiny, black snake, and being powerful yet gentle, it was a perfect ambassador of the department as well as the store. The children were allowed to interact with the snake but I knew better than to allow an untrained person to hold it. So, I demonstrated its calm personality by carefully supporting it high and away from the children's reach.

The children were in awe as I lowered the snake to a more comfortable height. And then, as I was explaining the passive nature of indigo snakes, I watched as the snake moved its head from side to side, opening its mouth. Soon it was engulfing and chewing my left hand. The children watched in disbelief as the blood began dripping onto the floor. I smiled and somehow managed to disengage my hand and place the snake back into its enclosure, all the while explaining to everyone how things like this happen when the snake becomes frightened and confused. The kids moved along to other things while I cleaned up my hand and then the floor, wondering if my demonstration would be the highlight of their field trip and all they'd be talking about later. It had certainly been the most memorable part of my day!

Toward the end of 1970, I left Animal Kingdom and went to work in the pet department of Amling's Flowerland on North Avenue in Melrose Park. The store was a popular upscale nursery that specialized in roses, exotic plants, succulents, and cacti. Years earlier this was also one of my regular pet store stops. It was a family destination business complete with gift shop, home improvements, plants, orchids, rare exotics, and a complete pet department with tropical and pond fish, exotic birds, and small animals. Don McLain was the pet department manager and the master of the tropical fish business. He taught me all about tropical fish retailing—who the best suppliers were, how to handle and acclimate new arrivals, tropical fish compatibility, water conditioners and medications, and, most importantly, the various water filtration methods.

While working the retail floor, I learned how easy it was to service customers who were interested in tropical fish. With few exceptions, they all wanted guidance on maintaining their aquariums. Selling product or additional inhabitants to their aquariums wasn't an issue. They sought advice from me and wanted to buy. I actually began to feel like the expert. I enjoyed my days taking care of Amling's tropical fish customers and there wasn't a time when I didn't imagine how it would be when someday I would be servicing my own customers.

When I wasn't working at Greyhound or at one of my part time jobs, I was revising my conceptual designs. I had improved all of my drawings of the possible layouts of the four departments. I added designs of large display birdcages and aviaries, puppy runs, and reptile habitats. I eventually received permission to use a back room of the basement in our apartment building so I could start building large bird display cages, the same types that were at Sedgewick Studio. After completing four of them, I realized something I wished I'd have realized sooner. They were too big to get out through the basement doorway. After breaking them down into manage-able pieces, I learned my lesson. It wouldn't be the last. The mistakes I made in creating my future career were all learning lessons, some serious but others rather funny in retrospect.

At the end of the year, Marie and I moved into a two bedroom apartment near Norridge, northwest of Chicago. Now we had a designated room for all the pets I'd been accumulating: Oscar, Beau and Franklin, my piranhas, my German warbler canary from Vahle's Bird Store, and Crackers my double yellow-head Amazon parrot.

But three months after we moved in, the apartment building was sold. The new landlord didn't want any pets. Our neighbor upstairs had a dog and decided to leave. Another tenant did the same. Marie and I were the last. The landlord, Mr. Boldoski, was aware of the doxies, but he didn't know about the other pets. To add to our dilemma, months before what would be our grand opening, I came across a beautiful, hand-tamed Mu-loccan cockatoo that talked and danced, and a tame and talking Greater Indian Hill Mynah bird. Only later, once in the apartment, did I discover that the Muloccan cockatoo had a blood-curdling scream that he often demonstrated when he got bored. We moved his cage into our kitchen to be with us as much as possible, but when he was left alone while we were gone for the day, not only would he scream as though he were being assaulted, but he soon learned how to unlock his cage door. He wasted little time in buzz-sawing several of the kitchen cabinet doors.

While all this was going on, Mr. Boldoski didn't hide his desire for us to move out of his apartment building, repeatedly telling us he wanted us gone. The straw that broke the camel's back was an incident that brought us both to the boiling point. Early one morning, as I was returning from walking the dogs, Mr. Boldoski confronted me at the back hallway door. Shouting, he once again told me that he wanted us out. We were terrible tenants, and he was tired of all the dog droppings in the alley. I reminded him that there were several dog owners in the area and for him to single us out was unreasonable. Boldoski's response was stupefying. With his bare hands, he picked up a pile of dog poop, stormed up to me, and smashed it into the front of my coat.

Somehow, Mr. Boldoski then went rolling down the three-step stoop to the ground.

Needless to say, it was time for us to move on. Soon afterward, Marie and I found a three-bedroom house for sale in Elk Grove Village. We had all the kitchen cabinet doors replaced and were preparing to move out of the apartment when I received a summons to go to court for the "assault" of Mr. Boldoski. Three court appearances later, the case was thrown out. I was relieved but still furious at this Landlord from Hell. But I also knew that I had more important priorities into which to put my energies.

By then, I had learned so much in my retail pet store experiences. I found little nuggets of wisdom everywhere, and I knew that if I took the best ideas and practices and improved upon them, I could be successful. And if I expanded upon them, I could extend my success with a mega "pet store of the future."

Working for stores like Sedgewick Studio, Animal Kingdom, and Amling's, I came across a common theme: customers were starving for information. They loved their dog or their cat. Their bird or hamster was a member of their family. Most weren't satisfied with just one reptile or aquarium. And they all craved a quality source of knowledge, food, and supplies. And then there were the curious customers, the ones who wanted to bring a pet into their lives but needed a little nudge. They needed answers to the whys and hows and which ones. All of this combined with my past retail and selling experiences at Ono's Gift Shop, the IGA grocery store, The Shores Restaurant, the Standard service station, and the Fuller Brush Company gave me a sound foundation to build on for being organized, working hard, and providing excellent customer service.

I had already decided to staff the four departments with top notch managers, each specializing in their respective department. Together we would train our staffs on how to provide great customer service by informing and educating, not hard selling. I began writing a checklist, a sort of a guide which would later become a written protocol for each responsibility from merchandising the shelves to greeting the customers, selling properly by providing a need, and, most importantly, concentrating on excellent animal husbandry.

I also planned to offer my customers products and pets that were probably never available to them before. I would explain the differences in bulk quality bird and small animal diets versus the limited choices of branded boxed and packaged seeds and diets available from the chain and discount stores. It was to be a state-of-the-art store, but I nevertheless wanted to create an old-fashioned, general store feeling by offering a complete variety of bulk fresh foods that would be scooped out of wooden barrels and weighed on the spot. I wanted to offer an array of products, giving my customers various sizes or styles, including feed, accessories, cages, housing, and aquariums. I planned to offer selections of many different natural aquarium gravels, rock, driftwoods, and decorations, the likes of which were never seen together in one place before. I would offer and display the best selections of live tropical fish, reptiles, birds, small animals, and healthy, purebred puppies.

And the entire business model was based on a simple concept: the health and well-being of our available pets would be our very top priority.

But of course we still needed a name. We brainstormed, toying with a bunch of different possibilities. Pet Paradise, Pet Kingdom, Noah's, Noah's Ark, Noah's Ark Pet Store, and others. The "Noah" concept resonated. After all, we'd have every animal imaginable. Or at least, every imaginable pet animal. We also hit upon the idea that we were bigger than a "shop" and would offer more than a "store." We were going to be a "center," a meeting place not only for pet lovers to find a quality pet, but to receive expert information, guidance, and advice. And thus, the name of our business was established: *Noah's Ark Pet Center*. The realization of my dream was getting closer.

15

THE GRAND OPENING

WITH THE NAME DECIDED, we needed a location. And nothing less than a perfect one. We canvassed heavily trafficked commercial areas through the northwest suburbs of Chicago, locating a few possibilities and finally finding the ideal spot in Niles on Milwaukee Avenue. It was only 4,000 square feet but, being in a location with heavy traffic and a highly visible storefront, it couldn't have been better. My mother, Ray, and I had a couple of face-to-face meetings with the landlord and came to an agreement. But we soon learned that the zoning had to be altered to allow a pet shop. The next month, we appeared in front of the Niles zoning board to present our intentions and they told us to expect a decision within thirty days. A month later, they presented us with the bad news that our request had been denied.

We were disappointed, but undeterred. We kept looking, all the while getting all our other ducks in order, including signage. Being a couple of young guys without a track record made it difficult for the big sign companies to give us the time we felt we needed, but a smaller company by the name of MK Sign Company on Elston Avenue responded and presented us with a few different designs along with a reasonable quotation. We chose the design we liked the most and advised that we would be in touch to make whatever adjustments would be necessary as soon as we had a place for the sign to go.

I believe things happen for a reason. Although we were disappointed in losing that Milwaukee Avenue location, we found an even better one. Ray and I drove around busy thoroughfares in the neighboring communities. We drove west on Oakton Street searching the suburb of Des Plaines until we ended up on Elmhurst Road, a busy four-lane road that looked promising, but after going both directions we found nothing. Then, in a final attempt, we continued further west on Oakton Street, which turned into a poorly lit two-lane road with a few light industrial buildings interspersed between corn fields. As we were preparing to make a U-turn we saw a brand-new building at 2469 East Oakton. It was a large commercial building divided into separate units with "For Rent" signs posted. The entire area was being developed with a mixture of retail and light industrial businesses. We jotted the telephone number down and called it the next day, speaking to a gentleman by the name of Bill Gamble who was a partner in the building development corporation that had just completed the construction of the building.

We had a few meetings with Bill and learned that an end unit of 9,270 square feet was available. Bill believed in our vision and determination and took a liking to us. In our last meeting, with my mother present, Bill not only agreed to finance the leasehold improvements, including the partition wall, office space, the entire glass storefront, a dropped ceiling with lighting, and basic plumbing and electrical, but he assured us that he would coordinate the plumbing requirements of our puppy kennels and pour the concrete for our custom kennel base. All of this in exchange for a reasonable five-year lease with a five-year option to renew at fair market value. I couldn't believe what I was hearing. We shook hands after he agreed to draw up a contract and we left literally screaming for joy.

But as the time to get our finances in order was fast approaching, reality started setting in. Our projected financial need to get the store open, including a two month cash flow (assuming no income whatsoever to start) was approximately $100,000. This was in 1971 and that amount would be close to a million today. My life savings? Around $15,000. Of course I was also eligible for an SBA loan, but that would be limited to $25,000. For Ray's part, he was able to cobble together no more than $5,000. The landlord agreeing to finance the leasehold improvements and our custom requirements added up to about $40,000 of what we needed. All totaled, we had about $85,000 accounted for, leaving us short by $15,000.

I talked to Mom about a loan and she said that I had to speak to Dad first. I called Dad and told him I had something to talk over with him and we met the next day at a restaurant. Dad was sitting at the bar when I arrived and after some small talk, I dove in, explaining everything to him, describing my vision as best I could. Dad listened to all my plans and my loan request for the money that I still needed. Without hesitating, he turned me down. I had expected, at worst, that he would tell me he needed to think about it. I was dazed by his outright "No." He uttered something about how he and Mom simply didn't have the money. Knowing better, I was absolutely dumbfounded. As with his absence at my wedding, the things that made Dad tick would become clearer to me only with time.

The next day, I told Mom about our meeting and she told me to sit tight. She'd see what she could do. Then she approached my grandfather and he immediately agreed to the loan. He wasn't a rich man, working as a barber all his life, but apparently he had saved for that rainy day. He loaned us what we needed. Not only would I pay him back within two years, but with interest. I still have my grandfather's original canceled check.

By then, it was the beginning of September and we wanted to open well in advance of the busy Christmas season. We decided on a grand opening date of Saturday, November 21, 1971. Ray quit his job working for Puppy Corral. I finally quit my full time job with Greyhound Corporation and gave a week's notice to Amling's.

Now we needed the people. Ray would focus on the puppy department exclusively. He had already made arrangements to hire one of the veterinarian technicians he had worked with at Puppy Corral. I would be responsible for the bird, reptile, and small animal departments. For the tropical fish responsibilities, I had an interested person in mind who would soon agree to join us. The rest of the staff would be hired closer to the opening. We had no trouble finding people once word got out within the industry that a new "gigantic" pet store was soon opening that was in need of experienced people.

I began modifying our drawings and plans to fit the new 9,270 square-foot store. Besides the four major departments, we had a backroom area of about 1,200 square feet primarily for storage, but also divided into three rooms, one for grooming/food preparation, one for use as a puppy holding/clinic room, and one for our office. We had an electrician, carpenters, and a plumber already lined up and they were able to start as soon as we signed the lease. For the next two and a half months, we worked nonstop, building puppy runs, birdcages and aviaries, aquarium racks, small animal, and reptile enclosures, three puppy "get-acquainted" rooms, and a clinic. Not counting the snake cages I'd built years before, I'd never done any major construction and surprised myself on what I was able to do by observing, and then trial and error. The carpenters we hired taught us quite a bit. It made all the sense in the world to build the two-by-four wall-framing on the floor and stand it up; how cool was that?

I already knew what we needed for supplies and store fixtures, so it was just a matter of ordering them along with the cash register, pricing machine, office and clinic equipment, invoices, purchase order forms, business cards, telephone system, music and paging system, and everything in between. We had fun getting accustomed to the phone and paging system once it was installed. It felt like a sophisticated, professional business to hear, "Mr. Krause, call on line one. Line one, please."

We met with five different wholesalers and wrote orders for all of our inventory of accessories, foods, seeds, bedding, cages, aquariums, and so forth. We learned that even though much of the merchandise that many of the wholesalers carried was identical, each wholesaler had a special niche that they were good at. Our initial orders were all supposed to be C.O.D. but for the most part we were able to negotiate thirty day terms once the wholesalers felt confident that we were worthy.

As for the live animal suppliers, those were the people I related to and enjoyed talking to the most, especially about our mutual passions. I had been pre-purchasing birds, reptiles, and various animals weeks before our anticipated opening, all the suppliers waiting for the go ahead. We couldn't wait to receive the baby kinkajou, the gentle mother wallaby with joey in pouch, the capuchin monkey, and all the baby handfed parrots we purchased from Pet Farm in Miami. I felt like I was in heaven upon the arrivals of the specialized shipping boxes of hundreds of parakeets, finches, lovebirds, and cockatiels from breeders in Oklahoma and California, and the crates of various reptiles from collectors all over. I couldn't stop smiling. The tropical fish suppliers were all local and we put them on notice, too.

The two weeks before our grand opening seemed like something out of a movie with us continually making runs to O'Hare International Airport to pick up the shipments. It felt like Christmas each time we'd open a shipping crate or a cloth bag. We created procedures to check their health and establish all the necessary guidelines for care, feeding, and handling. One day, as I was returning from the airport I witnessed our outdoor sign being erected. I got goosebumps all over and had to pull over and watch for a few minutes, giving me a moment to thank God for all what was happening.

But as we came closer to the scheduled grand opening date, we ran into a major complication. It turned out that the person I'd hired for the fish department simply wasn't the right guy. It became clear to me that he was in over his head, unable to handle the enormity of getting the 100-plus aquariums up and running. I also began to have doubts about his managerial people skills. I terminated his employment immediately. Later, thinking back about the situation, it occurred to me that I had felt all along that there was something wrong with him, but I hadn't been able to put my finger on just what it was. I learned from that experience that when you have nothing else, making decisions based on a gut feeling will usually serve you well.

Meanwhile, in the days leading up to the grand opening, people were constantly popping in, most trying to sell us some service or other, but some just nosey, wanting to see what was going on. One day, while we were rinsing hundreds of pounds of aquarium gravel, and me having pretty much decided that we were going to open with an unfinished tropical fish department, a man walked in the front door that I recognized from years before. He was Gary Murphy, the owner of Ultra In Tropics, a high-end specialty tropical fish store that I used to visit on North Avenue, but which no longer existed. His timing couldn't have been better when he asked if we were hiring. Gary carried himself with confidence and charisma. I believed in him and hired him on the spot. Ultimately, he saved our tropical fish department.

Of course no matter how prepared one is for the grand opening of a store, nothing happens if nobody knows about it. And so began our advertising push. We had already lined up radio advertising, along with display ads in the Chicago Tribune and local newspapers, as well as door hangers distributed by Boy Scouts in eight adjoining suburbs, all of which announced the opening of "NOAH'S ARK, THE WORLDS LARGEST PET CENTER." We mentioned our hundreds of puppies and kittens, thousands of tropical fish, hundreds of exotic parrots and birds, plus our enormous selection of reptiles, amphibians, and exotic animals. On the Thursday and Friday before our grand opening we hired people to dress in animal costumes and hand out flyers to commuters at the train station downtown who were traveling to the northwest suburbs.

Finally, the big day came and it was everything we had hoped it would be, as I got goosebumps again seeing all the wide-eyed people entering our store. Whenever I could break away from the crowds of people, I hung out near the entranceway to watch all the activity and to overhear all the complimentary comments as well-wishers came by to offer their congratulations.

Me in the bird department of Noah's Ark during our Grand Opening in 1971.

In addition to the customers, several pet industry people came in to see what they'd been hearing so much about. At one point, a few executives from Pioneer Pet Supply came into the store, led by the president, Giff Gardner himself. Not recognizing me, they all stood at the front of the store looking over the enormity of the entire scene. Finally, Giff turned to the others, shook his head, and flatly declared, "He'll never make it."

That one statement, those four words, would ultimately give me more motivation than all the well-wishes I received in those opening days put together.

16

SMOOTHING OUT THE WRINKLES

OVER THE GRAND OPENING weekend, along with all the supplies, we sold eleven puppies, along with several parakeets and cockatiels, a scarlet macaw, a few Amazon parrots, and numerous aquarium set-ups. And the days and weeks that followed proved just as promising. Seeing customers smiling as they carried aquarium set-ups to the register was validating. The numerous reptile and small animal sales were even more so. And none of that overshadowed the large number of continued puppy sales. To see each customer going home with all the proper supplies and care instructions was extremely gratifying. Working seven days a week seeing such successful results, it didn't seem like working at all. In fact, it was becoming a lifestyle.

I suppose, looking back, that it was naïve to think there wouldn't be problems. The first major one involved parking and access. We didn't have a parking lot but instead a circular drive that could handle up to six or eight cars. This was okay though because we were a couple of blocks from the busy business district and customers had no problem parking on the shoulder of the two-lane asphalt country road that led to our building. After all, there weren't any other businesses around at the time. But just a few months after our opening, in February of '72, road construction led to the barricading of the street. Traffic could now enter only from Elmhurst Road, a quarter mile away, creating a dead-end street. We immediately had large signs made up that we posted on the barricades, telling everyone that Noah's Ark, "THE WORLD'S LARGEST PET CENTER" was open during construction. The people kept coming.

But around this time, I had another problem, an even bigger one. It didn't take long before I noticed a lack of commitment from my partner. Ray wasn't willing to put the hours in that I was and he didn't seem to have the same passion. He took a busy Saturday off to attend an insignificant trade show with our vet tech, which I accepted, until they both stopped in later. They were dressed as if they'd just returned from a cocktail party and they paraded around the store like big shots while the rest of the staff and I were busy running around servicing the customers. Ray seemed to like the glory of being a business owner, but he didn't seem to care for the work required.

The lack of effort continued to show itself. I'm sure it didn't help that he was going through marital problems at the time. Before long, Ray ended up going back to the service station business. I returned his initial investment of $5,000 but after all the effort to get the store opened he felt he deserved more. I eventually paid him an additional $3,000 over the next six months.

Now I was alone in this gigantic endeavor. Of course I knew there would be challenges in dealing with live animals, fish, and birds, but I sure didn't sign up for all the unforeseen obstacles that I encountered, like the barricades down the street. Or having to sometimes push unhappy customers' cars out of the mud if they had to park off the side of our circular driveway and got themselves stuck. Or dealing with the frosted and dripping front windows, conditions caused by our inside humidity and inadequate ventilation.

Then there was everything else. Fortunately, Marie took care of the banking, bookkeeping, bill paying, and handling the vendors' phone calls, but I was out on the floor dealing with the overall management of the staff, making sure we were all working toward the same goals: quality live pets and excellent customer service. This included overseeing the purchasing of all pets and fish, training the staff, hiring, firing, communication, and security. Every day was a whirlwind of unforeseen responsibilities. All this while trying to maintain some type of personal life. The 8 a.m. to 11 p.m. hours became an accepted way of life for Marie and me. Being able to leave at 7 p.m. on weekends was our way of relaxing a bit, even though every conversation revolved around the business.

But the challenges only fueled my determination. Giff Gardner was wrong and I knew it. In spite of the many difficulties, we were able to keep our heads above water and pay our bills. We forged onward, building a team of dedicated employees that allowed us to increase and improve our product and pet selection as well as the service to our customers.

One day, in the spring of '72, I left the shop for an hour in the afternoon, the very first time I'd been away from it. It was a strange, uncertain feeling to not be there, to have to rely so completely on my employees, even for such a short period of time. Of course, I need not have worried. My employees were competent and conscientious and the store was, not surprisingly, still standing upon my return.

But at the time, I still didn't feel successful. I was keenly aware that I had a lot of work still in front of me. In spite of the early acclaim, both in the pet industry and in the marketplace, I knew that if I wanted to continue our growth, I had to ensure that we continued to have a strong management team. This continuity was tested not long after the grand opening. Gary Murphy was ready to move on. It was as if his job was complete after helping us get the fish department up and running. He let me know he'd be leaving and I contacted my old boss from Amling's pet department, the tropical fish guru, Don McLain. He took my call as if he'd been waiting for it, accepting my offer almost immediately.

Don was exactly what we needed. As soon as he started, he commanded the respect he deserved. He made weekly visits to Aquatics, Inc., in Norridge, to hand-select our tropical fish, goldfish, and aquatic plants. Being an excellent manager, he created efficient systems for his department, and began building a conscientious team of tropical fish enthusiasts who passionately serviced our customers. Our fish department looked fabulous, all the aquariums decorated and stocked with the common as well as the rare and unusual species of fish.

I was reminded not long ago by Chuck Breiter, a fish department employee back in those early days, how much he'd learned from Don working part time at Noah's Ark while attending high school. There's no doubt Chuck's background led him to his future career where he eventually became a PetSmart store director.

I had spent a considerable amount of my time setting up the procedures for the bird department, and now it was time to hand it off to the right manager. I had stayed in contact with Dave McKelvy, and when I learned that he planned to leave Sedgewick Studio, I offered him the position of our bird department manager. Dave fit right into our culture. Not only did he have animal husbandry experience in the avicultural world, but he seemed to know something about the behavior and attributes of many different kinds of animals. Dave was a born salesman and his personality attracted customers to the bird department. He was a charismatic and entertaining individual who could imitate the whistles, shrieks, honks, and calls of so many different species of birds. He was always making our customers and staff smile and laugh.

Now, freed up from the tropical fish and bird departments, I was able to focus on both the puppy and reptile/small animal departments. In short order, I discovered that puppies were definitely not dogs. They were babies and needed to be nurtured and cared for, especially the smaller, more delicate breeds. Handfeeding the little guys became a daily top priority.

When Ray departed the business, our vet tech left at the same time, but she departed leaving her assistant, Linda Moore, in charge. Linda was a dedicated individual who not only held the department together but established an excellent work ethic which the other puppy department employees followed. One time she sold a puppy while doing nothing more than handfeeding it and answering some questions a family was asking about it. This really gave her confidence and that moment became the start of her success with her customer service and selling responsibilities. She was soon ready to manage the entire department.

I knew the importance of offering only healthy, quality puppies. If there was one thing that could rapidly deteriorate one's reputation in the pet business, it was selling inferior puppies. That cute little golden retriever puppy is no longer just a dog; it almost immediately becomes a loving, inseparable member of a family. We began establishing a network of local quality dog breeders. Being extremely selective, we rejected several puppies that didn't meet our health requirements or weren't good representatives of their breed. On the other hand, we were fortunate to be able to purchase large quantities of purebred puppies, sometimes taking entire litters. Our standards attracted more and more quality breeders, some of whom drove in from all over the Midwest. During the early weekend mornings, it was not unusual to have two or three breeders with van loads of puppies waiting in line to have their puppies health-checked and then accepted or rejected.

As the department grew, we continued hiring and training new employees. One day, we hired a young lady by the name of Denise King for a cashier position, but with her passion and desire to work with puppies, we eventually transferred her to the puppy department where she worked in every facet of the department and soon became the assistant manager under Linda. Her quick learning made her an overnight asset to the department. I also hired a friend of mine, Don Wetherald, to help out on weekends, assisting customers who were interested in our puppies. Don was the husband of Marie's best friend Susie and worked fulltime as a salesman at a local Cadillac dealer. He was excellent with customer service.

During the evenings and weekends, the three or four employees we had working in the puppy department kept the "Get Acquainted" rooms full most of the time. I wanted to avoid any high pressure or unscrupulous selling tactics, so I didn't have a commission structure. I made it clear to the employees that they were there to inform and educate. The pets would sell themselves. And they did. It wasn't unusual to have a dozen or more puppies going to new homes on weekend days and even sometimes on weekdays.

Having a sound team in the puppy department allowed me to gravitate to my initial passion area: reptiles. I maintained a reptile inventory that paralleled the reptile houses at Lincoln Park and Brookfield Zoos. Our selection and expertise soon gave us an excellent reputation. Over time, I got to know our regular reptile and small animal customers. We attracted the beginning pet owners and the serious hobbyists, professionals, college professors, teachers, and veterinarians, many of whom were dedicated members of our local 4H Club and the Chicago Herpetological Society, both of which I joined and became a strong advocate for. I became personal friends with several, even maintaining relationships with them to this day. I was proud of the fact that not only did we carry a complete selection of every small animal from hamsters to the occasional exotic mammal, but our selection of all sorts of reptiles from around the world was extraordinary. We kept an inventory of numerous species of snakes, lizards, turtles, tortoises, and amphibians. Perhaps not surprisingly, given my personal interests, we specialized in turtles and tortoises. The variety of our inventory of hatchling turtles, everything from red eared sliders to Mata Mata turtles, was unprecedented. It was as though I had replicated my childhood laboratory but multiplied by a hundred. I was in my glory. I had species of turtles that I'd only seen in books and I took great pride in making sure our turtle displays were set up the proper way.

One of our regular turtle customers who always impressed me was Tom Lowden. Tom was a detail-oriented professional who worked for the world famous orchid grower, Hauserman's Orchids in Villa Park, Illinois. He was a soft-spoken individual who conveyed sincerity and expertise and had a passion for turtles as well as a basic overall knowledge of other reptiles and small animals. It didn't take long before I offered him a position as manager for our reptile/small animal department, which he accepted.

Basic animal husbandry came naturally to me and, in spite of the fact that I was still learning, the caliber of our growing management team in each department was beginning to pay off in attracting more and more quality employees. These employees, many of whom eventually made their careers working with animals, were at the front line, which in turn made us really shine in the eyes of our customers. But as I continued peeling the onion back, each layer presented another priority which had to be addressed. It eventually became clear that our biggest shortcoming was mastering the selection, ordering, and the maintaining of proper inventory levels of supplies and accessories.

Before I opened the store, I thought I knew which items to offer our customers, but soon learned there were many more that I wasn't even aware of. I had little experience with such things as quantities, sizes, brands, varieties, and styles. With the volume of business we were experiencing, we were always running out of stock. Without any real historical data, the solution for us became to carry everything. We had the room so why not? But I soon learned why not. Over-ordering became a nightmare, subsequently affecting our cash flow. We had plenty of inventory, but still seemed to run out of our best sellers.

The system I'd originally set up where each of the four department managers ordered, received, stocked, and sold their own live pets and dry goods began to exacerbate the problem, especially since each of the managers were required to do their reordering every week just to keep up. Making matters worse, it was necessary to purchase from several different vendors due to the variety of products I insisted on carrying. As a result, our department managers were spending the lion's share of their time either ordering, receiving, and pricing merchandise; or stocking the retail floor of their departments. Of course it was the live fish, birds, and animals they were passionate about, not the cartons and packages of product. I saw that they weren't happy spending so much time on the required paperwork and would often overlook the details of keeping our products in stock. I realized that we needed to solve the problem before it became obvious to our customers.

Then there it was: the solution was right in front of me. Don McLain's wife, Sandy, visited the store from time to time and I got to know her, learning in the process that she had the organizational skills we needed. I asked her if she'd be interested in a part time job assisting with the processing of our dry goods orders. She jumped on the opportunity and began coming in three days a week, working with our department managers.

Then came more help. One of our wholesale suppliers was a Chicago company called M.P. Krause and Sons. Two weeks before our opening, their salesman had written up what turned out to be a woefully inadequate order. Without any real experience, we had just gone along with it. Fortunately, another salesman from the same company by the name of

Joe Leonard recognized the inadequacy right away and asked if he could correct it. Trusting his judgment, we gave him the green light and he wrote an additional order doubling the quantities of key items and adding several items we were lacking. Then he had it all delivered the following day. From that point on, Joe became our M.P. Krause and Sons salesperson. Each time he called on us, he made sound recommendations, slowly guiding us in our overall order processing.

Joe earned my implicit trust and one day soon after I'd hired Sandy, he suggested that if we started ordering a lot of the everyday kind of items from M.P. Krause, instead of the other wholesalers, it would greatly streamline our order processing. He assured us that they would increase their inventory levels to handle our volume, extend us a favorable discount, and provide a consistent Wednesday morning delivery every week. This would then allow us to have our shelves nicely stocked well in advance of the busy weekends. The kicker was when he said that if we would do that, he'd be able to give us additional time to help guide Sandy in our inventory management. I told Joe he had a deal.

Meanwhile, we were continually increasing our live animal offerings as well as our supplies, foods, accessories, cages, and aquariums. It seemed like a day never passed without deliveries of some sort coming through our back door. We had our hands full just maintaining decent inventory levels of both supplies and pets. Sandy soon had to hire an assistant and I decided to split off the responsibilities of product merchandising to a new department. I offered Sandy a full time manager position of our new merchandising department, which she accepted, and before long, she hired two more part time employees, training them in every area of merchandising product. Sandy's department became the backbone of the entire store as it supported the sales efforts of each department by mastering the never-ending process of ordering and keeping the shelves and displays full.

Over time, by working with all the other department managers, Sandy learned their needs and her department was able to handle the entire process almost independently. Needless to say, my four other department managers were ecstatic. They were now able to concentrate 100 percent on animal husbandry and servicing the customers.

Joe recognized right away that Noah's Ark Pet Center had unbelievable growth potential, something I didn't necessarily see. Being so new to the business, I knew no other way and thought that our success was merely a result of working hard at putting all the pieces together. Joe approached me with the idea of coming to work for us on a part time basis. He resigned from M.P. Krause and Sons and we hired him. Mel Krause's daughter, Judy, soon replaced Joe and, being professional and accommodating in every respect, we continued supporting M.P. Krause and Sons in a large way. I learned to depend on Judy's expertise and in doing so, became close friends with her for years, even hiring her fifteen years later as a regional sales manager for another company I would build.

Meanwhile, I gave Joe the title of Merchandising Director. Sandy was happy to have him continue guiding us in product selection, buying techniques, and most importantly, negotiations. Noah's Ark Pet Center became famous for carrying everything and anything in pet and animal products, many of which were unheard of. Back in those days, many of the commonplace products of today hadn't even been thought of yet. We prided ourselves on not only carrying all brands of popular pet products, but unique items from the farm, agriculture, and zoo industries along with improvised items from the electrical, hardware, and construction fields. These items were used to provide improved diets, housing, and the environmental needs of the pets we offered, many of which actually became popular pet products in their own right.

As our sales continued to grow, we knew we could now handle it. We had a smooth-functioning department that not only supported the sales and marketing efforts of the entire company, but played a critical role in its phenomenal growth. But I wouldn't be able to remain comfortable for long. As it happened, I was about to enter one of the most tumultuous periods of my life.

17

NEVER A DULL MOMENT

NOAH'S ARK PET CENTER was a phenomenal success, and now entering our second year, our ever-improving business model was working and our sales were spectacular. Each morning when we opened the doors, there was a line of people waiting and on weekends, the line often went around the building. We had become known as animal husbandry experts and if our new customers didn't find us as a result of our relentless advertising, they found us by word of mouth.

Noah's Ark customers lining up.

All this time, I was learning to delegate better. I understood the value of having top notch employees and I knew that the only way I was going to succeed was to surround myself with quality people. Still, I thrived on being involved in every aspect of the company. Each day was different. If I wasn't gently placing a baby parakeet on the finger of an eight-year old as Mom and Dad looked on, or allowing a school of neon tetras to enter my net while letting a customer select the six they wanted, I was demonstrating how to properly clean the tile floor for a new employee.

The reality of operating a business always hit me during the early morning or late evening hours, the times I spent in the office doing paperwork, ordering inventory, counting the cash drawer, or preparing the bank deposits. Then, during store hours there were times in the office when, if I wasn't on the phone talking to suppliers, bird breeders, animal dealers, or reptile collectors, I was being interrupted with questions from my staff. I began thriving on what many people would describe as stress.

One of my means of cushioning the pressure was having a pet of my own, which sat high on a wall shelf overlooking the entire office. It was Otis, my young, gray phased screech owl who would fly to my hand for a cricket or the leg of a white mouse. Otis and the large aquarium behind my desk filled with hatchling turtles gave me periodic diversions that always put a smile on my face. To me there was nothing more enjoyable than watching my turtles diving off a log into the aquatic wisteria vegetation, spinning their little legs as they propelled themselves into the six-inch depths of safety. Memories of Camp Oconto would come flooding back.

I eventually added a pair of eastern indigo snakes from Florida. I had no interest in reliving the experience I'd had a few years earlier at Animal Kingdom, but indigos continued to intrigue me with their beauty and power, yet gentle nature. Meanwhile, my reptile department advised me whenever a new shipment of baby turtles arrived so I could cherry pick a new inhabitant or two. My office got a bit crowded but I had no one to answer to and, after all, it was *my* office.

In the meantime, as my life in the pet industry continued to evolve, so did the pet industry itself. Regulations began to crop up for both selling and owning animals. Baby turtles were banned in 1972 as a result of a salmonella concern. Puppy mills were becoming an issue. The Avian Bird Flu and Newcastle Disease affected availability. The importation and handling of tropical fish, birds, and animals were being scrutinized and international wildlife laws were being enacted. Animal rights activists weren't as prominent as they are today, but retail pet stores were still under the watchful eye of groups like the Humane Society as well as the Department of Agriculture.

Even back then, exotics were a particular concern. From time to time we handled several exotics, knowing that ours were captive-raised and that we were capable of giving proper advice on their husbandry requirements. At one time we sold seasonal baby raccoons, baby arctic blue foxes, and baby coyotes (marketed as brush wolves). We would occasionally have prairie dogs, flying squirrels, Coati Mundis, a tame baby kinkajou, an armadillo, or even a squirrel monkey, capuchin, or macaque. We often had ferrets and dwarf African hedgehogs, which were just becoming available and not the commonly kept pets that they are today. Although we never handled exotics like baby lions, cougars, and chimpanzees, back in those days they were available as well.

There were several exotic animal dealers and importers throughout the country, with most located in Florida but a few at other ports of entry into the US like New York and California. Then there were various people who dealt with native, wild-collected reptiles and animals from Texas to Minnesota on down to Louisiana and Florida. There were also a handful of local exotic animal breeders and dealers in the Chicago area, the most famous being Charlie Hume, a Purina animal food distributor who I did business with. In addition to developing exotic animal diets for Purina, Charlie raised mice and rats for both the scientific community and pet industry. He raised macaws for the bird industry, too, and eventually became the nation's most successful skunk breeder, raising thousands for the pet industry until the state of Illinois banned skunks as pets in 1968. Charlie's animal passion then led him to his eighty-eight acre Exotic Animal Ranch in Marengo, Illinois where he raised camels, zebras, and llamas, becoming one of the premier llama breeders in the US.

Lee Watson was another breeder of exotics and my personal favorite. I met Lee one Saturday morning a few months after we opened our store. I noticed a cowboy-type strolling down the aisle of our puppy department nodding his head as he glanced around at all the puppies in their kennel runs. After a brief conversation I could tell this man wasn't your normal kind of guy. In fact, when he told me what he did for a living, I knew he was *my* kind of guy.

Lee did anything and everything related to animals, especially the unusual. He lived on his farm with outdoor and indoor pens and enclosures of bears, cougars, a panther, vultures, and a lion. He ran a livery business renting out pleasure horses to the local community so they could ride in the adjoining forest preserves. But his big business was renting out his exotic animals for television commercials, movies, grand openings, gala events, and photo shoots. He worked closely with many other exotic animal people in the country, including the Hoffmans from Animal Kingdom in the heart of Chicago, and one fellow by the name of Don who kept and trained elephants in Wisconsin.

Lee bought and sold reptiles, too, and became a resource to our business in many ways. We immediately struck up a friendship when I visited his place in Hoffman Estates. I drove up his gravel driveway and laughed to myself as I noticed a three-toed sloth in a crabapple tree alongside the barn where there were several customers saddling up for their afternoon ride. Lee greeted me with open arms and after some small talk, gave me the grand tour of his facility, showing me his animals, all of which were well-kept and healthy. Afterward, while walking toward the farmhouse, we passed a gigantic chain-link enclosure that contained an adult black bear pacing back and forth. Alongside was a young lady sitting on a big oak log working with a bear cub on a leash. As I watched the behavior of both bears, Lee explained how he trained them and I was pleased to learn that they weren't abused in any way.

When we went into Lee's house, I could see that the tour wasn't over. There were several Neodesha reptile cages with snakes of all kinds, including venomous. We sat down with a cup of coffee and soon shook hands on doing business together. Upon my leaving, Lee presented me with the largest hermit tree crab I'd ever seen, which proceeded to take a chunk out of my left index finger. Lee would joke about that incident for years afterward.

From then on, every weekend we had one of Lee's handlers spend a couple hours during our peak periods walking one of Lee's animals up and down our aisles, allowing our customers to interact with a mountain lion named Roger, a bear cub, a three-toed sloth, or a young ostrich. This became so popular that people came from miles around for this experience alone. The increased business and word of mouth advertising was immeasurable. Then on special advertised sale weekends, we would hire Lee to set up an entire petting zoo in front of the store, along with free pony rides for the kids.

My relationship with Lee paid off in another, unexpected, way. One day an advertising agency approached us asking if we'd be interested in being involved in a MasterCard television commercial. I said sure, and with

Lee's contacts, we were able to provide everything the agency needed. Two weeks later, we spent an entire day while the store was open for business with media people and their cameras everywhere, lighting and microphone equipment throughout the store, and what seemed like miles of cable and wire running up and down the aisles. The commercial centered on a little boy and his family seeking an unusual pet. The commercial ended with a hand slapping down a MasterCard on our checkout counter, along with a chain, and then the little boy walking away from our front door with the chain now attached to a baby elephant. The tagline: "You can buy anything with your MasterCard." The publicity we got out of that commercial was priceless.

Of course, in addition to the presence of Lee's animals, we had Dave McKelvy continuing to imitate to perfection every bird from a European bull finch to an Indian peacock. Not only their sounds, but their behavior. Watching him run down the main aisle of the store bent over, flapping his arms, honking, and chasing our gray Chinese goose was a site customers could never forget.

There was obvious value in having our customers be able to interact with both common and exotic animals, especially allowing children to observe their behaviors up close and personal. We built a white picket fence around the center parrot tree in our bird room where we kept our resident goose, turkey, and a couple of ducks. At Easter time we added a second, larger one in the middle of the store where we created a barnyard scene with a baby goat, a potbellied pig, and several small critters like bunnies and guinea pigs. Our customers loved it, providing them with an enjoyable experience as well as ample photo opportunities.

We soon added permanent residents to our mascot menagerie. Years earlier, with my love of turtles, I was intrigued by the thought of owning a giant tortoise but knew I could never provide the environment needed.

Well, now I could and after doing some research, I located a reptile dealer in Michigan who had three of them. I drove there and picked out the most beautiful Aldabra tortoise, loaded him into our straw-packed van, and drove him back to Elk Grove Village where all our employees were waiting for the big arrival. The following weekend, we had a pizza party naming contest and it was unanimous that the tortoise should be named Methuselah. He joined our other mascots—Phoenix and Tucson, our handfed Hyacinth macaws; Magoo, our talking Greater Sulphur Crested Cockatoo; Zachary our hawk head parrot; and of course Crackers, our talking double yellow head Amazon. We always kept a large, tame boa constrictor around, too, and a continually changing inventory of interesting mammals like a wallaby, armadillo, or kinkajou.

All these mascots helped us to conduct immensely enjoyable school and scout tours over the years, not that every tour went perfectly. One time I was demonstrating the behavior of snakes when my five-foot-long boa constrictor bit a little girl on the forehead. You would have thought I'd learned from the indigo snake incident at Animal Kingdom. Fortunately, the only repercussion was the cancelation of all the scheduled remaining tours from that particular school. Luckily, the little girl only received a scratch and we made amends with the school and her parents without incident.

The same could not be said for an experience with a customer's beloved parakeet. One year we acquired a baby South American ostrich called a rhea. The bird was personable and tame and everyone loved her. She followed Chris Hoppe the assistant manager of our bird department, everywhere. One day, Chris was taking care of Mrs. Hanson's parakeet. Mrs. Hanson was elderly and one of our regular customers. She lived alone just a few blocks from our store and she provided her bird with the most varied diet and loving care imaginable. That day, she'd brought him in for a nail trimming and while Chris was carefully holding the parakeet and meticulously clipping each nail, our rhea stood close by looking on inquisitively. Then, in one shocking instant, the ostrich jumped straight up and snipped the head off of Mrs. Hanson's bird. Chris burst into tears and ran into my office, parakeet body still in hand. And you could hear Mrs. Hanson's sobs a block away as she slowly walked home. In spite of our attempts to make it up to her with a new parakeet and complete cage set-up, our relationship was never the same and it was just one of those sad moments of dealing with live animals.

You never really knew what was going to happen at the store from one day to the next. One Saturday morning, I noticed two women and a man walking through our bird department handling a few of our tame parrots. It was impossible to miss them. They were dressed extravagantly like gypsies. When I approached them I noticed heavy accents that I took to be Hungarian. The man was boisterous and overly friendly and he explained in his best English that they were in a traveling circus appearing at the carnival down the street with their primate act. I asked about the act and the man offered to show me.

We left the store and the man escorted me to a long Winnebago parked out front. I stepped up into the vehicle and right away noticed the foul smell of straw mixed with who knows what. The Winnebago had been customized with an aisle on the driver's side going all the way to the rear. On the left side were four large, built-in enclosures with sliding steel bar doors. We walked down the aisle and I suddenly found myself within inches of an adult gorilla, the bar doors the only thing separating us.

Then things got *really* interesting. The man gave a few voice commands for the gorilla to step back from the door. Then he slid the door open and the gorilla came out of his cage. Now I was face-to-face with him. He was as tall as me and weighed at least twice as much. I could feel my heart pounding. I loved interacting with animals, but this was a little beyond my comfort range. Finally, the man ordered the gorilla back into the cage. I meekly thanked the man for the introduction and made my way back into the store, walking unsteadily to my office where I had to sit down until my heart rate returned to somewhere close to normal.

Just another day at Noah's Ark Pet Center.

18

— • —

GROWTH

THE BUSINESS HUMMED ALONG, but soon came a huge change for Marie and me in our personal lives. We were blessed with a baby boy. Bob Jr. was born in August of 1972. What a wonderful time for us.

After leaving the hospital, Marie insisted on stopping by Noah's Ark to pick up some paperwork and of course everyone wanted to see our new addition. Not having a carrier or bassinet to place him in, we were obliged to hold him until it was just too much. I ended up bringing a new twenty-gallon aquarium into the office where our new baby fit comfortably and could gaze out through the glass. To this day, Bob Jr., who recently turned fifty, jokes about being the only person he knows of whose first glimpses of the world were from the inside of an aquarium.

With the baby, Marie began to spend more time at home, but still worked part time with finances and paperwork. My mother came in part time to help out with the accounting and banking.

As Noah's continued to provide the rewards of our accomplishments, we began to realize one of our valued strengths, which was offering fresh bulk foods, seeds, and mixes for birds and small animals. Up until this point our customers could only buy Hartz Mountain, 3 Vees, or Geisler brands of boxed or bagged diets, all of which were mass produced, warehoused, and shipped through wholesalers to grocery and specialty stores.

Besides the various diets for both   hard bill and soft bill birds, I carried over a process that I learned at Sedgwick Studio. We mixed certain unusual, hard-to-get seeds, like hemp, safflower, thistle, rape, and flax, creating specialty diets for the more discerning bird customers who were into breeding, weaning, or raising the rarer species.

A high school student named Greg worked for us part time and helped initiate a private label division by hand-filling, weighing, and labeling hundreds of plastic bags of aquarium gravel, pet bedding, and bird and small animal diets. In no time, Greg mastered our semi-automatic packaging system, which completely covered the corner of our backroom where our receiving area was. He was diligent and industrious and it's no surprise to me that that young high school student went on to become Dr. Gregory Stram, a highly respected veterinarian in Schaumburg, Illinois.

The popularity of the private-labeled products encouraged us to expand the program with more items that were never before available. We began packaging alfalfa, timothy, and straw from local farmers, as well as pine, red cedar, and ground corn cob bedding. We sourced and packaged river stones, pebbles, and specialty aggregates from local landscape rock suppliers for our more discerning aquarium hobbyists. Before the days of Reptomin and ZooMed diets, there were no commercially manufactured diets for aquatic turtles outside of the two brands of poor quality packaged dried insects labeled turtle food. We learned that Purina Trout Chow was a well-balanced aquatic turtle diet and soon repackaged and sold it to our turtle customers in one and three pound bags labeling it R.O.D. (Reptile Omnivore Diet.)

We also repackaged Purina fifty-pound bags of chinchilla pellets into three-pound bags of chinchilla diet. There was also a commercial product called Blue Sparkle, a pumice-type powder that was used by the chinchilla fur industry as a coat conditioner. Chinchillas instinctively dusted themselves in it. We purchased it in twenty-five pound bags and sold it in one- and three-pound bags labeling it "Chin Dust."

Ferrets were becoming popular in spite of the fact that there weren't any products for them, let alone a commercially produced diet. For customers interested in ferrets, we recommended a large rabbit-type cage and the only book we could find that had any kind of information about domesticated ferrets, a work published in the early 1900s for the game and fur industries and entitled *Ferret Facts and Fancy* by Arthur Harding. For diet, most of the small breeders we purchased our ferrets from used canned cat food. We researched a commercial pelleted mink diet that closely paralleled the dietary requirements of ferrets and repackaged it into three-pound plastic bags that we labeled simply "Ferret Diet."

Eventually, we built a department with three employees packaging close to a hundred different items, many of which could not to be found any-where else. Soon after, we created a "Noah's Ark" brand and logo and designed a full color packaging program. The bird and small animal diets became the lion's share of our bulk selection and the volume we were moving was phenomenal.

It was right about this time that the bomb dropped. In 1973, Marie was diagnosed with breast cancer and had to undergo a radical mastectomy. Marie's mother, Lucille, helped immensely during Marie's recovery as I divided my time between the business and taking care of Bob Jr. It was a very unsettling time, but Marie recovered and we were able to move forward with our lives.

Back at the store, Joe Leonard approached me one day with the idea that, since we were selling so many products in such high volume, we could start buying product directly from manufacturers that, up until then, we'd been buying through wholesalers. Obviously, without the middleman it would mean more profit for us. For the manufacturers who might be reluctant, not wanting to compete, essentially, with their wholesalers for our business, Joe explained that we could create another entity using a fictitious name.

I thought it was a great idea and jumped right on it, deciding to go a step further and create a pet product wholesale company of our own. I had our attorney, Ken Bellah, draw up the paperwork and we established a new corporation that we named NAPCO Distributing Co. Inc., NAPCO being an acronym for Noah's Ark Pet Center Operations. Later, however, when other companies would ask what the name meant, we just said North American Pet Company.

I designed a logo for the company, settling on the only concept that seemed appropriate for me: the "N" in NAPCO depicted a turtle sticking his neck out. While having invoices, purchase orders, letterheads, envelopes, business cards, and stationary printed, we put in a new phone line. I ordered a red phone and had it installed in the office right next to the store's black phone. The red color was a visual reminder to answer in a specific way: "NAPCO distributing company." Soon we were contacting manufacturers and buying a lot of our products directly.

While the store brought in pet-loving consumers from all over the Midwest and beyond, it also attracted curious pet retailers who had been hearing about this giant pet store called Noah's Ark Pet Center. Many of these retailers became close friends and several started asking where they could find many of the unique items that we carried so they could start carrying them in their stores. This opened the door for us to actually start wholesaling to other businesses.

Unfortunately, with all that was going on with the business, I found myself unable to properly balance my professional life with my family life. My business became my mistress, occupying my mind twenty-four hours a day. It was all I could think about. And so, in retrospect, it should not have come as a surprise that my marriage suffered. By the end of 1973, Marie and I were separated.

Being solo, however, didn't really agree with me. After work, several of us often went to Denny's Restaurant, eating late dinners and sharing the trials and tribulations of the day. Linda Moore from the puppy department always came along. Having so much in common with pets and animals, Linda and I were soon dating.

While I was splitting my time between running the world's largest pet center and building a brand-new wholesale company, Dave McKelvy convinced me that if I were to buy a small homestead, we could start breeding our own cockatiels, lovebirds, doves, finches, and several small animals. The idea was that it would provide us with a quality source of supply that would produce enough to cover the mortgage, taxes, and insurance on the property. Dave assured me that he and his wife could run the farm and he'd still be able to perform his full time management responsibilities in the bird department. In exchange, I'd allow him to live on the property rent free.

Since we were always looking for more and more suppliers of birds and small animals, this seemed like an exciting opportunity. I told Dave that I would think about it but before I knew it, Dave found a five-acre homestead complete with farmhouse, barn, and three outbuildings in an upscale, changing community. The price was right and I bought it. Dave and his wife moved in and we began building outdoor aviaries, along with cages and animal enclosures inside the barn and outbuildings. Within sixty days we were fully stocked with breeders and began producing pet rats, guinea pigs, dwarf rabbits, cockatiels, doves, finches, conures, and lovebirds.

All this time, while I was enjoying my success as an entrepreneur, my brother was working as a bartender at Johnny Held's Brown Bear Restaurant and Lounge. He also worked part time as a plainclothes store detective at Wieboldts department store where they had a continuous shoplifting problem. Tom volunteered to come in on weekends as a pretend shopper doing the same for Noah's Ark after convincing me that we, too, most certainly had the same problem that most self-serve retailers had. Tom soon learned a lot about the overall operation of Noah's Ark. In seeing this, Mom started pushing for me to hire Tom. She wanted to get him away from the nightlife environment he was in, but I thought that hiring him was a bad idea. Tom and I had different styles and I was afraid his employment under me would create a divide in the family and upset the business at the same time. Mom kept insisting and I finally caved after she agreed to cover the difference in the salary he needed and the amount I could justify, given what I paid the other store employees.

Tom joined the company and began his pet industry career selling puppies and I was happy to have been wrong about his coming on board. Tom was excellent at his new job. Being a people-person and with his magnetic personality, all he had to do was learn the traits and attributes of the different breeds of dogs and he was off to the races.

Soon, however, I started having problems with another employee. A key staff member. None other than Dave McKelvy. In less than a year, the farm operation turned out to be a complete disaster. I made some serious mistakes not only in being too trustful, but in again not following my gut feeling, this time whenever Dave would give me vague answers to my questions about the operation. I failed to implement a decent accounting system or a check and balance procedure on the actual investments in construction, live animal purchases, the buying of feed and supplies, and the expenses of upkeep. The farm ended up being the home of Dave's personal collection of exotic pheasants and waterfowl, as well as his wife's Arabian horse. Every night after work, Dave loaded his car with fifty-pound bags of feed of which we had no record. I soon had to sit down and have a serious talk with Dave and the end result was him leaving our organization.

Now I had a five-acre farm with birds and small animals that needed attention. Delegating such a responsibility to untrained individuals wouldn't work, so Linda Moore, Denise King, and I took charge. The first order of business was to exterminate all the escaped rats that had reproduced and established themselves in the walls of our outbuildings.

Once we completed the clean-up and restoration, we came to the realization that if we were to successfully produce any animals or birds, we had to specialize and focus on one specific area. During the Easter season, we sold hundreds of dwarf rabbits. We were always searching for additional breeders to meet our needs of Netherland dwarf, French lop, and Dutch rabbits but could never find enough. I moved into the farm with Linda Moore. By then, my divorce had been finalized and Marie and I had agreed on joint custody of Bob Jr. Shortly after, Denise King came along to the farm, too, and we began what would become our dwarf rabbit-breeding operation. We slowly acquired our breeding stock and started producing litters upon litters of dwarf rabbits. That following Easter season was a great success as we made sure all those little bunnies went home with proper caging, diet, and supplies.

In thinking about other things that impacted our business in a positive way, I have to say that we became an outstanding source of books on many different subjects as it related to pets and their care. One thing I had always known about our customers, whether they were buying rabbits or puppies or even a hamster or a turtle, was that there was always a thirst for information about the animals they cared so much about. Before the days of the internet, everyone's main source of knowledge came from either hands-on experience or books. Hands-on experience was invaluable and in the aggregate led to the creation of clubs, societies, and associations populated with people who all shared the same interests. But I knew from personal experience that books could be just as valuable and I knew that our customers would think so too.

There were primarily two major book publishers at the time that focused on pets: Howell Book House for purebred dogs, and TFH Publications for most everything else. Our elaborate book department inventoried every title they had, in addition to other titles we came across as we searched high and low for publishers who may have had a title or two on parrots or other caged birds, small animals, reptiles, or tropical fish. We carried books that were rarely available outside of museum gift shops. All told, we had the single most complete book department on pets and animal care anywhere.

Meanwhile, Tom's responsibilities began to grow. Soon, he was handling all the advertising. This consisted of newspaper advertising, including a color insert in the Sunday *Chicago Tribune*, coupon books that were handed out weeks before sales events, and Tom's personal favorite—radio advertising on WGN, the Chicago Cubs network. Tom not only wrote the ads himself but provided the audio with different voices and sound effects. Everyone loved them. Coordinating the purchasing of all sales merchandise became a joint effort resulting in the most successful sales of pets and products the Chicagoland market had ever seen.

As Noah's Ark continued to grow, so did NAPCO as we added more lines of pet products. Soon, we realized that our growth was being limited by the four walls of our 9,270 square-foot building. The backroom was busting out of its seams. The limited open area became nothing more than an aisle that you had to squeeze yourself through. The overhead door was out of use because it had become one of the walls of our private label packaging department. We had ladder-accessible walkways above the rooms in the back giving us a haphazard upstairs for merchandise overstock and it was a good thing OSHA never stopped by to inspect it.

As luck would have it, just as I was contemplating getting extra ware-house space somewhere, our landlord dropped by with an opportunity. He and his partners had just purchased the vacant property directly across the street and planned to develop it. He wanted to know if we'd consider moving into the entire front section of the building. We would be able to design the new store to our exact future needs. It was just what we needed. And the icing on the cake was that we would now have a parking lot with over a hundred spaces.

I didn't want to negotiate another lease and instead offered to partner with him by purchasing the front half of the proposed 46,000 square-foot building outright. He agreed, and together we created a commercial con-dominium concept. We didn't waste any time in developing a plan to move our entire operation into what would be a newly designed, state-of-the-art, Noah's Ark Pet Center, all a result of the lessons we'd learned in the four years we'd been in business. Our retail space would double in size while NAPCO would have its own 3,000 square-foot warehouse facility directly behind. We were already big. Now we were about to get much bigger.

19

— • —

WATCHING IT ALL COME TOGETHER

FOR THE NEW FACILITY, I hired an architectural design firm that specialized in state-of-the-art retail establishments and, over a six-month period,
while we remained in business across the street, we designed and built the
new Noah's Ark Pet Center. Our past successes, as well as the shortcomings
we experienced, allowed us to create the "Pet Center of the Future."

We created six custom-designed, live pet areas. We incorporated wider
aisles and an upgraded lighting system throughout. We put in departmentalized merchandising and aesthetically pleasing glass barrier walls to control air movement and noise. We installed a separate HVAC system for each
department. We had built-in temperature controls and zero condensation
on the front windows. We even included customer washrooms between
the double-door entrance and the turnstiles that permitted access to the
store. To ease traffic flow within the store, we designed two check-out lines
with the flexibility of adding a third. Upbeat and fun background music
played throughout the store.

The puppy department consisted of two walk-in display rooms, each
with twenty-two concrete block puppy kennels with rubberized grid flooring over drains for easy cleaning. In each room we had a pair of "get
acquainted rooms" where families could interact with the puppies of their
choosing. The kitten department had a custom-designed, ventilated kitten

room with built-in glass-doored compartments and a carpeted center room for litters of kittens to romp and play.

The tropical fish department was low-lit with a drop ceiling. We had every species of fish both common and rare, grouped and displayed in over 150 twenty- and thirty-gallon aquariums, as well as twelve display aquariums that ranged in size from 70 to 120 gallons for larger specimens. The racks were custom designed and incorporated a low maintenance subfloor central filtration system. We had a live plant section as well as a cold-water section of koi and goldfish. An in-the-floor koi pond was encircled by fish bagging areas for convenient service.

The bird department was a hub of sound and activity and consisted of eight seven-foot high, wrought iron parrot display cages on pedestal bases. These were for macaws, cockatoos, and various parrots, toucans, and larger birds. We had several walk in aviaries for finches, parakeets, soft billed birds, doves, quail, and dwarf parrots in addition to a "singing canary wall," reminiscent of Vahle's Bird Store. In the center of all this was an enormous tree that branched out, displaying our tamest parrots for customers to interact with over a garden setting.

The reptile department featured natural, built-in, rock-walled enclosures with secure glass doors, lighting, and pools, along with several screened-top aquatic terrariums. This allowed us to improve our displays of the largest and most complete inventory of turtles (I loved my turtles), tortoises, snakes, and lizards anywhere, plus our inventory of amphibians, tarantulas, and scorpions.

In the small mammal department, we offered a wide selection, and, for optimal conditions, built several spacious ceramic-walled enclosures with sliding glass and screened doors for our guinea pigs, dwarf rabbits, ferrets, seasonal bottle-fed Coati Mundis, and prairie dogs. We had smaller enclosures for our golden hamsters, dwarf hamsters, gerbils, degus, sugar gliders, dwarf hedgehogs, rats, and mice.

In my new office, we designed an area for two hatchling turtle environments that would keep me engaged while reminding me just how this whole world I was now living in got started. And of course directly behind the retail store was the space for our wholesale distribution company, NAPCO Distributing Co.

It was amazing to watch it all come together.

Soon, it was time to start advertising the pending move to the new facility. This is where Tom came in. He continued with his WGN radio spots and hit a home run with his ads featuring "The Lord and Noah." Tom was very creative and had a lot of fun doing the voices. He recorded "the Lord's" voice by echoing a deep and commanding tone into a coffee can. His "Noah's" voice was that of a trembling, obedient man who was obviously in fear of the consequences of disobedience, but who nevertheless questioned the instructions he was given. Tom recorded a series of these ads, with the first one being of the Lord commanding Noah to move the Ark with all its animals across the street.

Subsequent ads over the years would be of the Lord commanding Noah to build an Ark, make it a big one, then fill it with puppies, birds, tropical fish, and unusual pets from around the world. Then to park it on Oakton Street in Elk Grove Village, Illinois. Noah, would nervously question the Lord, even asking in one spot, "What's an Ark?" This would anger the Lord, resulting in an explosion of thunder and pouring rain. The ads would always end with Noah conceding and saying, "Yes, Lord." Tom's radio spots were huge hits.

Then the long-awaited day finally came. The collective efforts of all our dedicated employees working around the clock, filling our vans with merchandise, fixtures, and supplies, and crossing the street through the long evening hours was gratifying. It was a sight to be seen as we moved all the animals, even stopping traffic at one point to nudge Methuselah across, leading the symbolic procession.

In thinking back, who would have thought that in 1975 such a feat could have been achieved? Our Grand Reopening was huge. Our customers couldn't believe the new store. Many of them felt as if they were going to a miniature zoo, but even better. In our zoo, you could take home some of the enjoyment. It was exciting for us, but also a relief not to have to constantly address the unpleasant odors, the water on the floor, the need to escort people to the washrooms in the back, and the perpetual parking problems.

The new Noah's Ark Pet Center became a meeting place, a destination for pet and animal enthusiasts of all kinds—families, hobbyists, pet professionals, and even famous people including sports figures, entertainers, and authors. Famous jazz singer and band leader Billy Eckstine paid us a visit one day. So did singer-songwriter Todd Rundgren. Oakland Athletics' owner Charles O'Finley stopped by the store, as did Bruce Sutter of the St. Louis Cardinals and Randy Hundley of the Cubs.

Barbara Woodhouse, famous British dog and horse trainer, TV personality, and author made a trip to the United States one time and wanted to see the world's largest pet center. We received notice a few weeks beforehand and got the word out. Crowds of people showed up. We set up a fenced-in area for Ms. Woodhouse to demonstrate her techniques of training, which she was happy to do by performing her magic on a young Lhasa Apso. At the end of the applause, we ushered her and her entourage into our employee lunchroom. Denise King had done her homework and knew that it was Barbara Woodhouse's birthday. In the lunchroom, we surprised her with an elaborate birthday cake lit with candles.

One day none other than Muhammed Ali walked into our store and his presence spread through the organization like wildfire. Tom and I immediately greeted him and learned that Ali's wife was a bird lover. After floating around the bird department in his colorful fashion, Ali was taken aback by one of our store mascots, Magoo, the talking greater sulfur crested cockatoo. Ali wanted him. We explained that Magoo was not for sale and even if he were, he would be extremely expensive. That's all Ali needed to hear. In spite of my attempts to interest him and his wife in a tame Amazon parrot, he could not be swayed toward any other bird. He had to have Magoo. Finally, we made a deal.

That evening, Tom and I delivered Magoo, along with an elaborate cage and all the supplies, to Ali's south Michigan Avenue mansion. After spending some time explaining Magoo's requirements to Ali and his staff, we sat down to handle the finances. Ali excused everyone except two of his security people. Then he made a gesture and one of them placed a large envelope onto the table. Ali reached over and began peeling off one hundred dollar bills, counting them in front of me while joking and talking. When he finished, I picked up the bills and began counting them again which resulted in Ali asking me whether or not I trusted him. I smiled and continued counting, only to discover that he had overpaid me by a hundred dollars. When I brought this to his attention, Ali smiled and nodded while saying, "I was just testing you." Then he reached over and picked up a one-hundred dollar bill and slid it into his pocket. (To this day, I borrow Ali's line whenever I'm caught in a mistake, as I'm sure he was.)

A few days later, Ali called us on the phone. "Get this damn bird out of here!" As it turned out, Magoo's screaming was too much for him. We ended up trading Magoo for a complete 150-gallon aquarium set up and maintained Ali as a good customer until he moved out of Chicago.

Me, Muhammed Ali, Tom, and Magoo the cockatoo.

Magoo continued on as one of our store mascots but with an additional label of at one time belonging to the world-famous Muhammad Ali. He received all the love and attention he desired by greeting the thousands of guests who passed through our doors. When we would eventually close our last store in 1992, Magoo would become a Krause family pet until he moved to Miami and to live out his final days greeting visitors at the turnstile entrance of "Dr. Bern Levine's Jungle Island: Miami's Premier Entertainment Destination."

While the retail store was enjoying its success, things were happening on the wholesale front, too. As we were setting up the NAPCO warehouse facility, Ralph Diaz, the son-in-law of Mel Krause of M.P. Krause & Sons, approached me with the idea of working for NAPCO to build a true sales department. NAPCO could become a legitimate wholesaler and not just the buying arm of Noah's Ark. I thought it was a great idea and brought Ralph aboard. After establishing a wholesale price list and inventory, we created a list of potential customers in the Chicagoland area. Within a month, we were supplying a few select retailers and, soon after, opened up a cash-and-carry wholesale warehouse for out-of-town retailers, many of whom drove miles to visit the world's largest pet center, and many of whom became good friends. I spent my Fridays and weekends working Noah's Ark Pet Center and devoted a day to Bob Jr. on Mondays. On Tuesdays, Ralph and I hit the streets for NAPCO.

Among my pet store contacts was Amling's Flowerland whom I used to work for. On one of our visits, I met with Paul Wentland, the company president. After some small talk, and out of nowhere, Paul proposed a partnership. He told me that he had visited our store and was impressed with our merchandising and professionalism. He wanted to know if I'd be interested in leasing his four pet departments, even saying that we could advertise and market them as pilot Noah's Ark Pet Centers within the Amling's stores. Amling's was an upscale nursery and flower center and I was not only flattered, but felt the fit was excellent. Within a year we were advertising not only our original "World's Largest Pet Center," but we now had four additional stores for the shopping convenience of our customers.

Then came another idea. I noticed that our cash and carry operation did a great book business. Full service wholesalers couldn't support the TFH line of books to its potential because it was an inventory and ordering nightmare. But our cash and carry operation did well because we had inventory. Customers could go through it and physically pick out the books they wanted right on the spot. I thought about ways to more efficiently bring the books to the retail market and hit upon the concept of the "NAPCO Bookmobile."

We purchased a brand-new, high-top step van, had it painted with our bookmobile logo, and covered the interior walls with pegboard and wire book holders. We bolted two four-sided revolving wire book racks down the center and filled the truck with almost the entire TFH line of pet and aquarium books. The NAPCO Bookmobile established a regular route, calling on pet shops throughout the Chicagoland market and selling countless pet books.

Our driver was Linda Moore's younger brother Lee Scoville. Lee had come to work for us part-time back in '72 when he was in high school, bagging feeder goldfish on weekends. He'd always wanted to work in the pet shop and after he graduated, I hired him, eventually making him a salesman for NAPCO Distributing.

Lee was happy to take charge of the bookmobile and for a short period of time we became one of TFH's largest distributors of pet books. But soon we started experiencing major problems. Due to the size of our reorders, TFH began calling for payment of the previous invoices before they would release the next shipment. Meanwhile, while some customers bought heavy, there were others who wouldn't even take the time to climb the steps into the van. Sometimes the owner/buyer of the store wasn't present. And then there was the fact that the van could get hot and uncomfortable. The final nail in the coffin was when Lee had a near accident, swerving the van to avoid a collision. The books went flying everywhere. Enough was enough. Plus, I'd wanted to put Lee to better use calling on pet stores instead of just selling books. So ended the NAPCO Bookmobile.

NAPCO was doing well, however. We made our official introduction to the Chicago market at the October H.H. Backer Pet Industry Trade Show where we exhibited all our products, driving the other Chicagoland wholesalers nuts. All our varied and hard-to-get items were well received and we were now officially recognized as a legitimate wholesale distributor.

At one point during the exhibition, while I was talking to a customer, I noticed a well-dressed gentleman at our exhibit checking out our product displays. I glanced at his nametag and couldn't believe it: the one and only Milton Docktor, founder of Docktor Pet Center, the company I credit for turning on that lightbulb in my mind and encouraging me to enter the entrepreneurial world. I introduced myself and told Milton about Noah's Ark Pet Center and how he indirectly had been instrumental in putting me into the pet industry. In describing our newly opened 20,000 square-foot store, I could see he was intrigued. He told me he'd love to see it. Under no other circumstances would I have left that trade show, but I felt I owed it to such an icon in the industry.

We ended up leaving the show later that afternoon and driving to Noah's Ark so that I could give Milton the grand tour. He was impressed and asked if I had any designs or drawings I could share with him. Not knowing his intentions, I naively gave him a complete set of our live animal fixture enclosure designs and off he went. I later discovered he copied them exactly for another retail pet store venture he was involved in. But, considering that he had gotten me started in the business, I didn't spend a lot of time regretting it.

After a year in the wholesale business, we found ourselves in the favorable position of being approached by several manufacturers asking us to carry their line of goods. It was a proud feeling not to have to make speculative promises of performance. We were showing what we were capable of doing. And the business kept growing. We bought another 3,000 square-foot adjoining condominium warehouse space, thus doubling NAPCO's size by merely breaking two drive-through openings in the concrete block walls.

In the meantime, at Noah's Ark, we continued to package our own products. And the success necessitated a completely separate division with three employees handling our bulk feed, grain, bird and animal diets, aquarium gravel, rock, and stones. We had truckloads of bird and small animal feed delivered to us in fifty-pound burlap and paper bags from Kaytee Products Company. This represented the largest portion of our private-labeled products and I began to wonder if we could interest Kaytee in packaging the top-selling products we were buying from them into three- and five-pound full-color poly bags, thus saving us from having to spend the time and effort on the repackaging process. I made a phone call and set up an appointment with Bill Engler, president of Kaytee.

Tom and I drove up to the small farming town of Chilton, Wisconsin to meet Mr. Engler and the meeting resulted in a mutually profitable business relationship that not only increased our profit margins and contributed to our ongoing business success, but became an "Ah-ha" moment for Kaytee. Years later, Bill told me that it was this business we started together that made Kaytee decide to package bird and small animal foods in smaller poly bags themselves under the Kaytee label. The rest is history. Today Kaytee is one of America's leading brands of bird and small animal foods and bedding. The kicker? How could I have imagined back then that I would someday become the president of Kaytee?

In 1977, Tom and his girlfriend Bonnie got married. One day, he came to work with a very large carton and called me over to take a look. Inside was a fledgling great horned owl with a disfigured wing. Tom had found it lodged in the shrubs alongside his house. Apparently, it had fallen out of a nest somewhere, injured itself, and somehow made it to their house. I named her Ginny after the scientific name of the great horned owl, *bubo virginianus*, and took responsibility for her. Tom officially presented her to me as a gift on my birthday that June. I brought Ginny home to the farm and set her up in the aviary adjoining the house. It was very enjoyable to see her each morning and evening as she sat on the specially designed shelf outside of the kitchen windowsill, waiting for me to pay attention to her or feed her.

Meanwhile, during all this time, my personal life was changing. I was happy to see that Marie had moved on with her life. She had started dating a successful business executive and soon remarried. Linda Moore and Denise

King decided to move on as well. They both moved to Colorado where Denise began working at a local chain of pet stores and Linda took a job working for a racehorse breeding ranch. I remained on the farm and, at thirty-one years of age, found myself needing something more in life. I started dating again and met a pet-loving young woman by the name of Marilyn Schmidt. We enjoyed each other's company but, as always, my business priorities took precedence and the relationship lasted only a few months. Soon afterward, I started dating another young woman, Cathy Miller, but that too didn't last long.

The fact is, I missed Linda and soon renewed my relationship with her. She moved back to Illinois and into the farmhouse with me and I couldn't have been happier. We soon planned to marry and start the family life that I felt I was ready for.

20

—•—

MY FULL LIFE

IN JULY OF 1977, Linda and I married. For our honeymoon, we visited one of the sites of my boyhood memories: Crivitz in Wisconsin. Indeed, it was on that trip with Linda, camping out by the pond behind the antique store, where I got the chance to snorkel and had the close encounters with the midland painted turtles.

Back home, I sold the farm and Linda and I found a new home for us to start out fresh. It was a clean, well-kept, two-bedroom brick house on five acres that an elderly couple was selling. The roof was solidly built out of one-inch-thick panels from World War II shipping crates instead of plywood, an indication of the care that went into its construction. The house had a large enclosed screened-in patio that looked out over a giant cherry tree, a garden, a shed, and a four-stall stable. An attached chain-link kennel run allowed access through a dog door built into the rear wall of the garage. There was a back pasture area with a wonderful small pond full of bass and—wouldn't you know it?—painted turtles. During our negotiations, I added a line into our purchase offer giving the seller fishing rights for two years after closing. He later told me that they accepted our offer because of that condition, even though they never took us up on it.

We moved to the property with Linda's horse Mister, Blake our German Shepherd, and Ginny my great horned owl. Mister had his own stall in the stable and enjoyed his daily jaunts in the pasture. Ginny had her own stall as well until I was able to finish constructing her new aviary. I also put large basking logs in the pond for my favorite, shiny, dome-shelled inhabitants. It wasn't long before we were all settled in, including the midland painted turtles.

Linda and I were happy with our new home and lifestyle and were soon expecting our first child. Each of the five Noah's Ark Pet Center stores was doing well and our main store continued to set records. NAPCO Distributing Company continued to grow as well. Life was good. Late in Linda's pregnancy, however, she went into premature labor. Our son Eric was born in 1978, a tiny baby whose heartbreaking struggle to survive lasted only two short days. It was a painful, sorrowful time for us.

Then, in August of that year, I lost my father. He had been ill. In fact, he died of cirrhosis of the liver and I began to understand more and more about my dad, things about him that I hadn't taken the time to notice before, things that helped explain his behavior—his attitude toward Tom, his not taking part in my wedding, his refusal to give me a business loan.

Dad was a drinker and it started during his early days as a freight agent for the Canadian Pacific Railroad. Sears Roebuck & Company was his best customer and he and their buyer, Harry Sadler, spent a lot of time in the bar after concluding their business. Dad's drinking ultimately cost him his job. Afterward he became a closet drinker while blaming his staying at home on some mysterious "bursitis" ailment. When my sister was born the year before I got drafted, Dad had yet another reason to continue staying home: he had to "take care" of my sister.

Over the years, Mom was the face of our family, always there for us, even while working full time jobs. And she worked hard to present a normal family life to extended family members and friends, maintaining the image she wanted of our family. Tom was "doing well in the Army," even though he was serving time in a boy's camp. My sister was "busy working" when, during her teenage years, she became involved with drugs and was absent at birthdays and family gatherings. Mom always made excuses for Dad, too, while we all learned to deal with the raised eyebrows.

As a child I loved my parents and respected my father immensely. Dad was the rock of the family. At least that's what I thought. Looking back, it was easy to see that the rock was really Mom. As a preschool child, I craved what little attention my father gave my brother and me, even loving the attention he gave us while chasing us with an open jar of horseradish, demanding that we sniff it. Or, on that snowy afternoon when I was ten, when he insisted on taking an embarrassing photo of me dressed in an oversized snowsuit that he made me wear with hat, gloves, and scarf—in front of all my friends.

The times were rare when Dad was present in our lives. Not knowing any better, I imagined this to be normal. Yes, we took those family vacations out west and to Wisconsin, but I can count on one hand the times Dad got involved in Tom's or my school or outside activities. It was always Mom. I had always put Dad's temperament down to the fact that he was "a tough German," or "old fashioned." That's what people said, anyway. But now I knew better. Now I knew it was the alcoholism.

Three days before he died, I visited Dad in the hospital and was saddened at the sight of my once-proud father. And I was taken aback at the sight of his long, disfigured toenails, a reality check for me, signaling that Dad had given up quite some time ago. The next day, in a final effort to express some love for my father, I brought a manicure set to the hospital and trimmed Dad's toenails. Two days later, on August 1, 1978, he passed away. Dad was fifty-four.

True to form, Mom told everyone that he died of causes other than cirrhosis of the liver. For my part, I lamented that Dad would no longer be able to share in the joys, opportunities, and challenges that lay ahead for his family. I also couldn't help but wonder at our similarities. More than I wanted to admit, I was very much like my father in many ways. Looking back today, I can see how easily I could have fallen into the same trap that he did. Dad had the bottle; I had my businesses.

Not quite a year after losing Dad, the family gained another member. Linda became pregnant again and on July 21, 1979, Lisa was born, a perfectly healthy baby girl with the cutest little eyes I had ever seen. Shortly after that, Linda began pursuing her dream of raising collies while I kept forging ahead with the company.

That year, we opened store number six. The owners of Pet Ranch, a high-volume customer of NAPCO's in a regional mall to the south of us, were looking to sell. We jumped on the opportunity, bought the store, and converted it into a Noah's Ark Pet Center. Store number seven wasn't far behind. As it happened, our wholesale connections allowed us to easily identify more potential acquisitions. One of those was Mural's Pet Center in Crystal Lake. A few months after the purchase of Pet Ranch, Mural's Pet Center, too, became another Noah's Ark store.

At home, Linda and I added several animals into our lives. Besides Blake, Mister, and Ginny, we had another horse, a pony, a miniature Sicilian donkey, African pigmy goats, chickens, ducks, and a turkey. All in a beautiful country setting. Meanwhile, my pond now had numerous painted turtles, which I maintained in a wild state, making sure the logs, lily pads, and aquatic vegetation provided an ideal habitat.

Spending one day a week with Bob Jr. soon became every other week, but for a two-day weekend. Sometimes I'd take him with me to the office and sometimes we'd hang out with Linda and Lisa, fishing or spending time with our animals at home. I picked up a book on bee keeping, built two hives, and ordered Italian honey bees from Dadant Company. The following spring, we were in the apiary business and over the next two seasons gave a lot of honey away to family and friends. It was a great experience for all of us.

I continued taking care of Ginny, a marvelous bird that could never be released due to her crooked wing. Her ten-foot by thirty-foot aviary had several tree branches and a large box shelter and any great horned owl would have loved to call it home. Ginny would call to me with that great horned owl shriek and fly toward me every time she saw me. It became a habit for me to wear a certain brown leather jacket whenever I worked with her as she always flew to my outstretched arm for her meal. Even though I always wore a special pair of welding gloves, the left sleeve of that jacket, with scratch marks and shredded pieces of dangling leather, became a badge of honor for me.

For Ginny's meals, I brought home feeder rats from Noah's Ark. Sometimes, we'd receive older pet rabbits with permanent damage caused by overgrown teeth. To put them out of their misery these poor little guys would normally have been put down and either neatly disposed of or picked up by an animal removal service. Instead, they were put to good use and became a week's worth of protein for Ginny.

The rural area we lived in also provided an abundance of protein in the form of roadkill and I was never hesitant to pick up a freshly killed squirrel or rabbit for Ginny, so long as the body wasn't crushed or emaciated. I started keeping rags and newspapers in the trunk of my car and, at certain times of the year, roadkill became Ginny's main diet source. It wasn't something I necessarily wanted people to see but for the sake of Ginny, this practice became commonplace. I'd pull over and wait for any traffic to pass, then run over to pick up the animal, wrap it, and place it in my trunk where it would stay until I'd return home. In the winter time, I didn't have to wrap the bodies because they were stiff as boards. More than a few times, I'd forget I had something in the trunk, which led to some awkward yet funny moments for friends and family. For a reason other than retrieving the forgotten animal, I'd open the trunk in front of someone and suddenly remember about the dead rabbit or squirrel I'd put in there a day or so before. It didn't take long for people to just smile and accept such an unusual practice.

With all the different kinds of animals I interacted with on a daily basis, I never lost my love of turtles, still my favorite of them all. We continued stocking the books of TFH Publications and I was excited to learn one day of a new hardcover of theirs entitled *The Encyclopedia of Turtles* by Peter Pritchard. I couldn't wait to get my hands on it. In fact, as soon as it became available, I ordered a dozen of them and when the shipment came, I ordered two dozen more. Pritchard's book became the bible of turtle keepers everywhere and for the first six months it was hard to keep it in stock. I took two copies home for myself and refer to it to this today.

NAPCO continued to grow and eventually we purchased the last remaining condominium warehouses in the building, allowing us to phase into each one, and giving us (and the bank) complete ownership of the whole building. We had been acquiring an increasing number of product offerings from most of the major manufacturers, soon becoming a full-line pet product wholesaler. In addition to increasing our warehouse staff, Ralph and I decided to hire another salesperson to join him and Lee. Then we could cover yet another territory in the Chicago market.

By our seventh store, we were being approached by several shopping malls and strip centers wanting us to open a Noah's Ark Pet Center with them. But given the stresses and financial strains of our rapid expansion, we took a cautious approach. In 1980, however, we couldn't say no to the new development of an upscale regional mall called Stratford Square in Bloomingdale, Illinois. I hired the same design firm we'd used before and put together a 4,000 square foot beautifully laid out mall store which opened the following year on March 7, 1981. Our eighth store turned out to be another valuable asset in our arsenal.

And then it happened: that same year, one of our major suppliers, Pets International Ltd., which had a retail division called Chicago Bird and Cage Company, approached us with the single largest growth decision of our company to date. Sid Meyers, the president of Pets International built his company by importing commodity pet products from Asia and marketing them throughout the United States under his brand name Super Pet. He also leased pet departments from large department stores throughout the Midwest. This was a time when regional shopping malls were being built throughout the country and becoming the most popular destinations to shop. Sid and his son Barry had been opening retail pet stores in these malls in the state of Illinois, following the Docktors concept and naming them Pet World.

Lacking true passion for the pet industry and wanting to pursue his dream of real estate development, Barry eventually called me and asked if we'd be interested in taking over his retail chain of twelve mall stores. We negotiated a price with a six month buyout and established an agreed-upon transition plan. Within the next year we added the stores to our company. We had our work cut out for us with converting each of the stores, two per month, into Noah's Ark Pet Centers with new fixtures, merchandising, and signage, plus retraining the employees and hiring and training new ones. We built a team with Tom leading the charge. The stores basically paid for themselves. With new policies, training, joint advertising, and sales promotions, and keeping the stores stocked with quality live animals, birds, and fish, we rapidly moved forward. And now we had a total of twenty stores.

During this time, Marie had moved on with her life and things were looking up for her and her new husband, Don, after the birth of Marie's second child, Kate. But then came a devastating blow. Marie's cancer came back. Her treatments didn't help and her condition worsened. My first love, and the mother to Bob Jr., passed away on August 15, 1981 at the age of thirty-four.

Unfortunately, things became complicated when Don, who loved Bob Jr. as his own, decided he wanted full custody and filed a restraining order against my taking him, allowing me just one day per week with my son. For the next year, while Bob Jr. was cared for by his maternal grandmother, a custody battle played itself out that created an almost insurmountable level of stress for everyone involved. While this was going on, Linda became pregnant with our second child, and we decided to remodel the house, giving us extra bedrooms upstairs.

From 1982 onward, the business solidified its position in the Midwest as being the go-to place for quality pets and advice. We established a live pet wholesale division where our main store did all of the buying, holding, and distributing of puppies, kittens, birds, small animals, and reptiles. Denise King and John Farris were responsible for coordinating all the live animal procurement and distribution while each store did its own tropical fish buying through Aquatics Inc.

Besides having our own vet tech team, we built relationships with local animal hospitals to help us maintain protocols for animal health. We developed other initiatives, and without the technology of today, we created preprinted order forms and planograms for all the store managers to facilitate reordering merchandise from NAPCO. We began having structured monthly managers meetings. We designed our full-color newspaper advertising inserts, coupon booklets, in-store signage, and aquarium and animal enclosure labeling. We started a customer pet club and designed t-shirts and baseball caps. We hired an experienced pet industry merchandising director, Lanny Helford, and we put together several company manuals on such topics as merchandising, sales, and pet care. My brother Tom created a company monthly newsletter named the *Arkolography*, keeping all the stores informed and involved.

We also organized company picnics and an extravagant Christmas party every year where we had a deluxe dinner and entertainment followed by annual announcements and employee awards for exceptional performance. During a couple of Decembers we even offered a customer option to have Santa (Tom) and his helper (Tom's wife, Bonnie) deliver the family's new puppy on Christmas Eve at no charge. They made upwards of fifty deliveries on those Christmas Eves, and we ended up getting a lot of publicity, though that wasn't the goal. We just wanted to help people celebrate Christmas, and what better way than adding a puppy to the family?

In short, we became a top-notch, highly professional, twenty-store retail chain of pet centers, always thinking out of the box and trying new things. And every now and then, I couldn't help but find myself wondering what Giff Gardner might have had to say about it. "He'll never make it," he had said at the grand opening of store number 1. That had been nineteen stores ago.

On April 4, 1982, while living in a partitioned house with plastic sheets separating the three rooms we were living in from the areas under construction, our son James was born. At about the same time, the custody battle ended successfully and Bob Jr. moved in. Now we were a family of five: Me, Linda, Bob Jr., Lisa, and James.

Twenty stores, five family members. Plus all the animals. My life was full and then some.

21

— • —

INTERNATIONAL

ONE DAY, AROUND THE time our house was being remodeled, I was working at my desk in the warehouse office of our Elk Grove Village location and my secretary came in holding three five-inch by eight-inch, white, foamboard signs.

Warning: These premises patrolled by an attack hamster, read the first one. The second was identical but ended with "parakeet" and the third with "housewife." I chuckled as my secretary explained that there was a fellow up front in the retail store who was asking for the buyer.

Recognizing the sales potential of the signs, I went up and found myself shaking hands with an outgoing, happy-go-lucky guy by the name of Gerald Padulo. I asked what other titles he had. "Whatever you want," he replied. Then I asked him the price and he fumbled for the right number to answer with. I could tell he was naïve when it came to selling retail products, but he struck me as sincere, not to mention adventurous for his determination to cold call on a business like mine.

I told Jerry to come back to my office where we chatted and I quickly discovered that all he had was this idea, a catchy brand name ("Wacky Warnings"), and a cute logo. Nothing else. He'd stuck his neck out and had a few signs made with some different titles so that he could go out and knock on doors. His thinking was that when he sold some, he'd have them produced. Right away, I envisioned numerous titles, all of which would be great sellers, and saw the idea as a product line that could potentially be marketed nationwide. It would have been easy to steal Jerry's non-patented idea and have the signs produced myself. I had the distribution network in place and I knew the wholesale and retail markets. I knew which pets were cute and popular, the ones that would be ideal candidates for the comical product assortment. The signs would be the perfect impulse buys.

But taking Jerry's idea as my own wasn't the right thing to do. Plus, I had a lot of respect for him for trying something like this. Instead, I told him about the potential that I saw for his product but that the signs would need to be carefully created and marketed nationwide. I explained that I imagined fifty or sixty different signs using popular pets that were the furthest from being guard dogs. I saw the items retailing at $1.99. They had to be sold to wholesale distributors and had to be priced right. As we continued strategizing, I could see Jerry's excitement building. Mine was too. Jerry and I had three or four more meetings over the next few weeks and hammered out the details of a fifty-fifty partnership.

And yet another company was born.

I created the strategic plan and financed the entire operation. I had my attorney, Ken Bellah, draw up a simple partnership agreement and off we went. I learned that Jerry was a high school physical education teacher and, like me, rode a motorcycle. His quick and witty humor was marvelous and I knew right away that he'd fit into my group of pet industry friends. He and I went out and re-sourced some of our material, negotiating and re-negotiating volume pricing and terms. With Jerry's friendly, magnetic personality and my ever-growing business savvy, we were able to have our vendors bend over backward to help our little start-up get going.

We created a sixty-item product line, designed a catalog, and set up the whole company in a corner of my neighbor's warehouse, negotiating an arrangement at a very reasonable rent that allowed us to come and go to receive shipments and process orders. We hired four top-notch manufacturers' sales reps, one for each territory to cover the entire country, making sure that they had excellent reputations with the pet supply wholesalers in their territories.

Then, after calling in some favors, I was able to have Wacky Warnings join the American Pet Products Manufacturers Association (APPMA), the industry's premier manufacturers group. This was critical in my opinion. Belonging to the APPMA legitimized us. Plus, their famous annual trade show attracted buyers from everywhere.

That year's show, in New Orleans, which is where we'd make our big debut, was only a few months away. We had our work cut out for us. During the next ninety days we worked nonstop making all the arrangements, coordinating the logistics, building our initial inventories, placing advertisements in pet industry magazines, designing a trade show exhibit, and preparing for the show. Then, just as we were preparing to make our travel arrangements, Jerry made a rather interesting confession: he was afraid to fly! But nothing was going to stop Jerry, and aside from the stiffness he experienced from his very long train ride from Union Station Chicago to New Orleans, he was his same enthusiastic self.

We wrote a huge number of orders at the show and even had wholesale buyers seek us out. For marketing awareness, we produced several Wacky Warning signs, ending with the names of the presidents of the top pet product manufacturers and wholesalers. Then, before the show's opening, we walked around and handed them out as gifts, requesting that they be displayed in the companies' booths. Everyone laughed and enjoyed the signs and it was really something to see them posted throughout the show.

Jerry became one of my best friends. The next few years were a lot of fun and brought us together like brothers. We penetrated the national market completely, with all the major distributors putting Wacky Warnings into their product selection. We provided retail starter packs of our top eighteen sellers with self-serve spinning racks. To walk into a pet shop anywhere in the country and see our signs displayed up by the front counter was very gratifying.

Jerry and I also interacted very well businesswise, not only because of our similar personalities, but for the fact that we designed a seamless business model that eliminated any head bumping. Jerry had a straightforward and simple process for filling orders that allowed my responsibilities in Wacky Warnings to be minimal. I stayed busy growing my other companies while Jerry handled Wacky Warnings and we always found common ground in working out what few differences we had. When Jerry came in a few days each week to process orders, we always made time for each other, either going to lunch or just talking and strategizing.

After a couple of years, Wacky Warnings reached its peak and we decided to market the entire line through another company in the pet industry. Even though it would cut our profit margin, the decision made a lot of sense because it drastically cut our overhead in processing small orders and did away with all inventory of product, cartons, and labels. We also knew that partnering with the right company would get the line into new markets that we weren't able to penetrate. VO-Toys, a well-known manufacturer/importer of pet toys and accessories that I'd been doing business with over the years was the answer. The president, Gary Hirschberg was a friend of mine and I reached out to him. We ended up making a mutually profitable agreement and the new arrangement transformed the business into a hands-off operation.

I eventually sold my 50 percent ownership to Jerry for one dollar. Jerry continued running the company on his own, nicely subsidizing his income until, ultimately, he stopped having fun doing it. To this day Jerry and I maintain a close friendship, either riding our motorcycles or just getting together with our wives for dinner, all the while appreciating what brought us together in the beginning.

Meanwhile, I remained constantly on the lookout for new products and, late in 1981, an advertisement in one of our pet industry trade publications caught my eye. Koch Travel, a New York-based travel agency, was assembling a group to attend Interzoo, the world's largest pet industry trade show being held in May of '82 in the famous resort town of Wiesbaden, Germany. The possibilities and potential opportunities intrigued me. I figured it would be a great way to discover unusual and innovative pet products that I could import and market at my Noah's Ark Pet Center stores, and sell to other retailers through NAPCO Distributing. I wanted my brother to join me but he had no interest in going, and so I ended up traveling with Lee Scoville.

Our flight went through New York where we met up with the other people in the Koch Travel group, two of whom were Jean and Dave Merkel, owners of Great Lakes Pet Supply, a wholesale distributor in Milwaukee that Noah's Ark Pet Centers did business with. Jean, who had a reputation as a very headstrong woman, was definitely the decision maker of their company and made sure everyone knew it. Realizing that Noah's Ark and NAPCO were fast-growing companies, she considered me an adversary and didn't especially appreciate my attendance on the tour. In spite of my courtesy and politeness, she made it obvious that she felt I didn't belong.

We flew into Frankfort and boarded a bus to Wiesbaden where we checked into an historic hotel. I had never traveled abroad before and was immediately taken by the sights and sounds of my new European environment. Sidewalks, curbs, and narrow streets were all designed differently than what I was accustomed to. Cars and trucks looked unusually small and the distinctive sounds of the police and ambulance sirens reminded me that I was no longer in the US. At the hotel, the first thing I noticed was that the doors opened in the opposite direction than ours in the States. It was exciting to be in Germany and after checking in and exchanging some money at the desk, Lee and I explored a bit of Wiesbaden, popping into the shops along the main road. I ended up buying a unique, three-and-a-half-inch, bone-handled Solingen switchblade pocket knife, which to this day sits in my top desk drawer.

The next morning, we all met in the dining room of the hotel for a typical European buffet-style breakfast that I found more than satisfactory. But as we were all finishing up, I learned firsthand what the expression "Ugly American" meant. From a few tables away we heard Jean Merkel loudly expressing her displeasure with the coffee, which was not, apparently, up to her standards. At first I just shook my head but as she continued, I wanted to crawl under the table, embarrassed for us Americans. From that day forward, whenever traveling in a foreign country, I would always remind myself to be courteous, gracious, and respectful to my foreign hosts. I also learned the importance of at least making an attempt to speak a few words in the local language.

The Interzoo trade show was enormous, covering an exhibition center with several halls and buildings connected together. Our group split up and went their separate ways, which was fine by me. This was my first experience attempting any business communications with foreign-speaking people, most of whom spoke a bit of broken English. I tried to do my best to utter a few courtesies in both Italian and German, at least what I could remember from what I'd learned as a child and in my high school German classes. My efforts were met with appreciation, albeit also some laughter at my mispronunciations.

The three-day show opened the door to many opportunities. In those days, the show was primarily European, with exhibitors from all over

Europe and a few from Asia. Today, the Interzoo trade show attracts exhibitors from every corner of the world including the Americas, Asia, and the Middle East. But even back then, it was a huge show with hundreds of exhibitors with thousands of interesting and unique pet products, many of which could never be sold or accepted in the US market, others that could do very well.

Walking through all of the halls and seeing all the different exhibits representing so many different countries, I was struck by how big the pet industry really was. And how varied. Each market demonstrated a different way of caring for pets. The diverse products and philosophies of proper husbandry, coming from so many unique cultures was eye-opening for me. And yet, in spite of all the little differences, I saw that everyone was sharing the same fundamental interests: a love of animals and a desire to take that love and make a living from it.

If anything, with all the new products and ideas, the show made me realize how much I didn't know and how much more I needed to learn. One of the lessons I took home was that this was a time when the pet industry was evolving everywhere in the world. People in every country, from every culture, loved their pets and did the best they could to provide proper and loving care.

One of the largest exhibits, a venue in and of itself, was the Rolf C. Hagen and Company exhibit. This was fitting because Rolf C. Hagen was the largest pet product manufacturer in the world. I was flattered when Rolf himself, knowing that the Noah's Ark Pet Center chain, as well as NAPCO, were important customers, approached me at the show with an invitation to attend his company's special dinner celebration. He arranged transportation for well over 200 guests to a famous castle. The evening was spectacular and the graciousness of the Hagen family was unforgettable.

During the show, I introduced myself to several companies. They all seemed to respect my comments and opinions and could tell I wasn't new to the pet industry. Some of the manufacturers were no different than their counterparts in America in that they were very proficient at designing and manufacturing their products, but had no real experience with the actual animals they had designed the products for.

The exhibitors who were interested in expanding their business into the American market seemed to go out of their way to spend time with me. But the smaller companies, with many of the really unique and salable items, did business mostly with customers in Europe and weren't looking to expand into the US. The thought of selling to America was overwhelming for them. They had no idea how to do business outside of Europe. Currency valuations, the US dollar, overseas banking issues, export packaging requirements, freight forwarding, and overseas shipping requirements were all intimidating hurdles.

A few companies that were interested in expanding into our market I was ready to do business with immediately. There were so many Italian bird-cage manufacturers that my head was spinning, but the most outstanding discovery was a parrot cage manufactured by Stametal, a Belgian company. The cage was called the "Jock," and it was the most innovative and spacious parrot cage I'd ever seen. It had quality features never before offered, like an open-top playground, glass seed guards, oval perches, and an invisible, locking door.

I introduced myself to the only English-speaking person at the exhibit, Alphonse Vanderbroeck, who was their sales manager. Vanderbroeck told me that the company was primarily a manufacturer of high-end office furniture and over the years they'd developed cutting, bending, and welding processes that gave them a competitive edge in their furniture markets. A few years earlier they had acquired a small birdcage manufacturing company where Alphonse was employed. And so they put him in charge of sales and marketing. As it turned out, their line of birdcages wasn't anything special when he'd come aboard, but then they hired an experienced bird expert to design three large, innovative cages on wheels with steel tube framing and premium chrome mesh. These three cages turned the Stametal birdcage division into the proverbial Phoenix rising from the ashes.

The models were named the "Jock," "JR," and the "Florida." The names Jock and JR were taken from the American television show *Dallas*, which was popular throughout Europe at the time, while Florida was so named because the state was the most desirable US vacation spot for Europeans. I had a couple of serious discussions with Stametal and explained my marketing program and expressed my desire to introduce their three cages to the American market. There would be several issues to iron out, but I was ready to do business.

There were a few other companies I made contact with whose products piqued my interest including manufacturers of dog toys, aquariums, fancy cat and dog collars, and chew bones, each of which was unique in what I believed was a very marketable way. With the contacts I was making, I knew I needed to get up to speed on how to transact business internationally, starting with proper communication. This being a time before cell phones, emails, and the internet, several companies asked for my telex contact address. Unfortunately, I had no answer for them, but assured them I'd be in touch.

Our travels weren't over until Lee and I spent a day sightseeing. We rented a car and drove to Heidelberg where we toured the famous Heidelberg castle. We learned that the city was completely destroyed in World War II but thanks to the accurate records kept by the city's municipality, they were able to put it all back together, brick by brick, restoring it to its pre-war grandeur. We walked the city and came across the most enchanting antique shop where I found my first antique brass birdcage, in mint condition. And thus began an extensive collection that I've maintained to this day.

As we prepared for our journey back home, I could barely contain my excitement from what I'd experienced over the previous three days and the magnitude of all I had learned. I came across many products that would sell in the US and zeroed in on items that would fit right into our own Noah's Ark Pet Center stores. Then and there, I realized I had to learn all about importing. My first priority upon returning home to the United States? I got myself a telex machine. NAPCO International was about to be born.

22

— • —

Making a Difference

On my first day back at the office, I hit the ground running. My plan was to have NAPCO International offer select high-end pet products never before available in the States, products that I knew would be well received. I decided to kick it off with a line of birdcages from Belgium and Italy, led by the Jock from Stametal, the cage that had so impressed me at the show. Since the majority of the existing import companies were importing the fast-turning, low-end commodity products from Asia, I knew there was a market for what they were leaving behind. I bought my telex machine, had a dedicated telephone line installed, and we were in business.

It was now going into the fall busy season and one of the first companies I sent a telex to was Metheor, an Italian company that made designer canary and parakeet cages. I fired off a detailed message introducing myself as a pet product importer in the US looking for a range of birdcages and requesting information about their company and the products they manufactured. With the excitement of the possibilities, I could feel the adrenaline pumping through my body. Every morning, the first thing I did was check the telex for a response. Then one morning, I walked into my office and immediately noticed the roll of yellow paper extended, indicating an incoming telex, a response from Italy written in broken English. Metheor answered with all the details I requested. They also advised that they were sending me

a sample of their just-patented round birdcage base, along with photos and pricing. Two weeks later the cage base arrived with catalogs of
Metheor's entire line of cages and highlighting the newly designed styles.
They were absolutely striking. I sent back saying I was ready to fly to Italy
to meet with them. I wrote the same thing to Imac Gabbie, an Italian
designer of rectangular birdcages.

I sent more telexes to the companies I had visited at Interzoo, including
Stametal, explaining that I wanted to exclusively represent them in the
US. I told Stametal I wanted to introduce their cages to our wholesaler
network the following year, 1983. I told them I was prepared to meet with
them in their offices in Kortrijk, Belgium, but preferred they come to the
United States to better understand our company and its capabilities. I
explained that time was of the essence and I needed a response soon.

I created a logo for NAPCO International by inserting a globe in
the center of the "N," which already depicted the shell of a turtle, and
then ordered business cards, invoices, purchase orders, and stationery.
Then, it was time to create a brand name. Tom utilized the graphic
arts department of Noah's Ark to create several potential names and
logos. In a unanimous decision, we chose "Care Pet Products" and a
logo with a heart inserted in the center of the word "Care," the name
itself emphasizing our priority in quality. Then I began compiling a "hit
list" of all the companies that had items I was interested in, a list that
included companies in Belgium, England, Germany, Italy, Spain, Taiwan,
and Thailand.

Having received positive responses from Metheor and Imac Gabbie, I
flew to Italy in January of 1983. What an experience. I must have pinched
myself several times wondering, "What in the world am I doing?" There
I was on an Alitalia flight dressed to do business—shirt, tie, sports coat,
and my Hartman leather briefcase from my Greyhound Computer days,

putting on the pretense of a well-seasoned international businessman. In reality, I was still that simple guy who'd just wanted to open a pet shop.

At the airport in Milan, I met the Italian freight agent that I'd contacted to arrange my meetings and he took me to his office where Bruno Sabadini, the owner of Metheor, was waiting. Bruno was a tall, handsome man dressed in a worn, three-piece suit that he must have owned for twenty years. He was accompanied by an attractive young woman named Victoria, his interpreter—a college student and a friend of the family. Then Bruno, Victoria, and I headed out of Milan on our way up north to Lecco where Metheor called home.

In Metheor's factory, we climbed a long stairway to a humble office where we sat down with cups of espresso and discussed business. I talked about my company and my background and what I wanted to do in choosing a range of round birdcages and including them in my entire Care Pet Products program, marketing them throughout the US. It was at this meeting where I learned the importance of speaking slowly and with a clear and concise agenda, keeping subjects as simple as possible. I learned to pause between important points, allowing Victoria the time to carefully explain. In addition, I discovered that when conducting business through an interpreter, it gives you time to gather your thoughts. All this would become extremely useful in the countries and languages I would be dealing with.

Bruno described his business, too, explaining that Metheor specialized in the more intricate design of round birdcages, giving him a competitive edge since most other birdcage manufacturers chose the easy route of square and rectangular designs. He showed me his new patents and samples of his plastic cage base with pull out trays and built-in feed and water cups. He had just successfully entered the European market with these designs and was very keen to penetrate the US market as well. He didn't hold back in telling me that he'd be thrilled to work with us in accomplishing that goal.

In spite of my second strong espresso, I couldn't hide it any longer. My jet lag was beginning to show when I was caught nodding my head between topics and we agreed to finish our discussions the next day. I checked into the town's main hotel and entered the single-person, wire-caged, open-air elevator and slowly ascended to the third floor, peering down at the people in the lobby below. Once in my room, I opened the shuttered window and gazed down at the tiled rooftops of the village, while the sounds of distant church bells rang, all of this giving me the feeling of having stepped back in time. I slept the whole night through and early the next morning, after a café latte and biscotti in the dining room downstairs, I was picked up and taken back to Metheor's office where we finalized our business talks. Bruno agreed to my requirements for heavy export cartons and private labeling with our Care Pet Products logo on each cage. His pricing, coupled with the favorable lira/dollar exchange rate, gave me confidence that my projected wholesale distributor price and suggested retail price would allow everyone in the chain to make a fair profit.

Business done for the time being, it was time to relax and get to know each other. I met the entire Sabadini family and we all did some local sightseeing, enjoying a delicious meal afterward at one of the local pizzerias, drinking wine, and telling stories. It was a fun evening, with me trying out my limited Italian with limited success. When they returned me to the hotel, we all had a good laugh when I told everyone "Buon Natale" instead of "Buona notte," wishing everyone a Merry Christmas instead of a good night. Little did I realize at the time that this would be the beginning of a long and mutually profitable business relationship and, more importantly, a lifelong friendship.

Bruno and Victoria took me back to Milan early the next morning. We said our goodbyes and the agent and I took off on a two-and-a-half hour drive to Arzignano to meet with Imac Gabbie. Once there, we were greeted by the owner, his sister, and brother-in-law, all of whom worked for the company. Then we were given a tour of the manufacturing facility with my agent acting as interpreter. The company seemed organized and profitable.

We sat down to discuss business and everything was progressing nicely when suddenly the owner stood up, indicating the meeting was over. At least for the moment. Quickly, I grasped that, per culture and tradition, wine, cheese, and a typical Italian dinner was much more important. We continued our business discussions at a local restaurant where I laid out my requirements, and we ended the evening clinking our wine glasses with the popular Italian toast *"cin cin,"* anticipating our future relationship.

The empty seat next to me on my flight back home was just what I needed. My mind was filled with excitement as I spread out, working on my import plans and the creation of a high-quality range of European birdcages. It felt like I'd accomplished so much on the trip, even though it was all nothing more than plans and promises on each of our parts. Yet, I could actually see the future coming together.

Back in my office, I now had to plan for the most important meeting so far: Stametal. Alphonse Vanderbroeck had confirmed the meeting dates and advised that he would be traveling with the owner of the company. I soon found myself picking them up at the airport and after checking into their hotel, we went out to a popular steakhouse and had a deluxe dinner while getting to know each other.

Early the next day after giving them a tour of NAPCO and our main Noah's Ark Pet Center store, we sat down to discuss business. Their primary goal, they explained to me, was to penetrate the US market with their new models. They just weren't sure exactly how to go about it. I made it clear to them that I would not be interested in doing business unless I had an agreement in writing that I would be the exclusive sales and marketing arm for them in the US. They were reluctant to commit, explaining that the cages were brand new, without a track record, not to mention that they'd received several inquiries from potential customers. They mentioned that they'd even written a small order with a specialty bird food and accessory importer in Elizabeth, New Jersey, but being that I was familiar with the company I knew they weren't a major player. Stametal, it appeared to me, needed me more than I needed Stametal. They wanted to get into the US market badly and after I outlined my three-step distribution process, they saw that I had the most potential.

I agreed to keep the same names but insisted on offering the three models under our Care Pet Products brand. They were more concerned with volume than anything else and wanted a guarantee on number of units sold per twelve-month period. They were shooting for a 3,000-piece commitment but that was more than I was willing to agree to. I knew that I direly needed the Jock bird home in my line of cages, but I didn't let them know that. I knew that I had to give the impression that I was willing to walk away from the deal. After some strong negotiating, we finally agreed to a minimum of 2,160 units during the first twelve months of sales. I knew I could easily do that. We shook hands agreeing to a one-year contract starting in 1984, but with shipments beginning to arrive in September of 1983.

I finalized my birdcage plans and could clearly see that this program would become the core of my new company. My plans for having a full range of European quality birdcages and marketing them under our own private label were now happening and I was sure it would be a winner. Being a retailer at heart, I also knew exactly what was needed on the retail floor in the form of marketing support. My message would be that pet birds are members of the family and a "cage" just won't cut it. Our cages weren't cages. They were bird homes.

In the midst of all that was happening on the importing front, Noah's Ark was continuing to expand. In 1983, we picked up four more stores. These happened to be the last remaining stores of the Puppy Palace chain in the Chicagoland market. The Mars Corporation, which owned the national chain after purchasing them from Norman Docktor years earlier, decided to exit the retail pet industry and offered us a deal we couldn't refuse. We were now a twenty-four store retail pet center chain with an employee count of 270. We even upgraded our image with a brand-new logo.

After my meeting with Stametal, I felt it necessary to return to Italy to finalize our business procedures with Metheor. After a full day of meetings at the factory, dotting the I's and crossing the T's, I had dinner at the Sabadini home. Giovanni, their youngest son, spoke English about as well as I spoke Italian and we did a lot of laughing and, of course, drinking. Giovanni talked about his desire to travel right after high school. Even though it was a year away, I was happy to offer to have Giovanni live with us over the summer after his graduation.

On February 5, 1984, there was another addition to the family. Our son Andrew was born and our family now felt complete. With everything going on in my personal and business life, I still tried to maintain the type of rural family life I'd always wanted. Our little property now included everything from bees to a gentle, rideable buffalo named Buster that I had impulsively purchased while attending a live animal auction in Cape Girardeau, Missouri. We soon raised two Hereford cattle and added another horse and two pigs to our homestead, all the while making sure my turtles were doing fine. I always made time for turtling.

Our weekends, summers, and vacations always involved nature activities of some sort. In a grasp for memories, I took the family to Waubee Lake in Lakewood, Wisconsin where we rented a little cabin and did some fishing, hiking, exploring, and, of course, turtling. Camp Oconto had disappeared by then but the memories were still there. We rowed to the same location of days gone by. The coves sure seemed smaller but as we came closer, I was thrilled to see many of the same turtle-basking logs, still occupied by those shiny, dome-shaped objects, the same kind that were there years earlier. We caught several of them and enjoyed releasing them as they swam off.

There were also many weekends where we enjoyed fishing and turtling in Mercer, Wisconsin, where my friend Norris Graser had family. Norris was one of my old customers from the initial Noah's Ark days and not only was he an excellent bass fisherman, but he and I shared a fascination with turtles and, in fact, still do to this day.

Early that year, NAPCO International's merchandise started to arrive from overseas—our new bird homes from Italy, dog toys from Spain and Taiwan, chew bones from Thailand, and specialty dog and cat collars and aquarium and terrarium décor from the UK. With the soon-to-be-arriving Jock bird homes from Belgium, it didn't take long to realize we needed more space, and in the late summer of 1984, I rented a nearby 6,000 square-foot warehouse.

In October, we exhibited the Jock, Florida, and JR bird homes at H.H. Backer pet trade show. The Care Pet Products brand was very well received and before long, we were selling our Care Homes to distributors throughout the country. Over the next three years, we would exceed our annual quantity requirements and successfully penetrate the pet bird market, becoming one of the nation's leaders in quality bird homes, all led by the Jock parrot home.

1984 was also the year that I began to realize that, even with all our success and profitability, we were doing something that went way beyond mere business. Tom and I received a personal letter from Dr. David Bromwell, chief veterinarian of the Illinois Department of Agriculture. The purpose? To congratulate us on running a quality retail organization and spearheading a greatly improved atmosphere in the pet industry. After spending so much time on planning and analyzing and quantifying the income and expenses of the company, it was especially illuminating, and gratifying, to realize that there are some things that just can't be quantified. We were making a difference in the world of pet care. How do you measure that?

23

— • —

SUPER PET: SUPER OPPORTUNITY

PETS INTERNATIONAL, LTD., WAS a well-known commodity pet supply importer with the brand name of Super Pet. The company was founded by Sid Meyers in the 1960s to supply the pet departments he leased in discount department stores throughout the Midwest, as well as his Pet World stores in Illinois. As inventories started to build, he began offering his overstocks to pet supply wholesalers throughout the country. This is how Super Pet got started. I began doing business with the company in 1977 and after purchasing the twelve Pet World stores from Sid's son Barry in 1981, we developed a closer relationship.

We did a lot of business with Super Pet, but we also supported their direct competitors, VO-Toys and Ethical Pet Products. Back in 1983, Sid invited me to be his guest at Arlington Park Racetrack where one of his horses ("Super Pet") was running. Sid was more or less an absentee owner, living part time in Boca Raton, Florida while the day-to-day operation of his company was overseen by his vice president, Jim Chadwell.

During the races, we talked about business and it became subtly apparent to me that Sid wasn't happy that I was a strong supporter of his two biggest competitors. In not knowing what I'd been working on with NAPCO International and my importing of pet products, he kept massaging me, telling me what a great job I was doing with all the Noah's Ark

Pet Centers and NAPCO Distributing Co. With our companies literally down the street from each other, he said I should take full advantage by buying from Super Pet. He offered me extended dating and explained that by purchasing more frequently, but in smaller quantities, I could become more profitable by increasing my inventory turns. I agreed with him and assured him I'd give his thoughts serious consideration. As the afternoon moved on, I changed the discussion and came right out and told Sid that if he were ever interested in selling his company, he should call me. Sid kind of laughed and replied, "Krause, you don't have enough money to buy Pets International."

A year later, Jim Chadwell left Sid's company and was replaced by Don Dahlstrom, Super Pet's sales manager, who had often called on us. But even though Sid spent considerable time away from the business in Boca Raton, he micromanaged Don to the point where Don considered leaving the company. Sid, not wanting to jump back into the business full-time, implored Don to stay until he could work something out.

Eventually, Sid began talks with multi-business owner and investor Lou Lauch who, a few years earlier, had purchased Harper Leather, an established Chicago-based manufacturer of leather dog leashes and collars. Morrie and Luby Handiman had owned Harper Leather, and Morrie was one of the originators of the rawhide dog chew, initially fabricating the chew toys from the scraps of his leather tanning process.

Lou's strategic plan was to use Harper as a platform to enter the pet industry with the ultimate goal of competing with the mass market giant, Hartz Mountain. Tom Miller was general manager who, along with a close friend and colleague of mine, Harper's vice president of sales, Chuck Finucane, ran the day-to-day operations of the company.

In 1984, Tom Miller began doing business with Pets International and he soon established a solid friendship with Don Dahlstrom. Don expressed the frustrations he was experiencing with Sid, Tom mentioned this to Lou Lauch, and soon Lou and Sid were in negotiations for Lou to buy Pets International, thereby facilitating Lou's goal of giving Hartz Mountain a run for their money.

In the spring of 1985, word got to me about the possible sale and, needless to say, I was extremely disappointed that Sid never bothered to call me and that I had lost out on the opportunity of buying the company myself. But a few days later, I got a phone call from Chuck Finucane who told me that the negotiations between Sid and Lou had fallen apart. Sid had apparently flown back to Boca Raton in an uproar. Without wasting time, I called Sid's son Barry. Barry and I had a good relationship and I told him I was aware of the situation regarding Sid and Lou, and that I'd be very interested in talking to Sid about buying Pets International. Barry promised to talk to his father.

In the meantime, I consulted with my mother and brother, and described my vision of Tom taking over the entire retail business, me then phasing out of the wholesale operation, and merging NAPCO International with Pets International. My plan was to then build the new company by developing and offering new and unique quality pet products, eventually establishing sound and fair relationships with all the wholesalers throughout the country. Mom and Tom were on board.

That night, I couldn't sleep, thinking about all the challenges in front of me with starting up a completely new company. Sid was one of the first in the pet industry to import products from Japan, Korea, Taiwan, Thailand, and, especially, Mainland China, and had excellent contacts throughout Asia. But there were a few business practices I knew we'd have to eliminate once we bought the company. Not only was Sid known for being the low-priced commodity pet product importer, but he was notorious for blatantly knocking off other companies' popular items and selling them at much lower prices. As a result, he was disliked by many of his competitors. Even though Sid served on the boards of both APPMA and PIJAC for the overall betterment of the pet industry, he was not considered a fair competitor.

Even the larger companies who had established brand names were victims of his copying. In the late '70s, Penn Plax introduced their new line of Aquarium fish nets, which became a number one seller almost overnight. Penn Plax took the basic, inexpensive wire fish net and redesigned it with green, vinyl-covered wire frames and handles with green mesh netting and introduced it in five various sizes, branding them as "Quick Nets." In short order, Sid copied them to a T, calling his line "Swifty Nets," and offering them at pricing that was 25 percent lower than Penn Plax.

A few years earlier, Don Dahlstrom came running into our store one day saying he needed two of every wooden bird toy, ladder, swing, and accessory—products we were purchasing from a family-owned business in California by the name of Bob's Wood Products. He said Sid was departing for Asia the next afternoon. Sid took the wooden items to one of the China factories and had them knocked off exactly, adding them to the Super Pet line at a cheaper price. He even had the audacity to duplicate inventory numbers to make it easier for the wholesalers to switch the items over to Super Pet.

As bad as it was, I felt I could live with that stigma for a while until I could reestablish a new and respected reputation based on what I felt I could offer in the form of new and innovative products. I thought of Pets International as a fast-moving train but with half-empty box cars of commodity products just waiting to be replaced and filled with quality merchandise. I also knew that the acquisition would allow me to be fully integrated as a conglomerate. It was that little green turtle that kicked it off. I was an animal lover at heart turned retailer and wholesale distributor, and this acquisition would teach me how to import, each level with its own profit margin. It all made sense but only if we could pull it off financially.

Barry got back to me, advising that Sid was returning to Chicago the next week and he was ready to meet. The wheels started turning faster now. I strategized our game plan with Tom, while Mom consulted with Ken Bellah.

The meeting took place in Sid's office with Sid, Barry, and Don present along with my mother, my brother and me. We were surprised to see that Sid had a fair purchase price in mind based on inventory, fixtures, and goodwill. Sid wanted all accounts receivable, while agreeing to be responsible for accounts payable, until the day of closing. We asked for the right to refuse damaged, dated, and non-salable merchandise once we took a physical inventory, an assurance that Don Dahlstrom would remain with the company for a minimum of ninety days, and that Sid would accompany me on a trip to Asia to introduce me to his factory contacts. Mom had one more condition. She admired a piece of artwork hanging in Sid's office, a painting of an old Chinese scholar leaning over a table teaching a young child. Mom told Sid that when the deal was consummated, he had to present her with the painting as a gift. Sid agreed.

Looking back, I probably could have negotiated better, but I wanted the company badly. I was positive I could build it into a top-notch provider of quality pet products, knowing that my salvation in closing out a lot of the slow-moving merchandise was that I had twenty-four retail stores that I could funnel it through and still make a profit. Even though I knew that in the art of negotiating, you had to give the impression that you were willing to walk away, I didn't do that, but I didn't care. In my mind, I won. I now owned that half-empty train and I knew I could fill it with quality pet products that would sell.

We closed the deal on May 7, 1985, the largest single purchase of my life. By then, I had talked to Don Dahlstrom to inform him of my vision. He was on board, and relieved that he'd now be out from under the watchful eye of Sid.

I arrived at my new company early the next morning and told Don that I wanted to have a staff meeting. I explained to the six people in the room that it would be business as usual for the next forty-five days or so, but that we had great plans in the making. I assured everyone that the one thing I was excellent at was communication, and that they could depend on the fact that they would always remain informed. After asking everyone to do the very best they possibly could in their jobs, I asked them to do the same as I promised them, and that was to communicate with me as well.

Later that day, I called my best friend in the industry, Rick Savitt, owner of Prevue Pet Products who was a competitor of Sid Meyers. He always talked about "Copy Cat" Sid, the "crap" that Pets International sold, and Sid's deep discounting practices. I told him I'd just purchased Pets International and the Super Pet brand and wanted him to be one of the first to hear it directly from me. Today, we both laugh about his response, but at the time, I was disappointed and a little hurt. "I can't believe you just bought Super Crap!" he said. Well, that was a good example of the reputation I needed to get us away from. I knew it wouldn't be easy, but I also knew the rewards were going to be well worth the effort.

24

— • —

THE OTHER SIDE OF THE WORLD

PRIOR TO SELLING THE company, Sid allowed his sales team to slowly deteriorate, leaving me with only one sales representative who covered the entirety of the eastern US. I made a few phone calls and quickly hired two more salespeople: Bill Snodgrass, who had previously represented me with my Wacky Warning sign program, and my longtime friend and associate, Judy Krause, the daughter of Mel Krause of M.P. Krause & Sons, the wholesaler we did business with at Noah's Ark.

Leaving my baby behind wasn't easy but I felt confident that Noah's was in capable hands and that we had built a talented team of people to guide its continuous growth. Somehow, I knew I was moving in the right direction. Pets International was my inevitable destiny. But the one element I knew I would miss the most was my direct involvement with the animals, especially the reptiles and birds and, of course, my true passion, the turtles. Fortunately, I knew I was now in a position where, when the time was right, I could include turtles back into my daily life at whatever level I chose.

How was I to know at the time that my insatiable chelonian passion would soon give me a window on the world in so many phases of my life? To imagine that a boy's fascination with those little "shiny domed shelled objects" would not only lead to the creation of the world's largest pet center, but now allow him to see a much bigger picture, taking him to the other side of the world and in doing so learn so much more about life, especially his own? It was at that trade show in Germany where I first began to grasp how massive the pet industry was. Through the next twenty years of traveling abroad, I would learn much about business, while learning even more about myself in the process, and growing as a person.

Initially, Tom and I communicated daily and had formal meetings week-ly. We made sure to coordinate all of the individual priorities of both Noah's and the new Pets International. Soon, however, this level of com-munication became impossible, especially with the amount of traveling I was about to do. Understanding that there are different management styles, I trusted Tom to continue the direction we plotted for Noah's.

I was now busy with different priorities, like dealing with the fact that I had two brands. Should I discontinue what I perceived to be the tar-nished Super Pet brand and replace it with Care Pet Products brand? Not a game-breaking decision, I decided to temporarily continue with both, using Care Pet Products for my Jock Bird Home and the other high-end bird homes and merchandise, while keeping Super Pet for our commodity products. At the time, though, my very top priorities were preparing for my upcoming five-week-long trip with Sid Meyers to the Far East, and, even more urgently, to somehow reorganize our plans for the fast-approaching National APPMA Trade Show in June.

I had Don Dahlstrom contact the trade show organizers to see if it was possible to reconfigure our trade show booths, combining the four that Pets International had committed to with the four that I had reserved for NAPCO International. Don was successful at securing us a corner display of eight booths, an enormous display back in 1985. Two weeks after having our merchandise and display fixtures shipped, we loaded up a van with all the last-minute necessities. Don, his wife Sheila, Linda, and I drove fifteen hours to Atlanta to meet up with Judy and Bill and debut the new Pets International. How in the world did we do it? We wrote several orders for all the different merchandise, especially the big-ticket items like our new bird homes. The frosting on the cake was us becoming the talk of the show as we took first place for Best Booth Display. What a way to introduce our two brands: Care Pet Products and Super Pet.

Once back in the office, I worked non-stop, tightening up all my loose ends, knowing that in two weeks I'd be on my way to the other side of the world. Sid had planned his last official Asian trip, on my dime of course, by putting together his usual itinerary and then advising the companies overseas accordingly. I felt it extremely important that I establish my own agenda for each of the meetings we'd be having, making sure my priorities were addressed. I wanted to see first-hand the manufacturing processes of each of the companies and in doing so learn their strengths and weaknesses. More importantly, I wanted to deliver the message that I was not only going to continue supporting them as Sid had, but I planned to bring them new ideas and new business. I later discovered that this was exactly what they wanted to hear. I didn't realize it at the time but because of my pet industry background, I'd already had a respected reputation in Asia and many of the overseas vendors were eagerly anticipating our face-to-face meetings.

Sid's reputation overseas was that of a very wealthy businessman who was rigid and demanding. Once he advised all the vendors of our itinerary, each company was expected to accept our visit without compromise. I later learned that one of our most important agents, Heidinori Sugimoto of Bem Partners, happened to be in the US the week before we departed for Asia and had to change his plans. He flew back to Japan for two days of meetings with us, and then returned to the US to continue his itinerary in the States. I was embarrassed and felt bad for Mr. Sugimoto.

Sid had a special routine whenever he went to Asia. We left O'Hare International Airport early in the afternoon and flew to Las Vegas. Sid explained that he always flew from Chicago to Las Vegas first to get accustomed to the time change by staying up all night. That way, he'd be able to sleep for most of the long, overseas part of the trip. I think it may also have had something to do with Sid enjoying his drinking and gambling and being catered to at Caesar's Palace. In any event, from Vegas, we flew to San Francisco for the long flight to Korea.

Once we arrived in Seoul, we were picked up and driven to the Chosun Hotel by our agent, Mr. Cho of Dong Jin Industries. Then Mr. Cho picked us up the next morning and took us to his office. Quickly, I grasped the importance of trading companies. Dong Jin was an agency that offered a valuable service in connecting small manufacturing companies of various pet products with overseas customers. In addition to transportation and meals, Mr. Cho provided translation, negotiation, packaging expertise, handling, and shipping. I found him to be a patient, soft- spoken, and exceptionally industrious businessman. He also contracted rural farmers to grow catnip to supply his own manufacturing company where he produced thousands of cat toys.

After meeting with four different manufacturing companies, making introductions and discussing current and future business, I enjoyed my very first Korean barbecue, which I absolutely loved. Forty years later, it's still one of my favorite cuisines.

We met with one more supplier in Korea, and then flew to Osaka, Japan. Our agent, Heidinori Sugimoto from Bem Partners, having traveled back from the US, was awaiting our arrival. He was accompanied by Mr. and Mrs. Takimoto, owners of our primary cage manufacturer. The next morning, we toured their company. I was the only one wearing a jacket and tie and I quickly saw why. It was an archaic environment and I realized how determined the Takimotos must have been to operate under such conditions.

After showing us the manufacturing floor, the Takimotos led us outside where we climbed the stairs over a storage facility and entered what I unexpectedly discovered was their home. We all took our shoes off and slipped our feet into slippers, many pairs of which were at the door. Then we sat on floor cushions around a cocktail table where we drank tea and discussed business. Sitting uncomfortably on the floor, seeing Sid in a sport shirt and listening to Sugi and Taki speaking in Japanese, my mind began to wander. I was in Japan, pursuing business opportunities and absorbed in foreign cultures and traditions. I practically had to pinch myself again. It was one of many times where I found myself thinking, *All I wanted was a pet shop.*

After we finished our discussions we went to a very special restaurant on the outskirts of town for a late afternoon meal. Upon entering, I noticed what had to be a two-hundred-gallon aquarium on the far wall. We all sat down at a table and the Takimotos ordered our meal. Trying to be polite while the discussions in Japanese carried on, I couldn't help noticing a man in wading boots come out of the kitchen with a long-handled fishing net. He went over to the aquarium and attempted to catch a particular fish, splashing water everywhere. Once he made his catch, he disappeared into the kitchen while two young women came shuffling out of the backroom and mopped up the floor. Ten minutes later, they all came to the table with trays of several dishes containing various unidentifiable objects. In the largest tray was the fish the man had just caught, sitting upright on a bed of shaved ice with its sides scored into bite-sized slices, the most elaborate presentation of sashimi I had ever seen, or would ever see. The idea was that you were to peel off a slice with your chopsticks and dip it into your soy sauce wasabi mixture. The real show was watching the fish slowly opening and closing its mouth while you tried to enjoy your meal.

Early the following morning, Sid and I left Osaka for Hong Kong, the next leg of our journey. There were several pet product manufacturers in Hong Kong, but we were only meeting with the two largest, Alliance Pet Products and Wah Lok Pet Factory. Both of these companies specialized in plastic injection-molded products, including aquarium accessories and plants, and items for dogs, cats, birds, and hamsters. They competed with each other selling to several importers in the US, and what gave each a competitive edge was the ability to produce exclusive products for specific customers.

Emelius Wong, president of Alliance Pet Products, greeted us at the airport with a big smile and said, "Welcome to Hong Kong, Sonny." I had met Emelius when he had visited Noah's Ark Pet Center right before the APPMA show a year earlier. With my brother and mother, we'd had lunch. I thought it was amusing that he remembered my family nickname. After taking us to the Shangri La Hotel on the Kowloon side of Hong Kong, we agreed to meet later that evening for dinner.

Once we checked into the hotel, Sid called his contact at his shipping container company. It wasn't long before the agent came to the hotel and up to our room where Sid and he made small talk. I noticed Sid presenting him with a sheet of paper that I later learned was a listing of all the shipment numbers received over the last period. The agent went over the list and handed Sid an envelope containing $2,200 in one-hundred-dollar bills, one for each of the twenty-two shipments listed. Sid was teaching me how to cheat my own company. Instead of shopping around and negotiating the best freight rates with the many different carriers, Sid gave all his business to this one shipping company. In return, Sid would receive a kickback of

$100 cash for each shipment. It was one more way of doing business that the company, now in my hands, would be disassociating itself from.

Dinner with Emelius that evening was an extravagant affair in the restaurant on the top floor of the Holiday Inn of Tsim Sha Tsui, the world class shopping district of Kowloon. The next day I received a tour of Emelius's factory where we discussed business. I began to understand what an excellent supplier Emelius was, but felt that because of his strong dealings with my competitors, my business with him would have to be managed carefully.

Early the next morning we met Philip Lau of Wah Lok Pet Supply. Philip and I were close in age and there was something about him that I felt good about. He seemed sincere and I could tell he was a stickler for detail. I later met his cousin, Terrence Lam, the heir apparent to the company who was, at the time, fresh out of college and learning the business. My dealings with Philip and Terrence over the years would be very successful and we would develop many new items each year.

On our last day in Hong Kong, with a free afternoon, I simply had to see the world-famous Yuen Po Street Bird Market. This turned out to be a cross between Sedgewick Studio and Vahle's Bird Store, but on steroids. Thousands upon thousands of birds were crowded into hundreds of cages, birds from around the world, but most of which were wild-trapped Asian songbirds. There were hundreds of outdoor bird vendors selling anything and everything avian. Bird keeping throughout Asia had been an age-old tradition, which, in turn, spawned the captive breeding of many types.

The bird market was much more than just birds; it was an industry in itself. There were hundreds of exquisite, handmade bamboo and wire cages in various sizes and shapes, many of which were varnished with Asian shellac and adorned with elaborate brass, metal, pottery, and hand-carved ivory or wooden attachments. I found myself getting wrapped up in the frenzy and knew that I had to bring home a piece of the memory I was creating. I chose the perfect cage but ended up spending five times as long picking out all the unique handmade accessories, feeders, and attachments, even a mini flower vase that still adorns the cage today while on display in a showcase in my home.

Then I witnessed a most unique tradition. Strolling through the adjacent park were elderly Chinese gentlemen taking their birds for a walk. Many of these men could barely walk themselves but they proudly carried their cages by the built-in bottom handles as if they were presenting golden treasures atop satin pillows. Inside these exquisite cages were their proud possessions, hopping from perch to perch. The cages were then hung upon one of the many suspended bars and hangers that were provided everywhere. The proud bird owners would meet up with their friends and sit, chat, and smoke, as they enjoyed the early afternoon while marveling at the songs of their rare little birds. Another example of the role pets play in enriching our lives.

A pressing problem, however, was the illegal and lucrative bird trapping industry, which capitalized on the high dollars people were willing to pay for the rare and most melodious of exotic birds. It wasn't surprising that years later, in 2015, as the tropical forests slowly became silent, strong conservation strategies were created in an ongoing effort to help save the Asian songbirds from extinction.

From Hong Kong, it was on to China. In 1985, China was quite different than it is today. From overseas investments by multinational corporations, combined with the rapid growth of technology, much of Chinese manufacturing these days is very sophisticated and, with an unlimited labor source, the nation has grown to become an economic powerhouse. But on my first trip to China, it was like going back in time. Getting off the plane in Shanghai brought me into a totally new realm of reality. My perception was of complete chaos. The airport was dimly lit and everything seemed to be disorderly and confused, with people pushing and bumping into each other and yelling. After ambling through the lines to be cleared to enter the country, we grabbed our suitcases and made our way through the crowds. Once outside to catch our ride, I was dumbstruck by the scene before me—the gawking eyes of hundreds of people all dressed in gray or dark blue government-issued clothing that resembled military uniforms. As we gazed down from the steps I was stunned by the thousands of people peddling bicycles in all directions, with the occasional outdated truck or car moving between them and blowing its horn.

We were soon greeted and picked up by four Chinese government employees in a caravan of two old, black, Russian-made cars. I knew how Winston Churchill must have felt as we were ushered into the vehicles while all the people watched. After being driven to the famous, century-old Peace Hotel, located in the heart of Shanghai's waterfront, called the "Bund," we checked in and walked two flights up to our room and then understood why the old, damp lobby had been dark. The electricity wasn't working.

The next morning, we were driven to a dark, antiquated, rather dirty stoneware factory on the outskirts of the city. We watched the loud and labor-intensive production of dog dishes, as racks of pottery were rolled in and out of the ovens. We were then taken to the wicker factory where dog beds and woven bird nests were hand-fabricated. In the company's showroom were hundreds of woven products, and after noticing several items made out of natural twigs, leafy branches, and seeded sprays, I experienced a lightbulb moment. Why not create a range of natural finch and canary nests? In fact, we would do just that. The following year we would receive a first place award at the APPMA trade show for our new range of "Nature's Nests."

After lunch we arrived at the main government building to discuss business. It was me and Sid and eight government-uniformed, official-looking people, one of whom was our main contact, a woman who could somewhat speak broken English. The meeting took place in a large room with several open windows. We sat in very uncomfortable, heavy, and highly shellacked wooden-armed chairs lined up along the walls, in front of which were coffee tables, each with a basket of mandarin oranges. Not a word was said as everyone drank hot tea poured from old, dented metal teapots into their stained ceramic cups. Not being a tea drinker, I was reluctantly becoming accustomed to the taste. The room remained perfectly silent as Sid and I were stared at without anyone actually making eye contact.

Finally the woman began the meeting by asking if we had any orders to give them. This became Sid's cue to begin his performance, showing me how to be firm and demanding while squeezing another three cents out of the cost of the dog tie-out chain order we placed with them. Right away, I learned that it wasn't difficult to obtain a lower price just by sticking to whatever reason you gave them. Back in the '80s, Chinese manufacturers were starving to do business with the West and it was obvious that they were instructed to do whatever it took to write an order. Under government control, the team of people we dealt with never even understood their actual costs, and their selling prices turned out to be extremely attractive. Consistent quality, however, was another story.

Little did I realize what an important country China would become to my business. Over the following years, as a result of several trips to China attending the Canton Fair, digging out new vendors, networking, and receiving referrals, I slowly built strong and selective relationships with many Chinese companies. It took a lot of patience and persistence during all of those meetings, but over time it all came together for eventually achieving the finished products I sought.

Traveling the streets of Asia.

Years later, in 1997, when Hong Kong reverted its sovereignty back to China, the majority of the Hong Kong manufacturing facilities moved into China to exploit a much lower cost and unlimited labor source. This resulted in a dramatic improvement in doing business in mainland China.

From China, it was on to Taipei, the capital of Taiwan, which, because of the political cold war between Taiwan and China, we could only get to by flying first to Hong Kong. Taipei seemed like the New York City of Asia—a hustling, bustling city of finance, banking, and international trade. We visited with a couple of agents in Taipei, one of whom introduced me to a little piece of the future. After receiving a tour of his facility, he took

Sid and me into a small room where he had what appeared to be a copy machine. He handwrote a message on a piece of paper, placed it on the window of the machine, and pressed a few buttons. A minute later, an assistant came into the room and handed him an exact copy of what he'd handwritten.

The machine, the man explained, was called a "facsimile" machine, and it would soon replace telex communication around the world. He told us that not only could you transmit messages but you could now send copies of drawings, designs, and photos. I was blown away by the technology, but had my doubts about the machine's future. How many companies would really buy one of them, and how long would it take to convert the world? Let's just say, looking back, that my instincts about some things were a bit shortsighted.

Thailand was next, where we imported rawhide dog chews from Bangkok's largest tannery, Friendship Trading Company. With Thailand resting on the equator, I immediately fell in love with the beautiful, tropical environment. But being there on business rather than pleasure, I wouldn't be able to connect with any reptile enthusiasts who could have guided me around in search of, perhaps, the indigenous Burmese brown tortoise. Maybe some other time, I thought.

As luck would have it, all of the tanneries were located quite a distance away in what appeared to be an abandoned and forgotten district on the outskirts of Bangkok. These tanneries manufactured everything imaginable in leather, including clothing, handbags, gloves, and various accessories from prime grade materials, leaving the balance for the rawhide dog chew business, which was becoming more important as the pet industry grew worldwide. We knew we were getting close to the tanneries when the odor in the air became almost unbearable and we began to see bubbling chemical pollution in all the roadside ditches. How people could work, let alone live, in the area was unfathomable to me.

After returning to the city, we enjoyed the hospitality of our guests. I found the Thai people to be very respectful and gracious, and over the years, I would develop several new business relationships in Thailand.

I learned many things on this maiden journey to the Far East, most importantly the different cultures, traditions, and ways of doing business in Asian countries. At the same time, it became clear to me that I had no choice in letting go of my Noah's Ark Pet Centers and concentrating fully on Pets International.

I saw that all of the factory owners, were willing to invest in me, but I also knew that many of my major competitors were doing business with many of the same people. The agents wanted to give you the impression that they were loyal and wouldn't share information and new product ideas with your competition, but I would come to learn that sometimes this wasn't the case. While you were face-to-face with them discussing confidential business, they'd treat you like royalty. But as soon as you said goodbye, many of them would move on to other customers, some of which could be your fierce competitors.

I determined that my most critical importing priorities were establishing confidentiality to ensure my products wouldn't be knocked off, maintaining consistent quality, keeping my costs down, and building solid relationships. Eventually, I would learn which agents in each country I could depend on for bringing them new product ideas and designs. I would learn what each of their strengths were, and who I could trust and who I could not. I knew I couldn't replace some of them, but I also learned how to establish new vendors, concentrating on those without ties to the pet industry.

In time, I would have tons of new product ideas. I would even painstakingly buy products in component form from different suppliers, importing them and finishing off the item stateside with assembly and packaging. I learned the importance of patent protection. As our new product introductions became successful, I learned which companies I could rely on to partner with, and when I brought them a new product idea, whether in the form of a prototype, an engineering drawing, or even a sketch on a napkin, they believed in me.

It didn't take long after I began successfully introducing these new products to the market that everything started to snowball. These companies began investing in me in the form of tooling and R&D, all based on my track record. This groundwork, which I laid by improving the ways Sid did business, allowed my Asian partners to see a bright future in our relationship.

But coming back to the US, all of this was still in front of me. I had no idea that my first trip to the Far East would turn out to be a five-week-long harbinger of what would become the most significant twenty years of my career. At this point, I only knew one thing for absolute certain: I had *a lot* to learn, not only in the different ways of doing business, but in the everyday encounters.

There were moments when I'd wished I had done my homework a little bit better before the trip. I would have loved to have brushed up on simple things like greetings and courtesies in their languages, and improving my knowledge of world events, economies, customs, cuisines, traditions, and cultures. I soon began putting together my own little booklets on exchange rates, populations, economies, and conversion tables, plus names, spellings, pronunciations, restaurants—anything I could think of to help me establish good relationships and build my own personal ways of conducting business. Eventually, after traveling for years throughout both Asia and Europe, I compiled a "Travel Tips Document," listing all the small but important, and sometimes humorous, tidbits of information that can be helpful in navigating through a foreign country. These were later given out to my employees and friends who traveled overseas.

All that experience would come in time. This first trip was to open the door. To new worlds and new ideas. And when I finally returned to my office, I hit the ground running. There was much to do. My first order of business? The purchase of that technological marvel I had been introduced to in Taiwan: a facsimile machine. I was off to the races.

25

ASIA REVISITED

IN LATE SUMMER OF 1985, I was preparing for the arrival of Bruno Sabadini's son, Giovanni. He had taken me up on my offer to host his visit to the US. But I had one priority I needed to tend to first. I had just received three alligator snapping turtle hatchlings from one of our suppliers and my goal was to create the ideal display aquarium in my office.

I'd wanted an alligator snapping turtle for years. I had always been intrigued by their interesting way of angling. In addition to foraging for food like other aquatic turtles, the alligator snapping turtle, even as a hatchling, has a unique habit of sitting with its mouth wide open, wiggling a small, pink appendage on the tip of its tongue, thereby attracting passing fish to prey upon.

I set the hatchlings up in a twenty-gallon aquarium with a few inches of water and arranged everything in a naturalistic fashion, with logs and aquatic plants. I put the aquarium right next to my tank of two baby alligators and it became a terrific conversation piece. Whenever I had a visitor in my office, I just had to demonstrate the fishing expertise of the turtles by dropping in a few guppies.

When Giovanni Sabadini finally arrived, I picked him up at O'Hare. Through the crowd, I spotted him, looking apprehensive and uncertain as he made his way through the mass of travelers. When he saw me, I could see the relief on his face, and it made me think of how that same experience must happen to so many people during their first foreign travels.

In short order, Giovanni became a member of our family. He took it upon himself to improve his English as he adjusted to the American ways. He accompanied our family to several functions and met many people who, even today, remember the wonderful experiences they had with him. I also included Giovanni in a few business functions, including a trade show that fall in Texas. After the first day of the show, we were all gathered in the hotel lounge enjoying some drinks when all of a sudden Giovanni stood up and called out in Italian, *"Petro, Petro, non posse creditci!"* He was directing his excitement toward a well-dressed gentleman coming down the stairs, and when they approached one another, the man dropped his briefcase on the floor and they embraced, both speaking in Italian.

The man was Peter Geboers, a very close friend of Giovanni's. Peter was from the Netherlands and had been doing business for several years with Metheor, the company Giovanni's father owned. He was on a buying trip in America and had decided to attend the trade show in Texas. Peter joined us that evening for a company dinner and that began a lifelong friendship between him and me that remains to this day.

Peter owned and operated a wholesale/import company in the small Dutch village of Geldrop, about two hours south of Amsterdam. He serviced pet stores throughout the Netherlands, Belgium, and Luxembourg with pet supplies from various manufacturers as well as his signature live, fancy goldfish that he imported from the States. Peter and I had similar backgrounds and shared the same enthusiasm about growing our respective businesses. He told me there were so many more unique Italian manufacturers that I should be looking at and he said he could help me, especially since he'd learned to speak fluent Italian. Meanwhile, he was interested in doing business in Asia and I told him I could help him there.

Before we parted, he invited me to visit him in the Netherlands to further discuss how we could help each other. I assured him I would plan a trip.

Giovanni and I returned from Texas, and soon it was time for Giovanni to return to Italy. We said our goodbyes knowing, since I was doing business with his father, that we'd be keeping in touch.

Before long, it was time for me to start planning my second trip to Asia. I'd be leaving in early January, 1986. The main priorities of the trip would be to establish new ground rules with each of the companies I was doing business with, put the past ways of doing business behind us, and take a few new product design ideas with me.

Lou Lauch of Harper Leather and Rawhide Company contacted me and asked if I would mind having him come along so that he could visit a few of the companies we both happened to do business with. I soon learned that Lou was a master delegator. He cheerfully let me handle his itinerary, passport, visa, and factory appointments. When the trip came around, I met him at the airport. I was, as usual, dressed for business, with my briefcase of paperwork, files, and folders, as well as my suitcase with shirts, ties, slacks, and another sport coat. Lou showed up with nothing more than a small leather binder and dressed like he was going to go play golf. Thirty-five years later, that's how the majority of business travelers dress and travel. How could I have known that Lou was so far ahead of his time?

Our first stop was Seoul, Korea where I worked with our agent Mr. Cho from Dong Jin Industries for two days. I met with our aquarium fish net company. I had brought a prototype net with me with the idea of introducing three sizes of bird nets. I figured that if they could produce fish nets, why not larger, long-handled, soft, nylon bird nets? I knew such nets would be in demand. At Noah's like other retailers across the country, we used large fishing nets purchased at sporting goods stores or ridiculous, small tropical fish nets, or even towels to capture escaped birds.

I had another project, too, one that I called Zipper Nippers. I wanted to upgrade the ninety-nine-cent catnip, cat toys that were everywhere in the market. I wanted to create a refillable catnip toy with a zipper. My meetings in Seoul turned out to be very productive. My concepts would become real products, and the next year, our Zipper Nippers would win a first place award at the APPMA show.

Our next stop was Hong Kong where we were again greeted by Emelius Wong. By coincidence, several pet product importers/customers were in Hong Kong at the same time and while accompanying Emelius on various factory tours, we happened to run into both Rick Savitt of Prevue Pet Products, and Jonathon Zelinger of Ethical Pet Products.

It was always a challenge for the factory owners and agents to keep their business with competing companies private, thereby separating competitors whenever possible to show respect and confidentiality to each of us. Emelius invited us to dinner at the same restaurant he took Sid and I to months earlier in Kowloon. Understanding that he had to choose whom to take to dinner, I told Emelius that since I had a long and friendly relationship with all his customers from my Noah's Ark days, I would welcome them to join us. Emelius was very surprised, and pleased by my offer.

Later that evening, we all entered a private room, which featured a large, elaborate, round table with seating for twelve, complete with revolving turntable that would rotate all the special dishes of Cantonese and Mandarin cuisine we were about to enjoy. Many toasts were made, a Chinese custom meant to show respect. As the evening progressed, the beer toasts made way for whiskey toasts, another tradition, this one meant to see who could drink the most without getting blasted. Rick and I sat next to each other, laughing and joking and making bets about anything and everything. At one point, a plate of roasted, spicy chicken cut up into bite-sized pieces and crowned with the chicken's head was placed in front of me. As everyone reached toward the plate with their chopsticks, Rick challenged me to eat the head. We bantered back and forth, daring each other, and I said, "Let's flip for it. The winner gets $100 but he has to eat the head." Rick accepted. I took out a shiny Hong Kong dollar and Rick called heads, appropriately enough. And heads it was. I gladly paid him the money and we all watched and laughed as, without hesitation, Rick chowed down on the chicken head. I was fortunate to take a photo to document the occasion, Rick holding the head with his chopsticks and sliding it into his mouth. I still don't know how it happened, but months later, that photo somehow found its way into *Pet Business* magazine.

Fun in Hong Kong. Lou Lauch, me, and Rick Savitt, who's about the eat the chicken head.

That night began the Hong Kong dollar coin-flipping tradition. Later in the year, Rick would commemorate the experience by having the coin drilled and threaded with a chain necklace. From then on, that coin would come with us whenever we would go out to dinner where it would be flipped to determine who would pick up the check in steak houses, Korean restaurants, Japanese sushi bars, Italian delis, Mexican cantinas, and every other kind of restaurant all over the world. The winner would always assume the honor of wearing the necklace to the next dinner.

From Hong Kong we were off to Thailand to visit the tanneries. In one of the factories, I observed a production line for the manufacturing of leather welding gloves, thousands and thousands of them being made and packaged. This turned out to be another lightbulb moment. I knew that pet shops across the country used welding gloves for handling bronco parrots and other untamed animals. I even used them myself for handling Ginny, my great horned owl. I asked the owners to bring a couple of pairs into our meeting after the tour. On large sheets of cardboard, I traced out an improved size with reinforced finger pockets and an extended sleeve length. In a few short moments, another product was born: Animal Handling Gloves.

I had the gloves dyed green, designed a header card, and had them packaged in six-pack inners. The following year they too would be successfully added to our new product offerings and welcomed by customers nationwide, not to mention used in the stores. The experience proved to me that if you understand the needs of your markets, you can spot opportunities when you might not even be looking for them.

The many new products, processes, and procedures I was establishing in doing business in Asia would eventually pay off. Over the years, our business dealings in the Far East would grow by leaps and bounds. Meanwhile, Noah's Ark kept growing. We opened two more stores, one in Davenport,

Iowa, and one in Orland Square Mall in a south suburb of Chicago. Now we had twenty-six.

It wouldn't be long after my first trips to Asia when I would enter the European landscape. A whole new layer of that gigantic onion was about to start peeling away.

26

—•—

CONTINUING TO ROLL

IN FEBRUARY OF 1986, a month after I returned from Asia, I took off for the Netherlands to meet with Peter Geboers to learn more about the European pet industry and to discuss how we could work together. Our plan was to go to Italy but first Peter showed me around his hometown of Geldrop, birthplace of Vincent van Gogh. We toured the van Gogh museum and then stopped at Geldrop's local garden center. It was enormous, the size of a Home Depot, but only for plants and gardening.

It was at the garden center that something caught my eye. I noticed a free-standing, point-of-purchase display containing sixteen, full-colored cardboard bins, each with a beautiful photograph of a different kind of tulip in full bloom. Each bin dispensed different tulip bulbs to match, though the bulbs themselves were nondescript and rather unattractive. Attached to the full-colored header was a packet of self-serve poly bags. How eye-catching and convenient. And yet how simple.

I thought about the way pet shops sold rawhide dog chews, bones, and munchies. The majority of them used a goldfish bowl or a small cardboard box to display them in. How unprofessional compared to what I was looking at with the tulip bulb display.

After the garden center, I couldn't stop drawing sketches of a new rawhide display. Six months later, those sketches would result in our Super

Pet Gourmet Chew Display, a 1987 APPMA award-winning point of purchase display of sixteen full-color bins of different rawhide munchy chews, each with a beautiful photo of a different dog breed. We created a program that allowed retailers and wholesalers to order the complete set-up and to reorder the different chews in appropriately sized poly bags.

The day after touring Geldrop, Peter and I left for Italy, with Peter driving his Mercedes Benz on the Autobahn and *autostradas* of Germany, Austria, and Italy at the usual high rates of speed and still getting passed from time to time.

After spending a full day discussing business with Metheor and enjoying a home cooked meal with the Sabadini family, we traveled to two other Italian manufactures, Terenziani, a cage manufacturer, and Marchioro, a plastic-injection molder. Peter introduced me to both Sandro Terenziani and Nico Marchioro who were young, sincere, hardworking men who strived to grow their businesses. They both welcomed our proposals to work together designing and creating new cages and pet products and giving us exclusive sales rights in our respective markets.

The trip to Italy was successful and over the next year, both Peter and I were able to prove ourselves to Terenziani and Marchioro. In 1987, we all decided to meet in Barcelona, Spain at the Sizoo Pet Trade Show. In the famous Barcelona Colonial Hotel, Peter and I and Nico Marchioro and Sandro Terenziani all agreed to work together in an unprecedented manner. Peter and I would bring new product ideas and designs to Marchioro and Terenziani along with sales projections. We would assist in developing each item, down to each detail. For this, Marchioro and Terenziani were willing to invest up front in any and all tooling as long as we guaranteed the volume at acceptable pricing. We signed an agreement where Peter had the exclusive sales and marketing rights for northern Europe, and I had the exclusive rights for North America. Since the Far East market was in its fledgling stages, they weren't concerned about it, so I insisted on including it in my territory. With my contacts there, I knew the potential.

We started out with two very successful programs, an innovative range of quality rabbit and ferret homes with Terenziani, and a new cat litter enclosure system with Marchioro. The arrangement worked well and over the next six years, we would introduce several new products worldwide.

I traveled to Europe two to three times each year, coordinating my travels with the many pet product trade shows in the UK, Germany, Italy, France, and Spain. If Peter and I weren't busy developing new products with various manufacturers, I was exhibiting at a trade show and acquiring more new product ideas. At the same time I was establishing a respectable and well-known name for us throughout the European landscape.

In June of 1987, while our sales were increasing throughout the US, I welcomed Mr. Um, the principle of a company called Guppy Plastics from Malaysia, and his English-speaking associate, Miss Sim Bee Lin who took the English name of Evelyn. Guppy Plastics was a Malaysian plastic injection molding company that Peter had told me about. A few years earlier, the Hagen Corporation introduced a line of plastic terrariums that were selling well throughout the US market. Our Noah's Ark Pet Center stores promoted them big time and it was a product line I was very interested in for Pets International, knowing that its sales potential hadn't even been tapped yet. Peter was getting the same terrariums directly from Guppy, the manufacturer, and at significantly lower pricing. I contacted Guppy and it turned out Mr. Um had been planning a trip to the US and was happy to include Pets International in his itinerary.

Nothing came of the meeting as Mr. Um decided to continue to work with the Hagen Corporation, and now exclusively, but at least we had a nice dinner and I found myself impressed by Evelyn who conducted herself in a professional and organized manner, speaking perfect English, reflecting her advanced business schooling.

One day that same year, I was contacted by Marshall Meyers, CEO of the Pet Industry Joint Advisory Council to see if I had any interest in joining the board. Being that PIJAC was the Washington DC-based national pet industry organization, working to promote animal well-being and responsible pet ownership, I was honored and accepted his invitation to be elected. The meetings I would attend over the following years would allow me to voice my opinions about the changes I believed were needed in our industry, as well as enlighten me on the much bigger picture of what it took to be a part of the pet industry. It sure didn't take me long to learn that Marshall Meyers was one of, if not the most, influential and hardworking individuals in the entire industry. Years later, in 2022, PIJAC would go through a rebranding and become the Pet Advocacy Network, pushing for additional initiatives in promoting animal companionship.

While never underestimating the importance of my continued business in the Far East, my trips to Europe started making the continent feel like a second home to me. Through the development of several new products for the American market—like our Jock parrot homes; our exquisite, Italian-designed, small bird homes; our entire range of rabbit hutches (the "Original" and our newly introduced "Peter Rabbit Homes"); and our filtered, covered, cat litter pan system ("Kitty Comfort Station")—I was building friendships in Belgium, Germany, and Italy. Peter introduced me to several more of his Italian friends as we enjoyed side trips to Milan, Florence, and Venice. Staying in people's homes, attending dinners and family parties and even a wedding, all added to the closeness of friendships that I treasure to this day. Of course, we also welcomed these friends to America as our guests. Georgia, the daughter of Sergio Rabito, owner of Euro3Plast, a large plastic injection molder, stayed with us one summer, teaching us how to prepare several new pasta sauces while we introduced her to our ways of life (including my collection of turtles).

In October of 1988, Peter came to the US to attend a trade show and happened to join me in a meeting with Heidinori Sugimoto of Bem Partners of Japan, who was also visiting the States. Sugi often traveled to the US accompanied by the president of one of his most important Asian manufacturing partners, Mr. Katsutoshi Tominaga. Tomi had never been interested in doing business with Pets International due to Sid's non-cooperative reputation and, even with a new owner, he remained reluctant. But that evening, I invited Sugi to join Peter and me in my home for a light dinner and Sugi brought Mr. Tominaga with him, introducing me to the man who would ultimately leave one of the biggest impacts on the growth of the Super Pet brand.

After dinner, we sat around the dining room table talking and laughing. My brother-in-law had introduced me to a crazy drink that I offered my guests. You take a slice of lemon and top it with a half-teaspoon of fresh ground coffee and a half teaspoon of sugar. Then you put it in your mouth, start chewing, and, before swallowing, you chase it with a shot of vodka. It didn't take long before I had the Japanese wearing cowboy hats and taking turns riding Mister, our quarter horse, up and down the gravel driveway. That evening Tomi got to know the new owner of Pets International and from that day forward, we became the best of friends.

During this time, Noah's Ark was putting the finishing touches on the opening of store number 27 in the south suburb of Oaklawn. It was a large store, 6,000 square feet, designed to be a south side smaller version of our flagship store in Elk Grove Village. It had all the same features, just fewer of them. Led by our VP of operations, Bob Brown, and my brother Tom, the entire team worked around the clock to meet the grand opening deadline in November.

Two months later, in January of 1989, I took Peter to the Far East, introducing him to several factories I'd been doing business with, manufacturers of everything from aquarium pumps and accessories to rawhide dog chews and birdcages. Peter established some nice contacts while learning a totally different way of doing business. During this visit, Sugi took me to Tominaga Industrial to again meet with Tomi. I was impressed. The company consisted of a team of professional designers, tool makers, and engineers, with manufacturing facilities in both Japan and China. Tomi's company helped design and produce products for the houseware, electronic, communication, automobile, and pet industries worldwide. I saw right away that Tomi had all the potential of becoming a most valuable supplier. We commenced our business relationship then and there, starting out with plastic terrariums that were identical to Hagen's.

Two days later, we met with Mr. Takimoto, our cage manufacturer. Here, Peter saw a different side of me. I'd been having quality control problems with Takimoto and yet my costs were continuously inching upwards. Sugi did the best he could to keep the peace but our meeting became more and more adversarial. I chalked it up to the language barrier and sort of accepted it. Then, between discussions, I started reviewing Takimoto's own birdcage catalog and discovered to my dismay that my designs and logos had been copied and were being marketed to the Japanese market without my knowledge, let alone approval. He even had the audacity to proudly show me a Japanese version of my full-colored birdcage hang tag, explaining to Sugi in Japanese that everyone was very impressed with his new designs and company image. I abruptly ended our meeting, knowing I needed to start looking for a cage source somewhere else.

After returning to the States, I started thinking of alternatives. I had always admired the designs of Mexican wrought-iron cages, even though their fabrication was crude and lacked some functionality. Their decorative cages made beautiful planters or home décor, but weren't adequate for housing a bird. Nevertheless, if I could find the right Mexican fabricator and show them what was really needed, we could do some serious business together. Then, out of nowhere, I received a random mailing from a trade show organizer in Mexico about a general merchandise expo being held in six weeks. I thought this to be the perfect opportunity.

Right around this time, my mother broke a rib in a freak accident. She was bending over at her desk chair trying to pick up a lit cigarette that she'd dropped. But the X-rays showed more than a broken rib. Mom was diagnosed with colon cancer. She began chemo treatments, which she handled without any complications, and we came to regard that freak accident as God-sent. Although I always had a great relationship with my mother, my relationship with her took an even more positive turn at this point, allowing me to appreciate and love her in a more enriching way.

In March, I flew to Mexico City to attend the expo and found it a waste of time. But during my flight home, I reviewed some of the literature I'd picked up and came across a crude directory of different companies written in Spanish. One of them stood out: "Grugar Industrial, *Manufacturacion de Alambre*." My Spanish/English travel dictionary told me that *Alambre* meant wire. Back home, I contacted Grugar, a family-owned business in Mexico City that made welded wire milk crates and store display racks for a large bread and bakery producer in Mexico. I thought if they could make wire milk crates and wire display racks, they could make cages as well.

I explained my interest and within a month, I found myself welcoming Jose and Alfredo Garcia Pina who had agreed to come to Chicago to meet with me. We spent two days together learning about each other's businesses and what I had in mind. The next month I flew to Mexico City to see firsthand what Grugar Industrial was all about. The company consisted of about 150 employees running two shifts but with very old manual systems including foot-pedal welding machines, hand operated wire chippers, benders, and cutters. As disappointed as I was, I still felt that some sort of potential still existed.

Back in my office, I received a phone call from PetSmart, which we were beginning to do significant business with. My main contact had been Jim Dougherty, the president. He had stepped aside and hired Sam Parker as the new chairman-CEO. Sam was a twelve-year veteran of the Jewel Food Store chain and wanted to pay me a visit. He came in July and it became clear that he was very interested in the retail pet business of the Chicago market, asking me if I could give him a tour of a few of our Noah's Ark Pet Center stores. I liked Sam from the start and enjoyed the time we spent together, especially when it came to lunchtime when he insisted that I pull over at one of Chicago's popular Vienna Hot Dog stands. I had a feeling I'd be dealing a lot more with Sam.

I soon received a surprising fax from Evelyn Sim of Malaysia, the assistant to Mr. Um who had impressed me so. She said she'd left Guppy Plastics not long after they had created a joint venture with the Hagen Corporation, and was starting her own trading company. She told me of another plastic injection molder of houseware products by the name of Mah Sing Plastics and said they had a lot to offer a company like mine. She invited me to come to Kuala Lumpur on my next trip to the Far East to discuss the possibility of doing business together.

I started putting my itinerary together for my next trip to the Far East in January of 1990. I had a few things in mind for this trip, including the search for a manufacturer for a bird perch program I was developing. As it happened, years earlier in my Noah's Ark Pet Center days, I'd become close friends with a veterinarian by the name of Theodore Lafeber, owner of Niles Animal Hospital in a northwest suburb of Chicago. Dr. Lafeber developed the very first pelleted psittacine cage bird food, becoming an icon in the captive parakeet and parrot nutrition industry. He was one of the most sincere and dedicated professionals I ever knew, and I learned a lot from him. He brown-bagged his lunch and rode his bike to work every day during the months that weren't too cold and treacherous. I had occasion to spend some memorable times with him, including one time when I brought him in a deceased blue-fronted Amazon parrot for a post-mortem. The bird was one of several babies that we'd just imported and Dr. Lafeber was willing to take the time to determine its demise. He performed the post-mortem during his lunch, all the while eating his sandwich. My kind of guy.

Dr. Lafeber and I had always talked about enhancing the lives of caged birds and during this visit, we talked about the poor birds that are forced to stand on their feet their entire caged lives, on the same perch day in and day out. Eating, drinking, playing, standing, or even sleeping—same perch, same diameter, same shape. Dr. Lafeber explained that this was unnatural and contributed to many foot disorders.

His observations had always stuck with me and here I was years later and finally in a position and ready to pursue the idea of something I called "The Comfort Perch," an oval perch in three diameters, each with heavy duty plastic end caps designed so that the perch could be rotated, offering a flat or a vertical position of comfort. Then by providing two different diameter of perches, or for some avian species all three, the bird would have a choice of foot positions.

In Hong Kong and in China, I met with my suppliers on a few other new product programs and I inquired of each about their capabilities in providing a wood component to another new product I was designing. All of this as an attempt to determine who I would select to partner with while not divulging the Comfort Perch program.

From Hong Kong I flew to Penang, Malaysia and spent two days with a new vendor who would provide us with unlimited quantities of Malaysian driftwood. This was a popular selling decorative and natural aquarium accessory that we marketed in the tropical fish sector.

From Penang, I flew to Kuala Lumpur to meet Evelyn Sim. During our meeting, Evelyn filled me in on her relationship with Mah Sing Plastics, and assured me that she could help me with developing many new products in Malaysia. After a nice lunch, I decided to go over the whole Comfort Perch idea with her. She was excited, and certain that together we could do it. After meeting Mah Sing Plastics and negotiating a business arrangement, I hired Evelyn to assist me with my Comfort Perch pursuit. She and I shook hands and she became my exclusive pet industry agent in Malaysia. By the end of 1990, we were importing all the components for the Comfort Perch, and we introduced the program in the spring of 1991, receiving an APPMA new product first-place award that June.

Meanwhile, I was continuing to roll, committed more than ever to developing more and more products for the industry that I was madly in love with.

27

—.—

More Than Just Business

My professional goal of turning Pets International into a world-class producer of unique pet products was becoming my priority in life, probably just short of an obsession. And it was taking its toll, especially on my personal life. In 1990, just after Bob Jr. went off to college, I noticed an unmistakable distance between Linda and me. I justified the hours and the traveling as my way of supporting my family, not really allowing it to sink in just how damaging all the work was to my marriage. Before long, Linda and I separated.

Though the business kept rolling, I was becoming painfully aware of the old adage that it's lonely at the top. And not just because I was separated from my wife. The fact is, I lacked someone within the organization to bounce my decisions off of. Someone to play the "what if" games and to serve as the occasional devil's advocate. Tom was no longer there for me as he now had his hands full with the challenges of running all of the Noah's Ark Pet Center stores. And even though I was a firm believer in creating and building strong management teams while delegating even the most important tasks, there were many things I couldn't share with my employees. It seemed that the more complex my various enterprises became, the bigger the decisions became. And I began to realize, with a sense of intimidating alarm, that I was all alone in making them. There were even times when I felt like I was in over my head.

Where I could, I sought help and advice from other business owners. I kept attending the Elk Grove Village Chamber of Commerce meetings, and I worked with my bank advisers and my accounting firm. But things were changing rapidly and it felt to me as though the tail was wagging the dog. One morning, going through my mail, a piece of junk mail caught my eye. It was titled, "Are you lonely at the top?" I laughed out loud, wondering where the fly on the wall was that had witnessed my frustrations. I kept reading. "Do you have business decisions you cannot share with your employees?" the mailing read. "When you're at home are you thinking of business rather than engaging with your family?"

The mailing came from TEC, "The Executive Committee," an organization of independent CEOs who helped each other in strategizing and dealing with the challenges of growing their businesses. I decided to attend an introductory business breakfast they were having in our area, never hesitant about trying something new. At the breakfast, the room was filled with business owners and executives from every sort of business imaginable. It was explained to us that small groups of ten to twelve members took turns hosting monthly all-day meetings. There were morning speakers on various topics and then after lunch each member would have an opportunity to discuss openly and confidentially any of his or her critical issues about any facet of running their business, especially those things that were keeping them up at night. The group would then respond and in doing so, help one another navigate their business or personal challenges. The group was headed by a chairperson who was trained to facilitate, making sure the agendas were focused and the proceedings didn't wander off course.

I joined right away, hopeful, but not realizing that my professional career was about to move into high gear. I was forty-four years old and what was in store for me over the next fifteen years I could never have imagined.

Our newly assembled group consisted of Jim Tesch, our chairperson, and twelve CEOs of privately owned, non-competing businesses, each with annual revenues between ten million and fifty million dollars. Suddenly, I felt a lot less alone. In fact, I would become close friends with my fellow members. We had our monthly meetings, one-on-one personal meetings with Jim, and something called "SWOTs," office visits by fellow members to identify Strengths, Weaknesses, Opportunities, and Threats. All of this allowed me to share the challenges I was experiencing in both my business and personal life. As painful as some of them were, miraculously, the right answers now always seemed to surface.

In running my business, I used to question myself a lot. Then I'd sometimes find myself procrastinating and losing opportunities or making the wrong decision altogether. Our TEC group worked hard in not allowing that to happen. We learned not to be shy with one another, never hesitating to have fierce conversations and telling it like it was, all the while holding each other accountable. We all learned much about other businesses and methods of growing companies while understanding that we were very much the same. We were hardworking, determined professionals all of whom had families we cared about. In essence, we became a family ourselves, even socializing and learning to appreciate our personal lives.

As for my own family, I was struggling to maintain a relationship with my four children after years of being an absentee father. I couldn't see, nor admit, that it was my personal ego that had fueled my drive and determination to build my business. I rationalized my behavior, telling myself I was still in my children's lives with my weekend custody visits, after-school activities, and vacations, as well as my financial support. At one point, I bought a two-bedroom townhouse near the office. Bob Jr. moved in and would stay with me when he wasn't away at school, and Lisa, James, and Andrew would spend occasional weekends.

During the first quarter of 1990, after traveling to Mexico City several times to meet with them, our Mexican partner Grugar Industrial began producing four sizes of puppy-training crates for us. We received them in small runs primarily for our Noah's Ark Pet Center stores. Unfortunately, some of the first shipments came with broken welds and inconsistent powder coating. I wondered if I had made a mistake. As dedicated, hard-working, and sincere as the people at Grugar were, they just couldn't assure me of consistent quality.

During my retail days, I was the single biggest customer of a small local wire mesh fabricator in Illinois by the name of Circle K Industries. We'd purchased hundreds of wire mesh guinea pig and rabbit cages over the years but the company downsized and eventually became a direct consumer supplier. I kept in touch with the owner, Emmet Krist, as my retail stores still did some business with him, and in one of our conversations, I learned that he was thinking about selling his business.

I had doubts that the business was a good fit, but in June of that year, I pursued it anyway. During a visit, I saw something that intrigued me. Two years earlier, Emmet had purchased a state-of-the-art, Swiss-made, automatic wire- welding machine, called a Schlatter, that was his company's biggest hard asset. He demonstrated its performance and I was impressed. The machine automatically formed and welded perfect wire panels.

I passed on buying Emmet's business, but the visit gave me an idea. I contacted Alfredo Garcia of Grugar and he agreed to partner with me on the purchase of a brand-new Schlatter machine. After meeting one of the principles of the company who flew in from Switzerland, we purchased a custom machine, waited six months, and finally had it delivered to Grugar's Mexico City factory. Then we began to produce several sizes of welded wire panels. Grugar would ship the panels to us, now without any of the prior quality issues, and we would package them with attachments and cage bases in full-color display cartons for various sizes and styles of rabbit, guinea pig, and ferret homes, introducing new award-winning designs and features to the pet industry.

Our business with Grugar exploded and over the years, I became close friends with Alfredo and his family. Factory visits to Mexico City were certainly much easier than visits to Asia; it was the same time zone and a four-hour direct flight. I attended several family functions including birthdays and Alfredo's wedding. I even took Alfredo to Hong Kong and China on a Far East trip so that he could learn of different manufacturing processes. We soon began traveling around Mexico together looking for ideas and opportunities, and it was then that I began marketing and selling the Super Pet brand in Mexico City. Along the way, I met other people in the pet industry who impacted my business and my life.

One of those people was Antonio Estrada, a young biologist who taught me a lot about the pet business in Mexico, particularly the tropical fish segment. Then there was Rosalia Amparo Simon, a hardworking businesswoman who singlehandedly ran a pet product wholesale company, marketing products in Mexico City, and concentrating on department store sales. I admired her never-give-up attitude. Our business with her grew swiftly and every time I visited Grugar, she would set up meetings with department store buyers and I would make time to work with her to further develop the market for Super Pet products. As our business continued to grow, Rosalia became our exclusive agent for the Hispanic markets, representing our company in both Mexico and Spain.

Throughout the years in building my organization, my strengths were sales, management, and product development, and I had been primarily concentrating in those areas exclusively. To that end, and only after strategizing with Tom, we offered one of our regional managers from Noah's, Brian Kindl, a growing position as Pets International's Midwest sales manager. At the same time, it was becoming clear to me that one area that was not of my expertise was the area of finance. We were continually at wits' end on what and where to invest our dollars. Our payables were always running past sixty days and we had vendors and suppliers constantly calling for payment of their invoices. Every Friday afternoon about 3 p.m., my bookkeeper would come into my office with an armful of invoices with checks attached, each waiting to be signed and mailed.

"How much do we have in the bank?" I'd ask, knowing we couldn't pay them all. Then I'd wonder aloud, "Who's going to win the lottery?" meaning who was going to get paid that week. Our priority became to first pay the vendors that we needed to place more orders with, and/or the ones who were screaming the loudest.

While I was preparing to search for a financial person, Don Dahlstrom came into my office one morning and told me he had decided to retire. Don had been my go-to guy when I was out of the office, and I asked him if his decision was firm. We talked and Don mentioned that he'd been thinking of retiring for quite a while but had been struggling with how to tell me. I reluctantly accepted his resignation, knowing that I was going to have to pick up his priorities, as well as put my job search for the financial person in high gear.

In October, I hired a financial person to help us properly continue the growth we were experiencing. Mark Procter was a big help almost immediately. Two days after he started, Mark came with me to a scheduled meeting with our bank. There, I was hit blindsided when they told me that if we weren't able to infuse some fresh capital into the business, they were going to call in our loan. The meeting was pretty cut and dried; they were concerned with our ability to remain solvent.

Then, during a coffee break, one of the bank officers happened to walk by and he recognized Mark from some previous business dealings. Mark's presence made all the difference in the world. The bank softened its demand and gave us ninety days to improve the situation. Over the next eighteen months, Mark's expertise turned our company around and we actually started accumulating cash reserves while budgeting our growth. I didn't stop "sticking my neck out," but now we did it in a more financially controlled way.

One day, a man, somewhat untidy in appearance, came into my office with a woven bird nest, telling me that he was from Bangladesh and that he could supply me with unlimited quantities of the nests. Shafique and I talked and I soon learned his complete family history, including the struggles he and his family had endured in one of the poorest countries in the world, and his involvement in a civil war that cost him several fingers of his right hand. He told me he was now in Chicago getting his Master's Degree at the Chicago Art Institute and was calling on some businesses on behalf of his family back home. I admired his tenacity, especially after he told me he had just come from Noah's Ark Pet Center down the street to buy the nest he'd brought in. He assured me he could produce the exact same nest at a much lower price than what I'd been paying.

We agreed on a price that was just two cents cheaper per item than my Chinese supplier. I gave him samples of four different nests and asked him to send me three samples of each size and style for approval. I told him that if all looked good, I'd place an order with him. I didn't think much more about our meeting, but three months later, a package arrived from FKF Trading Company in Bangladesh. The contents were perfect. I kept my word and placed the order.

Six months later, in November of 1991, I went back to Asia for another business trip, this time including a stopover in Dhaka, Bangladesh, to meet Shafique's family and see their company. My three days in Bangladesh were life changing. I knew I'd be visiting a very poor country, but it would have been impossible to prepare myself for what I experienced. What made conditions even worse was that two months before, a devastating cyclone had hit the area, resulting in some of the worst floods in Bangladesh's history and thousands of deaths. As my plane approached the airport, I could see the aftermath. Much of the infrastructure was still in total disarray and many areas were still without electricity or potable water.

I was greeted at the airport by Shafique's family, including his older brother, Kuhrul Alam. They all shielded me from the swarm of desperate people as we walked from the terminal to our vehicle. We drove to my hotel and I saw sights that are ingrained in my mind to this day. The traffic consisted of oxcarts, bicycles, and motorbikes, interspersed with beat-up old trucks and cars. Some of the oxcarts were stacked with wrapped bodies of flood victims, loaded like firewood. Meanwhile, thousands of homeless—thin, dark-skinned men, women, and children in soiled, ragged clothing ambled along the streets. They seemed to be going nowhere, lost and abandoned. Beggars gazed at me with extended hands turned upward. At one point, a woman tapped on the car window and, inches from my face, unveiled her dead baby.

When we finally reached our destination, the guards pushed the people aside, clearing the main gate of the luxury hotel that I would call home for the next three days. When the iron gates closed behind us, it felt as if I had just awoken from a nightmare. Through the courtyard of the hotel there were marble statues and fountains, palm trees and tropical plantings. It was hard to reconcile the setting with what I had just witnessed on the other side of those courtyard walls and I couldn't hide my tears. In seeing my emotions, Kuhrul explained to me that their country was slowly recovering but over the past few weeks it had become a common practice for beggars to find a deceased infant and use it to exploit foreigners for money.

Meanwhile, I knew I had to stay focused and concentrate on the purpose of my visit, which was to meet the people I was doing business with, examine the production, and do a quality control inspection of the products they were making for me; all of this while establishing a relationship.

The next two days I was treated like a dignitary, with my hosts accommodating my every move. The first evening I was served a special dinner in Kuhrul's home where I was introduced to his wife and three daughters, each of them dressed as if they were attending a ceremonial function. The meal consisted of assorted dishes of curried chicken, fish, and vegetables, accompanied by white rice. I noticed my place setting was the only one with a fork and spoon and I asked if I could join them by dining in the same traditional fashion as they, by using one's hands and flatbread. I knew I made the right decision when they all smiled at the request. But back at the hotel, I kept asking myself, *What in the world am I doing here?* I was there to find another supplier of woven bird nests at a better cost, but that all suddenly seemed so insignificant against the backdrop of the tragedy I was seeing played out on the streets of Dhaka.

The second morning, we took a small prop engine plane 180 miles inland to a town called Jessore where we were picked up in an old rattletrap of a car that lacked a front windshield. I'm not sure which was more annoying, the wind and dust in my face, or the continuous loud honking of the horn the driver made use of during the entire twenty-mile ride to warn the crowds of people carrying baskets or cloth bags on their heads to move out of our way.

When we finally arrived at our destination, it was nothing more than a tiny tropical village of little grass huts with dirt floors, and a small community of basket weavers that Shafique's family had selected to produce the little canary and finch bird nests for Pets International. We were greeted by the village leader while children from out of nowhere swarmed us, all wanting to take a look at me. They had never seen a foreigner before, especially a white-skinned one. Then I was given a demonstration of the weaving and assembling processes. I knew that the workers had no under-standing of, or even interest in, the purpose of these ridiculous little articles they were making. But they were clearly proficient, careful to pay attention to every detail, and capable of producing the perfection I was looking for.

When we concluded our business, I felt it time to show a bit of hu-mility and friendliness by talking to the children. Through one of my interpreters, I asked if they could sing me a song but they were shy and I initially received no takers. Then, out of the crowd, a little boy with a big smile raised his hand. I gestured for him to come closer and I noticed that he only had one eye. The boy sang a beautiful little song and I almost cried. I wished I'd had a way to record it.

If I could have adopted that little boy, I would have.

On my flight back home, in thinking about the whole Bangladesh experience, I realized that I now had another purpose besides just having a new supplier for my finch and canary nests. I wanted to make a difference, at least in some small way, in the lives of a rural population of extremely poor people who were barely able to make a living in a third-world country.

Over the years, I like to think I did just this. Recently, I heard from Kuhrul who expressed his gratitude for the business we had done together, touching on several experiences we'd shared during my visit. He also mentioned his appreciation for how despondent I'd felt about the devastating situation his country was in, even though he couldn't relate to the sympathy I'd expressed for all the baskets of turtles I'd seen the fishermen carrying into the marketplace.

He reminded me that in our busiest times, I had helped improve the livelihood of around a thousand people. Today, more than thirty years later, there's still a community of a few hundred "nest makers," some of whom have been profiled in local media outlets. Kuhrul's words were beyond gratifying, reminding me that sometimes there's more to business than just the buying and selling of commodities.

28

—•—

Priorities

WITH ALL THE NEW products we were introducing, and the modifications we were making to competitors' products, we were starting to be recognized as one of the fastest growing manufacturer/importers in the industry. We introduced hundreds of new products, many of which were award-winning. One I was especially proud of was our Puppy Housebreaking Kit. The packaging we designed for it included a picture of a toddler, and that toddler happened to be my son Andrew.

Of course, I continued to miss the live animal side of the business. Even though I set up aquariums of baby turtles and alligators in my office, and adorned the walls behind my desk with my lifelong butterfly collection, I'd still find myself driving down the street to spend time at Noah's Ark, checking out the new critters that had just arrived. And when I wasn't at the office, traveling overseas, or attending trade shows, I'd make every attempt to spend my weekends with the family doing animal activities, or go on wildlife hikes, even squeezing in the occasional turtling trips back to Wisconsin.

My new office.

Since I was always looking for ways to interact with nature, I suppose it was a foregone conclusion that I'd eventually find myself involved in taxidermy. This started during those times when I'd pull my car over to pick up the body of an unfortunate rabbit or squirrel for Ginny, my great horned owl. Many times I'd encounter other animals or birds that hadn't been flattened into obscurity. I always felt that it was not only a terrible way for a life to end, but a waste of some sort. As long as they were fresh specimens and not disfigured in any way, I started accumulating them, and having them mounted for my collection room. Over time, I accumulated a menagerie of critters from raccoons, beavers, and red fox, to skunks, and coyotes. I'm sure my boyhood experiences at Camp Oconto, where I learned to trap, skin, and tan chipmunks had something to do with the development of this rather unusual hobby.

At one point, my high school buddy, Bill Mazurek, who had been living in Hawaii, paid me a visit and ended up staying with me for a time in my townhouse. He'd also been having marital problems and I not only let him stay with me, but he would often accompany me to work and hang out. One afternoon, when Bill and I were pulling into the parking lot after having gone out to lunch, we noticed an attractive young woman parking her car. I recognized her as our previous accounts receivables manager, Denise Razaitis, who had left the company a few months before to go back to school. She was swinging by to have lunch with one of her old friends in the office and I couldn't help notice a somber look about her. We got to talking and it turned out that Denise had just buried her fiancé. I felt terrible for her and expressed my condolences, and Bill and I went on our way.

But I kept thinking about Denise. By then, I had been separated for a couple of years and, being so busy with the business, I missed female companionship. I knew Denise had just lost her fiancé, and I also knew she was a lot younger than me. But I couldn't get her off my mind. I heard she was in the middle of a job search and a couple of weeks after I'd seen her that day in the parking lot, I called her up, using the excuse of offering to write her a letter of recommendation. We talked some more and I asked her if she'd like to grab a bite sometime. With a bit of hesitation, she accepted and I did everything I could not to reveal my excitement. I knew that to Denise, it wasn't a date, but it sure was to me. And I ended up going overboard, buying tickets to a concert and making reservations at Lawry's Steak House in downtown Chicago. Denise got cold feet and two days before our date, she called and canceled. Something had "come up."

As disappointed as I was, a few weeks later, I tried again. We agreed to meet for a drink at a local bar and then drive downtown for dinner. That evening, I waited for her in the bar, nervous as hell. I sipped on a glass of wine, looking out of the window at the parking lot, waiting for Denise's arrival. I fidgeted around, rehearsing in my mind what we were going to talk about. I checked the time. She was late. Was I going to be stood up for the second time?

And then...there she was. I watched as she parked her car and got out. She was wearing a beautiful green dress and looked stunning. She came in and we had a glass of wine. I couldn't hide my nervousness, which later, I would discover, made her feel more comfortable. We had dinner at Eli's Steak House and had a lot of fun getting to know each other. From that day onward, we slowly developed a meaningful friendship. What more could I ask for? She was young, beautiful, intelligent, and loved animals. I also learned that she had a strong family background and appreciated the little things in life. Denise made me feel complete. Best of all, she even accepted my other love affair: the one with turtles.

My divorce with Linda was finalized in 1994 and the following year, my relationship with Denise became a new priority in my life. In the beginning, the seventeen years' difference in our ages concerned the both of us but after dating for a year, our ages became a non-issue. We fell in love.

I can't put my finger on exactly when it hit me, but I was beginning to see that there was more to life than working hard and building a business. Maybe it was the day Denise and I were out driving and we passed a large raccoon lying on the median yellow line. I had learned that the movement of a roadkill's fur as the wind blows is an indication of it having been recently hit and this one sure fit the bill. I made a quick U-turn and it turned out to be an extraordinarily large specimen with a slightly disfigured forward right quarter but an intact and immaculate, long, bushy tail. I opened the trunk, retrieved my Rapala fishing knife out of my tackle box, and surgically removed the tail, all to Denise's disbelief. But she accepted my strange behavior. That's when I knew for sure this was the woman for me. I ended up tanning the raccoon tail and later presenting it to her as a gift.

I continued my involvement in TEC, which changed its name to Vistage, and over the following years, my business continued to grow significantly. In 2002, Jim Tesch decided to move on, which was a blow to me as Jim had been such a wonderful mentor. His replacement was a man by the name of Bob Berk, a successful jeweler with several stores. I found him to be hardworking and sincere but young and, compared to Jim, a bit of a rookie. Other members shared my sentiments and after a long discussion in a private meeting, we all agreed to give it ninety days to see what this new guy could bring to the table. Could Bob really be the person to guide us all toward fulfilling our personal and professional goals?

Turns out he was. After two short months of interacting with Bob in both group and private meetings, I decided that I liked his direct, inquisitive, thought-provoking approach. He asked the right questions and challenged me constantly. Over the following years, Bob not only guided me through the tough decisions that needed to be made in a company that was growing at an annual rate of 25 to 30 percent, but he kept me focused on the big picture. He taught me how to work *on* the business rather than *in* the business. He helped me identify both my strengths and weaknesses and taught me how to concentrate on each of them in totally different ways.

My overall strength, which catapulted me into the business world, was my passion—my love for the animal and everything involved with its well-being. He would always remind me to focus on that, and never compromise my beliefs. My weaknesses were tending to those business activities that I had no interest or expertise in. Bob reminded me of the importance of recruiting the best people I could find to fill those areas. "Do what you do best, and hire the rest," he would say.

The TEC (Vistage) family.

He also emphasized the importance of balancing my life, enjoying the journey, rather than waiting until I reached some "destination." I felt at times that, for me, that piece of advice might have come a little too late. I was twice divorced. I couldn't admit to it, but on some level, I knew that everyone was right in saying Pets International was my mistress, and I became determined not to screw up again.

But it would never be easy. Once, we had a speaker at one of our Vistage meetings who asked everyone to write down on a sheet of paper what their "walkaway" number was. At what dollar amount would we be willing to sell our businesses? Everyone read off their numbers, everything from $7 million to $50 million. My turn came and I said zero. I was having too much fun in growing my business. There was no way I could put a value on it.

Within the group, I became a sort of model for passion. But it certainly wasn't anything I could help. One time, our group enjoyed a retreat in South Carolina. As we were heading back to the airport, I jumped up and insisted that the bus driver stop in the middle of a rural road. The confused driver reluctantly came to a stop, and I hopped out of the bus to move a turtle to the side of the road. And then I returned to the bus to the chuckles and nodding heads of my fellow Vistage members. I sat back in my seat, feeling certain that they were all beginning to understand.

29

—•—

INDUSTRY DEVELOPMENTS (SOME NOT SO GOOD)

HAVING FREQUENTED PET STORES my entire life, I could see that the retail pet industry was changing from the mom and pop pet stores of the 1950s and '60s. These shops were typically owned and operated by serious hobbyists turned business owners, some catering to niche markets—aquarium, bird, or reptile stores. They had always been my free-time destinations, places I would spend hours. Then in the 1960s and '70s came the large, full-line stores that stood out from the rest. My favorite, of course, was Animal Kingdom, Chicago's inner city zoo and home of the television pets.

Soon franchises like Docktor Pet, Puppy Palace, and Petland were cropping up throughout the country, along with privately owned chains like Shasta Pet Centers, Pet Supplies Plus, Pet Supermarket, Petland Discounts, and Pass Pets. This was the time when, unknowingly, the seeds were being planted in my mind for the creation of the world's largest pet center, Noah's Ark Pet Center. I opened the store in November of 1971 and it evolved into a twenty-seven store chain in the Midwest.

All the while, the pet industry continued changing. In the late '80s, we were just beginning to see super stores opening in markets around the country, led by the soon-to-be national giants PetSmart and Petco. I observed this growth firsthand by the size of the orders Pets International was receiving from these companies. And I knew it was only a matter of time before we would see them entering the Midwest market.

Even before this development, Noah's Ark was beginning to struggle. Some of the stores were becoming burdens on the entire organization. We decided not to renew the leases of non-profitable or even marginally profitable stores. We started pushing our accounts payable beyond ninety days, resulting in poor inventory levels. And then we started falling behind on our rents. A few of the mall location landlords threatened to close the stores. We negotiated plans to close several stores while making every attempt to hold on to key employees as long as possible, even offering important positions at Pets International to some of them. Soon, it was like a snowball of cash flow problems, growing bigger and bigger as manufacturers began demanding cash with our orders. On the Pets International side, I did everything imaginable to help, keeping the shelves as full as possible and extending dating on all purchases. But the key products from the other manufacturers had become unavailable to us.

It became too late. After closing store after store, our flagship store, my original Noah's Ark Pet Center was forced to close on November 14, 1992.

It took several years to financially recover. Not only did we owe our vendors, we owed the IRS in back taxes. We also had an outstanding mortgage, along with real estate taxes on the Oakton Street building, plus several broken retail store leases that had to be satisfied.

There were only two main stakeholders, my mother and me. And the financial burdens were enormous. Filing for bankruptcy was out of the question because we'd signed personal guarantees. We ended up hiring an attorney who specialized in turnarounds, bankruptcies, and company restructuring. Eventually, we were able to negotiate payment plans that, over the following two years, allowed us to satisfy our debts in every respect. I blame myself for the failure of Noah's Ark, not only for walking away, but for not demanding the financial controls I knew we needed years earlier. It was an extremely painful time for the Krauses.

The year 1993 saw me continuing to face my challenges at Pets International while Tom liquidated all the remaining fixtures of Noah's Ark, prepared the empty store for rent, and took some time to figure out a new direction for himself. Tom needed his own passion to pursue, not mine. As it happened, he and Bonnie always loved antiques, frequenting barn sales, flea markets, garage sales, and antique malls every chance they got. Their home was full of beautiful antique furniture, lamps, vases, and art objects, all of which they were passionate about. After cleaning up the retail space, it didn't take long before Tom and Bonnie started talking about getting into the antique business. The empty 20,000 square feet of available space was an ideal location.

It was 1994 and we were almost six months away from satisfying our entire debt when Tom and Bonnie opened the Oakton Street Antique Mall, a dynamic business that still stands today. Essentially, they became landlords, renting out several 100-square-foot spaces to other antique dealers. They kept six or seven spaces they ran themselves and built a thriving business. At about the same time, our mother passed a milestone in her struggles. She was five years cancer free. And Pets International was now focused and sales were increasing. We all had much to celebrate.

Three years later, in 1997, Denise and I got married in a spectacular wedding where our family, closest friends, employees, and business associates all joined in and shared in our happiness. I sold the townhouse and bought a beautiful home in South Barrington where we set up house. One of the first things we did was design a new patio and garden setting, complete with a waterfall and a koi pond. After planting the entire area with shrubs, evergreens, perennials, and several hostas, I encircled it with sixteen-inch-high wire panels to create my box turtle habitat. We kept several eastern and three-toed box turtles, and it was great fun watching them as they'd dig into their favorite hiding places, go in and out of the water, sun themselves in the open areas, and hibernate in the winter.

Everything was beginning to move in the right direction for the Krause families.

Then, the following year, on July 5, 1998, at one o'clock in the morning, Denise and I received a terrible phone call. Tom, just fifty-four years old, had had a fatal heart attack. Later that day, I had to sit his children down and explain to them that their father would not be coming home.

Tom's passing hit me hard. He had so much to live for. With the differences we had throughout our lives, we deeply loved each other and there are times to this day that I regret not being able to have done more, if not by helping him with the business, then by just spending more meaningful time with him. It took me two weeks after the funeral before I could even return to my office.

I supported Bonnie and my nieces and nephews for a few years in every way possible, and then the Antique Center finally made the turn and was able to stand on its own. Sad as it may be, however, my brother's family and ours split up as a result of finances, which to this day, as much as I personally contributed, is something I could never figure out. The one happy exception is my nephew Joe, Tom and Bonnie's oldest son, whom I have maintained a close relationship with. Joe has followed his passion and is in Florida successfully working for one of the largest commercial reptile breeding organizations in the world. I couldn't be more proud.

Meanwhile, the pet industry continued charging ahead. Big box super stores had already been rapidly changing the retail environment in other industries—toys, hardware, sporting goods, housewares, and office supplies to name a few. But due to its live pet inventory and its perception of being an insignificant mom and pop market, the pet industry was one of the last to experience this phenomenon. But that all changed.

Ten years earlier, while I was busy traveling the world, designing and developing new pet products, a progressive pet retailer by the name of Brian Devine decided to take the plunge and open his first Petco super store on the West Coast. Then, almost simultaneously, a young entrepreneur by the name of Jim Dougherty was hired by the Tetrault family, owners of Universal Feed, to run two new concept retail pet supply super stores called Petfood SuperMart, one in Las Vegas and one in Phoenix. They were both poorly lit, concrete floor, warehouse concepts, selling only pet foods and supplies at discount prices directly to the public, but located in industrial parks, rather than the high rent districts of shopping centers. Their success opened the door to Pacific Coast Distributing Company from which Jim and his wife Janice single- handedly built a company called Petfood Warehouse.

I met both Jim and Brian, and we started doing business together. In supporting the entire Super Pet line, they became two of my most important customers. Apparently, my timing was right because they were both in the beginning phases, and needed us just as much as we needed them. Both companies kept improving their business models. Petco believed in carrying tropical fish, birds, and small animals, while PetSmart focused exclusively on pet foods and supplies. Both hired mass-market professionals, and it was at this time that Dougherty changed his company's name to PetSmart. Soon, he followed Petco by including tropical fish, birds, and small animals in the stores' inventories.

PetSmart and Petco became extremely successful and, after receiving investment financing, started opening more locations throughout the country eventually going public.

Both organizations soon had several followers replicating their business models, and, as pet super stores started appearing all over the country, many independent retailers were afraid of what the future held for them. The mom and pop stores were going to disappear. Many didn't want to face the fact that they were going to go by the wayside unless they either upgraded their stores or found a specific niche to concentrate on. Many refused to do either.

Soon the entire pet industry was in an uproar. The manufacturers were at a crossroads. Should they remain loyal to the independent market and sell only through wholesale distributors, or open the door and sell directly to the super stores, most of which were capable of supporting the lines better than the wholesalers? The wholesalers tried to put pressure on the manufacturers, threatening to discontinue their products if they decided to sell directly to the super stores.

PetSmart and Petco continued to grow through new store openings and acquisitions fueled by shareholder value, ultimately resulting in the consolidation of the pet super stores nationwide until they became the only players in the market. One key ingredient that fueled their growth was the premium brands of dog and cat food they sold. The super stores went after the pet owner who wanted something better than what he or she could find in their local grocery store. This attracted a totally new consumer to the pet industry.

As PetSmart and Petco jockeyed for position in markets throughout the country, their business models were simple—to provide a fun place to visit where you could bring your pet; provide quality brands of pet foods at very competitive prices; sell fun and exciting pet products, toys, and accessories; but refuse to sell puppies and kittens, working instead with local shelters for pet adoption. However, they also felt it necessary to start

limiting inventories in the high-maintenance areas of live birds, tropical fish, small animals, and reptiles.

Many of their consumers never before frequented pet stores and
were excited to enter these giant stores with thousands of new and
exciting pet products. They loved being able to bring their dogs and
cats into the stores, something that was practically unheard of for retail
establishments at the time. And many of these consumers became new
pet owners after being introduced to the other animal offerings. Soon,
grooming, dog training classes, and veterinarian services were added
and the super store concept grew even more rapidly.

Just like the McDonald's business model, one of the critical ingredients of a successful super store is consistency. But with live animals,
that's the one thing that is a constant challenge. Consequently, PetS-
mart, as well as Petco, continued simplifying their live pet inventories.
Their selection of tropical fish, for instance, became limited to the
"bread and butter" species. This worked well for them, and for the
vast majority of consumers, but the more advanced and discerning
hobbyists demanded more. This gave the specialty tropical fish retailers
an opportunity, and today there are many specialized, quality, tropical
fish stores in upscale urban areas throughout the country offering large
selections of both freshwater and marine specimens.

Something similar happened with birds. With not being sure if imported birds were wild caught or captive raised, PetSmart discontinued carrying imported birds altogether, and eventually even eliminated US-raised
macaws, cockatoos, and parrots from their inventory. Their selection became limited to parakeets, cockatiels, lovebirds, conures, and a narrow
selection of canaries and common finches. The availability of beautiful,
home-raised, hand-fed baby parrots, cockatoos, rosellas, colorful singing

finches, and other interesting birds was left to specialty pet stores and, in time, to the ever-growing online sales segment.

Other changes in the industry have come from animal rights groups. Due to their increased pressure, PetSmart discontinued the sale of rabbits and ferrets. Their customers were required to sign an agreement specifying that the purchase of a rat was not for the purpose of feeding it to a snake. Eventually, the sale of rats was discontinued. The more unusual little guys like dwarf hedgehogs, degus, mice, and sugar gliders were soon no longer offered either. Selections of popular children's pets like hamsters, gerbils, guinea pigs, and chinchillas were limited. As a result, small animals became a much more important component in the inventory of the independent pet stores, as well as Petco, as both capitalized on the animals that PetSmart was no longer offering.

Reptiles and amphibians, meanwhile, fell into the same dilemma as birds. Reptile imports were eliminated with one or two exceptions. Captive breeding of reptiles, a booming industry in itself, provided an abundance of new selections but, for the most part, the super stores concentrated only on what appealed to the beginning hobbyist. This also helped fuel the growth of specialty pets in independent stores.

Perhaps the most significant, long-standing improvement in the pet industry was the super stores' decision to work with local humane societies and shelters by initiating pet adoption programs for dogs and cats. Many local and state laws today forbid the sale of puppies and kittens in retail stores. However, this, along with the internet, opened up a new avenue for retail puppy sales. Puppy breeders have sprung up all over the country, enjoying increased revenues by selling directly to the consumer as the demand alone shot prices skyward. Then, an additional market was created for what we now call the designer pet category—the breeding of two different purebreds to create a specific trait.

As breeders of puppies went the direct route, the demand for reptiles, small animals, and birds sure didn't disappear. PetSmart and Petco established a handful of approved wholesale suppliers who could meet animal husbandry, handling, and shipping requirements to designated stores. And they visited and inspected these suppliers regularly. As a result, progressive enthusiasts came out of the woodwork and started breeding specific species to supply these authorized suppliers. Then over time, as they continued to modify their business models, limited "green lists" of birds, small animals, and reptiles were established, narrowing the availability but increasing the volume. This was a boon for small business enterprises and family businesses that soon invested big dollars to expand their breeding operations to meet the demand.

But as the wind blew in one direction, it soon blew in another. With live animals, there are always operators who do not adhere to the best standards of animal care and husbandry. These represent a small minority but are often unfortunately used as examples by animal rights activists to demonstrate how bad the industry supposedly is. The majority of people in the pet business care about the pets and strive to do the right things. But PETA and other militant animal rights groups have become relentless in their attempts to stop people from owning any pets. As a result, the super stores have, many times, been kowtowed into discontinuing the sale of certain animals.

As an entrepreneur who has been in both the private and public sectors, I can understand giving in to the pressure rather than run the risk of bad publicity and poor stock performance, whether that pressure comes from groups like PETA or from other sources. On the other hand, the consequences have been unfortunate. An example is the cockatiel, at one time, one of the most desirable and attractive pets. Cockatiels live fifteen to twenty years, tame easily, love human interaction, can learn to mimic

sounds including the human voice, and have been successfully domesticated and bred in captivity for decades. A cockatiel makes for a wonderful,
educational, and affordable first pet for a child, providing much enjoyment
and enriching the child's life.

From a strictly business perspective, an initial cockatiel sale along with
proper housing, food, treats, toys, and accessories is in the $250 to $350
range. With a conservative average sale of one cockatiel per week, 1,000
stores can find homes for 52,000 cockatiels per year, generating more
than $13 million in annual sales revenue at retail. More importantly, these
customers return to the store two or three times per month for food, treats,
and supplies. Being long-lived, cockatiels can generate perpetual income.
It's also a fact that most pet owners have one or more different types of
pets. The cockatiel owner has the chance to be introduced to tropical fish,
cute little hamsters, or a singing canary on each visit.

And yet, at one time, PetSmart discontinued cockatiels due to a mis-
informed fear of an anthropomorphic disease. The decision to stop selling cockatiels was immediately decided upon by upper management not
wanting to take any chances of a national outbreak and running the risk of
a significant drop in shareholder value while investigating the legitimacy of
the problem. While understandable, consider the outcome of this decision.
All of a sudden, the authorized suppliers had an overabundance of cockatiels, some even having to accept returned birds. All cockatiel shipments
from the numerous breeders throughout the country were halted. In a very
short period of time, there was a backup of thousands of young cockatiels
that couldn't be sold. Many of these birds were eventually discounted to
other customers at below the breeders' cost or destroyed. Then, a lot of
these small businesses were forced to discontinue their cockatiel breeding
operations and ran into financial difficulties. Many were forced to close
their doors.

A few short months later, when it was learned that cockatiels weren't a problem after all, and PetSmart wanted to resume sales, there were none available to supply the demand. As a result, prices increased until the demand could be met again, which took years. In the meantime, a generation of children came along that would never know the joy of having a cockatiel as a pet. And the cockatiel market today has never recovered to what it once was. This scenario, with pet stores being strong-armed by outside forces, can potentially apply to any pet, from tropical fish to hamsters, and from parakeets to leopard geckos and bearded dragons.

The pet industry itself has reached a point where many negative impacts are having their effects. If it isn't the well-funded, extremist animal rights organizations, it's the puppy mill concerns, or the contagious disease fears. Today, there are countless animal, bird, and fish restrictions, everything from handling and shipping to importation and interstate transport. There are numerous federal, state, and local laws being enacted regarding pet ownership. There are invasive species and conservation concerns that are always popping up, so many that it seems uncontrollable. Advocates such asPETA and the Humane Societyhave "no-pet agendas," from goldfish to dogs. They are relentlessly chipping away at the choice people make to own pets.

While the availability of many species of tropical fish, birds, and small animals has been adversely affected, the reptile category, on the other hand, has grown. But in a different direction. With demand increasing, direct internet sales, reptile expos, and swap meets have been popping up all over the country. These have led to more and more hobbyists getting involved in the captive breeding of many different species. For many families, reptiles have become the answer for an easy pet to care for, a modern-day representative of the charismatic dinosaur that children seem to love so much. Reptiles are interesting and educational. They have no offensive odor and they don't require the attention that dogs and cats do. And they fulfill the desire to obtain the rare and the unusual. It doesn't hurt that they're often portrayed as loveable and with human characteristics in TV commercials!

But, naturally, as the reptile hobby raised its head above the radar, it was spotted by the animal rights activists and soon came a bombardment of unfair legislation. Fortunately, there are organizations that have formed to advocate for the pet industry, such as the Pet Industry Joint Advisory Council, which was formed in the late 1960s and is today called the Pet Advocacy Network. But even this organization was overwhelmed with all the newly proposed reptile legislation. Additional organizations like the United States Association of Reptile Keepers (USARK) were formed to educate and inform both the ever-growing reptile segment, and government lawmakers at the state and federal levels, providing reasonable guidelines for animal care, transporting, and ownership.

This is a promising development in an industry that, due to onerous and overreaching regulation, is in danger of not being able to provide the supply of educational, faithful pets that is in demand by animal-loving families everywhere.

30

— • —

THE LITTLE CRITTERS

IN THE LATE 1980S, seeing that the retail pet industry was changing with the onset of the super stores, along with the various directions the availability of pets were taking, manufacturers were changing as well. We started to notice more concentration on dog and cat foods, treats, and accessories. And the larger companies were getting bigger and stronger, much of which was the result of acquisitions and consolidations. At Pets International, we knew our uphill battle was only going to get steeper.

With the lion's share of the market being dog and cat products, many of the new and unique items we had introduced in that category years before had been copied. Our larger competitors had much deeper pockets and did everything they could to hold onto their market share. Another problem we were experiencing as we kept expanding and adding new items to our ever-growing selection of Super Pet branded products was that our cash availability was becoming stretched. As a result, we were constantly running out of some of our key items, Hamster Runabout Balls being the main one.

There were other reasons for our deficient inventory. We were importing most of our items, and our lead times for replenishment were often several weeks. Being unsure of the potential success of some of the newer, unproven products, we had a difficult time keeping our customers in stock because we weren't willing to risk overstocking. The problems were exacerbated due to the limitations of our warehouse space. All of this in addition to being undercapitalized. Even our domestically produced items suffered due to the cash flow problems we were experiencing. It was a totally new game for us, and not an easy one. As a result, we felt that our customers were starting to lose confidence in our ability to be a reliable vendor.

The Super Pet Hamster Runabout Ball was an especially well-received item with our customers and very few orders left our building without it being included in their overall purchases. It was inexpensive and consisted of an injection molded, ventilated ball made from clear, strong, flexible K-Resin, and with a locking, plastic access door. Our molder was a Chicago company called Integrated Molding Corporation. The ball was a popular accessory for families because not only did the hamster enjoy it, but it provided fun and entertainment for children of any age.

The inventory difficulties were cutting into its success, however. Terry Coleman, a top-notch salesman I had hired, would return from sales trips, review our customer invoices, and invariably discover that we'd been unable to timely fulfill the orders for the Runabout Ball. I'd hear him groaning, "Why, why, why, can't we even stay in stock on our *key* item?!" He'd always rant about us needing to concentrate on items like the Runabout Ball and forget about all the me-too fish nets, cat toys, and dog tie-out chains, all of which were being supplied by our biggest competitors. I knew Terry was right. On the other hand, my retail stores needed all of the commodities as well as the new items, not to mention the fact that I wasn't ready to give up competing with the big guys just yet.

On Christmas Day, 1993, Santa brought a model train set for my children. We all enjoyed watching it chug around our Christmas tree but as we did so, I had another lightbulb moment. Why not develop a custom track for our Runabout Ball? Retail stores throughout the country had already been conducting promotional hamster races with our ball, lining up two-by-fours on the floor. The track could be marketed as fun and interactive for the hamster as well as the child. In addition, we could sponsor pet shop hamster races. We could sell the product in complete starter kits with a ball included as well as individual tracks, all available in full-color, fun packaging. I began writing notes and drawing different concepts. After the holidays, I sat down with our graphic artist, Eva Barriga, and explained everything. She produced several conceptual drawings and eventually we settled on the perfect design and began making prototypes.

Strangely, over the years, I've noticed that when I'm working on designing a new product, someone else out there has a similar concept. So it was with the track idea. While cutting out cardboard prototypes, I was contacted by an individual who had been designing a similar concept that he wanted us to purchase. I told him that we were coincidentally working on the same concept and after revealing our prototypes to him, I examined his drawings. They were excellent. To keep him from approaching any of our competitors, I told him we'd finance the entire project, apply for patent protection, and, once the product was introduced, pay him a quarterly royalty over the lifetime of the patent, which was seventeen years. He accepted and we applied for a trademark, naming the product Hamtrac. Soon, we were finalizing new designs for patent applications.

We produced several prototypes and the product performed perfectly. In test runs, the hamster propelled the Runabout Ball on the track to the delight of our employees who looked on and enjoyed the show. I knew then and there that we had a winner.

I met with Larry Sternal of Integrated Molding and explained the entire project, showing him our drawings and prototypes, and emphasizing the necessity of having the product ready in four months, in time to introduce it at the June 1994 APPMA Show in Cincinnati. Then, after meeting with Istvan Heim, their head tool maker, I was assured that they could do it. The designs were simple and consisted of just two molds—a straight piece of track and a curved piece of track. The connecting points had to snap-lock together while at the same time being easy to disassemble. Their work began.

As the time for the show neared and our displays, signage, and other products were being shipped to Cincinnati, I personally joined in and worked around the clock doing whatever I could, even helping to polish the finished molds. It was getting down to the wire, just three days before the show opening, I did everything I could to help, even having pizzas and sandwiches brought in to save time. Then, hours before our deadline, we ran into a major road block. The tool for the straight piece finished off perfectly, but the tool for the curved piece would not perform. The product would never make it to the show.

Meanwhile, our marketing staff had arrived in Cincinnati with brochures, order forms, handmade prototype packaging, and several cages of hamsters. They were setting up the whole exhibit, working on all the displays but concentrating on our elaborate, circular centerpiece display for Hamtrac, not knowing that the display might have to be trashed.

The evening before the trade show opening, we again worked all night at Integrated, completing the tool for the straight section, and then producing a few hundred samples in various colors. I boxed them up and went directly to the airport to catch the very first flight to Cincinnati. Mark Procter picked me up at the airport and we sped off to the show just hours before the opening. Our revised plan miraculously fell into place. An hour before the show opened, we modified our Hamtrac display and converted it into a miniature racing venue of six straight runs, each a different color. With our signage, music, flashing lights, and the hamsters racing back and forth, we became the talk of the show. The laughter and commotion attracted a continual audience. We even had unofficial betting going on as people applauded for their favorite hamster. Hamtrac took first place as best new product for APPMA 1994, adding to our proud list of past first place awards. Every customer wanted it and we returned from the show with enough orders to keep the machines of Integrated Molding Corporation running 24/7 for several weeks. And Istvan was able to solve the tooling problem with the curved piece before we returned.

Hamtrac, first-place award winner at the 1994 APPMA Show.

Within thirty days, our Super Pet Hamtracs and Hamster Runabout Balls were now on every order leaving our warehouse. We were shipping hundreds all over the country and even opening the door to new business. To top it off, that fall our marketing department came out with a retail pet store Hamtrac contest kit complete with instructions on conducting races, scorecards, trophies, and stuffed animal give-aways. Hamtrac represented a turning point for Pets International and the Super Pet brand.

I didn't especially need the lesson, but one evening, out with some employees and their spouses, Ed Pawelko, the fiancé of our marketing manager, Diane Woltz, told us a little off-the-wall story that I've always found relevant, in its own amusing way. Ed was the divisional CFO of a Spanish-owned corporation with their offices in the northwest suburbs of Chicago. His division's performance was falling short of projections and the CEO was due to arrive from Tudela, Spain in a week to sit down with all the US executives for a meeting. Of course everyone was nervous as they prepared for the visit, compiling their specific reports.

The CEO arrived and the meeting began. After the typical formalities, everyone presented their reports with Ed concluding the presentations with the uncomfortable responsibility of reporting the underwhelming bottom-line figures. He closed his folder and the room went silent waiting for the CEO's response.

The CEO stood, paused, looked around the room, and, in his thick Spanish accent and very limited English, raised his voice and said "Fut ve all neet is tu *fukus*!" Then he repeated it. "Ve neet tu fukus!" You could hear a pin drop as he continued. "Dah goal is to fukus all dah time. Customers, fukus! Marketplace, fukus! Innovation, fukus! Team members, fukus!" Then the meeting was adjourned. Afterward, there were chuckles in back-room conversations about the CEO's mispronunciation. But everyone knew what he meant. And they knew he was right. Everyone, in all areas of the company, needed to *focus*.

As we moved into the mid '90s we had already begun introducing several new products in the small animal category. Being a very small area in comparison with the dog, cat, and tropical fish markets, it wasn't an area of concentration for most of the other manufacturers. We immediately saw that the category was undervalued, and we saw far more opportunities waiting to be discovered as we continued building upon our arsenal of products like the Hamtrac and the Runabout Ball. It struck me that it was better to be the big fish in a small pond than a small fish in a big pond. I made the decision. We immediately improvised a two-year plan to discontinue all products in the other categories, including the retirement of the Care Pet Products brand.

I took a page out of that Spanish CEO's book and decided to "fukus." We were going to concentrate the Super Pet brand exclusively on products for the warm and fuzzy little critters.

Over the following months the success of our new, small animal product programs allowed us to close out the other merchandise and fuel our new product development. Around this time, I started looking at the UK market. In my European travels, I had learned that the UK pet industry was strong, and I'd been intrigued with the idea of penetrating the market but didn't know how. Now, with our small animal products, I felt I had the answer.

I called Bryan Sharples one morning, one of England's top manufacturer's representatives. We'd never met but Bryan knew of me and we had a very promising conversation. Bryan had already heard about Hamtrac and expressed immediate interest in representing Pets International in the UK. I flew to London and spent three days with Bryan, not only learning the ins and outs of the UK pet industry, but what a straightforward guy Bryan was. He was a likable, hardworking man, energetic and hungry to do business. He knew his market well and was capable of penetrating it with our Hamtrac. As it happened, hamsters happened to be the single most popular child's pet throughout the UK. And Bryan explained that the market was starving for new and innovative small animal products. We agreed on a business arrangement and Bryan was soon representing not only Hamtrac but the entire Super Pet Line. Hamtrac was an immediate success, as were other products in the line, and it wasn't long before I began traveling to the UK regularly, visiting wholesalers and retailers alike.

Back in the US, our new direction was validated by how our customers were welcoming our products. We started branding our company as "The Number 1 Source for Superior Small Animal Products." Our motto was, "Creating fun products that enhance the relationship between pet and the pet owner."

At one point, Bryan called to tell me that the buyer for Pets at Home, UK's new super store chain, was planning to attend the 1996 APPMA SHOW in New Orleans, Louisiana, just a month away. Bryan planned to accompany her to the show and asked if I'd be able to arrange a once-in-a-lifetime experience for her, assuring me that in doing so, I would help in solidifying a strong business relationship. I put two swamp tours together, one strictly ecological and educational, and the other a little more fun—an evening alligator encounter. What better way to showcase a natural environment that the buyer from Pets at Home was guaranteed not to ever be able to see back in the UK?

The New Orleans show was a success, and afterward we rented two cars and headed for the swamps of Louisiana. The first car carried Denise and me and my son James, along with our good friends Bill and Barb Chew from Scottsdale, Arizona. The second car had Bryan, his girlfriend Amanda, and the Pets at Home buyer. Our first stop was the eco-tour company but we had a heck of a time finding it out in the back country of Louisiana. We must have driven three or four times up and down a remote dirt road that ran alongside a bayou for miles before we realized that the location we were seeking was a small, weathered, frame house.

There on the front porch, standing in the doorway was an intimidating looking fellow in bib overalls, staring at us through a broken screen door. After introducing ourselves, the man stepped out onto the porch followed by another man with a long gray beard. They walked us to a rickety wooden pier that extended out into the bayou and we boarded two wooden flatboats with small outboard motors. It was funny watching Amanda getting into one of the boats in high heels. Our tour guides slowly maneuvered the boats, one in front of the other, through the swamp and began pointing out all of the various fauna and flora. They told us which floating aquatic plants were edible and which ones would make us deathly sick. After witnessing my excitement in seeing several basking eastern river cooters, they didn't hesitate to threaten to leave us stranded in the swamps if we attempted to take a frog, turtle, or even a plant home with us. The Pets at Home buyer sat open-mouthed and speechless the whole time.

The second tour was with a family who ran a bed and breakfast at their alligator farm in the heart of the swamp. Upon arrival, we were led down wooden piers to our cabins, which were suspended over the alligator-infested water. Then all eight of us and the owner's son, who was the tour guide, fit nicely into their boat and we shoved off twenty minutes before dusk. The sun was setting and the humming of the motor became the background music as we glided through the smooth, serene, and picturesque channels. Soon it was pitch black and we began slowly sweeping our flashlights across the water. In the distance we could see pairs of eyes reflecting from the water's surface. The guide explained that you could tell the size of an alligator by the distance between the eyes. By that rule of thumb, we saw several that were well over ten or twelve feet long.

Then we cruised the shallows until we came across a three-footer. Our guide lunged over the side and grasped it just behind the head. With a lot of splashing and commotion, he brought it on board where we all took turns taking pictures of each other carefully holding the alligator behind the head as our guide had done.

The next morning, I chatted with the owner over breakfast and we became fast friends, swapping turtle and alligator stories. He learned of my turtle passion, and then I told him of the two alligators I had raised the past year, and that they were getting too big and in need of a new home He said he'd be happy to have them, and I promised to send them as soon as I got back, a promise I kept.

We all did some exploring that day in the area, had a memorable deep-fried alligator dinner at a local restaurant, and turned in for the evening. After breakfast the following morning, we started heading out when the owner approached me, saying he had a gift for me. He led me to a corner of his workshop and pointed toward an alligator snapping turtle shell that was over two feet in length. "It's yours," he smiled. I couldn't believe it. He said he'd had it for several years, dating back to the days when alligator snapping turtles were commercially hunted and made into turtle soup. Today, that shell is one of the most prized possessions in my artifact display room.

As for the Pets at Home buyer, Bryan let me know that their business relationship had been cemented by our excursions. Our Louisiana swamp experience was something she appreciated and talked about always.

31

CRITTERTRAIL

IN 1996, I WAS ready to start building a complete new product development department. As difficult as the decision was, I felt I was prepared to
turn over the reins of developing new products, and in doing so, I created
a new position: director of marketing and product development. To fill it,
I needed someone who understood the pet industry, someone who knew
animal husbandry, and someone who could take charge and continue the
growth that we were now experiencing. And so in November, I hired a past
district manager of Pass Pets from St. Louis, Missouri, Dave Hitsman.

Dave shared my values and had an excellent work ethic with strong
leadership capabilities. On his very first day at the office, he brought in a
crude metal litter pan which was designed to fit into the corner of a cage.
He explained that it was fabricated by a ferret enthusiast in Missouri who
happened to be an experienced metal fabricator in the HVAC business.
It was easy to see that the raised back wall design would definitely reduce
the mess ferrets make when backing into a corner while eliminating. We
took the sample and redesigned it by not only enlarging it, but increasing
the height, as well as smoothing out all the edges. Knowing that ferrets
were becoming more and more popular, we didn't waste any time in sitting
down with Integrated Molding to develop an injection molded High-Cor-
ner Litter Pan for ferrets. Soon, we were selling them nationwide. Then we

added a few more, but different sizes, marketing them for dwarf rabbits, guinea pigs, and chinchillas.

We soon introduced a whole new range of some really different housing for rabbits, guinea pigs, and ferrets; housing that the industry had never seen before, complete with ramps, shelves, and tunnels. The success of this program was followed by numerous small animal interactive toys, chews, feeders, and accessories. Dave and I enjoyed working together, always contributing improvements to one another's ideas.

As our business rapidly grew with PetSmart, Petco, and our wholesalers throughout the country, our business in the UK was creating another major revenue stream. In fact, Bryan and I decided it was time to hire another salesperson. Robin Grant soon became a key ingredient in the success of our UK sales strategy. During my frequent trips there, we'd spend many evenings hammering out the challenges of penetrating the UK market. Robin would many times ask for my advice, mostly, it seemed to me, looking for validation. I'd always respond the same way. "Robin, if I were to ask you to get yourself to New York, and on a specific day, I wouldn't want you to ask me how I thought you should plan your trip. I hired you to get to New York. Your job is to figure out how. Just get there." I knew Robin already had the answers. He just needed a nudge to confirm his thinking and build his self-confidence.

The increased volume of UK business and the amount of support and follow-up needed had us creating a new department within the company, an international sales division. I promoted my administrative assistant, a long-time loyal employee from Noah's, Tina Drews, to run it, and she was soon traveling overseas regularly to attend open houses and trade shows.

Of course, I was still traveling to international trade shows, too, and that year, I had attended the Germany Interzoo Show. While there, I'd come across a small manufacturer of bird accessories. I was especially intrigued by one specific item, a tiny canary/finch waterer the size of a perfume bottle that was flat on one side so as to fit snugly up against a wire birdcage.

There it was again, the lightbulb moment.

The pet industry only offered three sizes of small animal water bottles. They were all typically round and hung on wire attachments, none of them ever fitting securely. In 1997, after searching for a custom plastic blow molder in the Chicago area, I found a company by the name of Arrow Plastics that had a division that specialized in blow molding. I sat down with the president of the company, Bob Klekauskas, and told him about my idea. He and I hit it off and over the next month, we designed four sizes of blow molded, small animal water bottles, each with a completely flat side. The Flat Bac small animal water bottle program, as I called it, was an instant pet industry success and another award winner.

Soon, we were on the cusp of another great product breakthrough. As it happened, back in 1971, Mattel Toy Company developed an interactive hamster enclosure with connecting tubes, tees, and elbows that allowed a child to enjoy a whole new experience with their pet as it scampered through the clear plastic tubes. They named it Habitrail and successfully entered the pet industry during its early stages of growth. A few years later, however, Mattel felt they were losing focus and restructured the company. One of their decisions was to concentrate exclusively on the toy industry and in 1974, they sold the Habitrail brand to Metaframe Corporation, one of the largest aquarium product manufacturers. Metaframe was looking to enter the small animal segment of the pet business, and Habitrail allowed them to do just that. For twelve years, Metaframe enjoyed the sales of the Habitrail line until they started running into financial difficulties.

In 1987, the Rolf C. Hagen Corporation not only bought the Habitrail brand, but purchased the entire Metaframe company. Even though Habitrail only had a few years left on its seventeen year patent, it had been such a great seller that the Hagen Corporation felt it made all the sense in the world to buy it, and they swiftly filled the pipeline, selling the product very well over the following years.

In the meantime, Penn Plax, who had been expanding their aquarium product range, was also reaching into other pet categories. Knowing what a great seller the Habitrail line was and that the patent was soon to expire, they began developing a similar program, unveiling their SAM—small animal module—at the 1989 APPMA show. It took a first place award for best new product, and the entire Rolf C. Hagen team spent considerable time walking past Penn Plax's display in the new product section of the show.

Although SAM was somewhat different in looks and had a few unique features, I felt it missed the mark. It didn't offer anything functionally different. The tube attachments and connectors were similar to the Habitrail. So was the overall shape and size of the unit. Even the red and yellow colors resembled the original. Nevertheless, Penn Plax was successful with their new product.

These two companies, two of the largest and most popular pet supply accessory companies in the world, would fight fiercely for market share. Even though dog, cat, and tropical fish supplies were the main emphasis for both, I'm sure that pride and ego came into play. The year after Penn Plax's introduction of SAM, Hagen fired back by hiring a European designer to come up with a totally new version of Habitrail. They invested considerable resources and money to regain their strong market position. Their new innovative design combining wire panels with plastic components was truly different, and they successfully solved their one main drawback, which was inadequate ventilation.

Still, it didn't completely hit the nail on the head. It all looked very "European," lacking the excitement and bright colors that American children loved. Its drab earth-tone green and beige colors with packaging to match didn't market the product well, and it didn't perform as projected at the consumer level.

While all this was transpiring, our company kept chugging along and making phenomenal in-roads within the small animal category. I subscribed wholeheartedly to the message I always heard at our regular PIJAC meetings. Alan Levy, president of Wardley's Pet Products, would proclaim that, "Nothing happens until the pet is sold." And with my retail experience, I knew he was right. It was the sale of the small animal that created the sale of all the products from housing to food, treats, and accessories.

While closing out all our commodity fish, dog, and cat products, our new, small animal homes and accessories kept the first place new product awards coming year after year at pet industry trade shows. The entire industry was taking notice—retailers, wholesalers, manufacturers, and, especially, potential competitors.

But when it came to competitors, I always respected and kept friendly relationships with them. After all, a few short years earlier I was a good customer of theirs. If I wasn't sharing a meal with them, I'd make sure to stop by their trade show booths to shake hands and say hello. At the Interzoo trade show in Germany one year, Rolf Hagen interrupted a sit down meeting he was having when he saw me walking by. He made it a point to come over and shake my hand and tell me what a great job I was doing with Sid Meyers's company. And then with a smile, he said, "I've got to keep my eye on you, Bob." Occasions like that not only made me feel proud, but gave me added incentive to work even harder.

Once Hamtrac was successfully introduced in 1994, our company started ed really gaining momentum in the small animal arena. In spite of our phenomenal growth, our goal of becoming number one in the small animal segment lacked one key item: a unique, functional, and exciting home for the most popular small animal, the hamster. We needed a product that would not just compete with Habitrail or SAM, but one that would take the market by storm.

And so, in 1997, we introduced Crittertrail. And it promptly went nowhere. What turned out to be our first version was admittedly put together hastily and it fell short of expectations, failing to penetrate the market after a year of sales and marketing. The product was too expensive due to the amount of raw material we designed into it. It was overbuilt and heavy. And though functional, it didn't scream, "Wow."

The product had been a joint effort by us, Bem Partners, and Tominaga Manufacturing out of China. The following year, in 1998, Bem Partners and Tominaga introduced me to their number one customer in Japan, Sanko, Incorporated, explaining that we should all work together in developing a totally new design of housing for hamsters. After two long days of some very involved meetings, we all agreed to share in the cost of developing a program. Super Pet would market it exclusively in North America and Europe, and Sanko would have exclusive sales rights in Japan. It was our goal to become number one in hamster housing by hell or high water. We knew we had to not only build on what was already on the market, but bring it to a much higher level in every respect. We needed to "knock it up," instead of "knocking it off." In my TEC meetings, we had a concept called "B-HAG": Big Hairy Audacious Goal. This new hamster program became my personal B-HAG.

Our team of marketing, new product development, and manufacturing experts, led by Dave Hitsman and Larry Sternal, took what was already on the market, addressed the bad points, improved on the good ones, and added features that hadn't even been thought of. We were constantly flying to Japan and China, changing and improving the prototypes, making sure that we addressed every conceivable potential problem. The enclosures had

258

to work. They had to lock properly and safely. The tubes had to be securely attached yet able to be easily unattached by a six-year-old child. The size of the units had to be an ideal maximum. All add-ons had to be designed with sufficient ventilation. We strived to incorporate patented features that served important purposes in animal care, the major one being our "petting zone," a multipurpose, removable feature that served not only as an important area where the child and pet could easily interact, but as a sleeping/nesting area and a safe holding container while the enclosure was being cleaned.

In the final stages of development we hired a young college graduate, Jason Casto, as our marketing manager. He fit in perfectly. His marketing knowledge combined with his several years of retail pet experience were exactly what Dave needed, allowing Jason to contribute immensely to the fine details of development, and subsequent responsibility in bringing the program to market.

In 2000, we were ready. The "Crittertrail One" was born. This time, it was not only functional and eye catching, but expandable, with a design that we could build on with new models and features every year. It was child-friendly in every way. We addressed the needs and habits of the hamster and incorporated fun, attractive designs into our rainbow-colored attachments for feeding and playing. There were seesaws, wheels, ramps, and slides. There were hiding places and tubular bubble-shaped tunnels which we marketed as "funnels," and the consumer could expand and connect their hamster's "play land" at the pace they desired or could afford.

The modular and expandable design enabled us to economically market a complete program, rather than just one new item. The design allowed for different heights of wire mesh panels, and we were able to offer three sizes, one-, two-, and three-story models. The customer not only had a choice but they could modify and expand their existing Crittertrail. Each year our product development department added new models with unique moving exercise features and creative add-on accessories. Our graphics art department constantly improved our kid- friendly packaging, and our marketing department had a blast designing eye-catching new product displays for the trade shows.

Eventually, we introduced twelve unique modular homes. In 2001 we brought out Crittertrail Two and Three, representing the different stories. In the years following, we added Crittertrail Xtreme, a best-selling model that my son James was instrumental in creating; then Crittertrail Y and Crittertrail Z, each one having a new major feature in the form of interactive movement by incorporating wheels, spinners, and exercise balls.

We pushed the envelope a few times, one of which was our unsuccessful introduction of what we named Crittertrail Revolution where the entire home revolved in an internal rotating system. On the other hand, we successfully introduced Crittertrail Pink to support the Susan G. Komen Breast Cancer Foundation, where we donated one dollar for every unit sold. We also introduced mini versions, going after the mouse and dwarf hamster market while remaining focused on the fact that any item with the Crittertrail name had to be connectable.

From a sales and marketing perspective, we were quickly assembling a strong and professional sales force. My son Bob Jr. joined the company after working for both Noah's Ark Pet Center and a fast-growing tropical fish wholesaler by the name of Apet Inc. Outgoing, with a great personality, Bob Jr. excelled in the sales field, and, while in his new West Coast sales manager position, he put together direct container programs for our customers nationwide. We established suggested quantity orders which could be easily understood and financially justified by our customers, especially those not accustomed to ordering large container orders. We unleashed the program nationwide. We would ship directly from our

Chinese manufacturing facility with dependable arrival times, all the while passing on significant savings and maintaining our gross profit margins. All the major wholesalers in the US capitalized on our program. So did PetSmart, Petco, and companies in the UK, Germany, Denmark, Belgium, the Netherlands, France, Hong Kong, Malaysia, and Australia. It was an exciting year for us. We were positioned for growth that no one could have imagined.

Our Crittertrail program grew into the single biggest program of our company's history, eventually representing close to twenty-five percent of our total annual revenue and becoming our calling card in all future trade shows. Perhaps the greatest Crittertrail achievement was the fact that the entire process worked so well. Not only was the Crittertrail brand a financial success, it became a product that transformed our company, and, in doing so, performed extremely well for everyone involved in its success from the manufacturing process to the end user. Including the hamster.

Crittertrail

32

— • —

MY FRIEND AL

BACK IN MY RETAIL days we carried several unusual and hard-to-get items at Noah's Ark Pet Centers including various natural aquarium and terrarium woods, cork bark, driftwood, manzanita branches, drilled tufa, and rock. We marketed them as aquarium and reptile décor, with a few marketed as small animal chews. And we were always searching for new suppliers. Knowing the items were scarce, and having reliable sources, we began wholesaling many of them to other pet shops via Napco. Then, when I formed Napco International, we sold some of the items to whole-salers throughout the country. When I merged Napco into our acquisition of Pets International, some of these products were added to the Super Pet brand.

One of these products was our brand of cholla logs and our main sup-plier was a company by the name of McLaren's Desert Woods located in Apache Junction, Arizona. The owner, Al Lawrence, applied for annual permits to harvest the remains of dead jumping cholla cactus skeletons on government land, and he made a living doing so.

Jumping cholla was a name given to this cactus due to the flexibility of the cactus's branches. Its spiny growth grabbed hold of any passing object whether it be an animal, a person, or even a vehicle. In this way, it dispersed small balls of cactus spines, a very unique way of propagating, and, hence the "jumping" moniker. As the cacti ended their lifecycle and the outer skin and spines fell to the ground, you'd have skeletal remains and this is what Al would collect. In turn, he would clean and process them and sell them to local artists and small craft/furniture accessory customers.

When we first started doing business, I told Al that we'd buy all his leftover scraps as long as he cleaned, bleached, and cut them into four-inch pieces. We agreed on a price and began a profitable business relationship. Upon receipt of each shipment (usually a dozen or two large cartons), we would inspect, label, and shrink wrap each piece into a finished product.

Once Pets International came into the picture, the volume increased significantly as we sold this product to almost every wholesale customer we had throughout the entire US, plus PetSmart and Petco. Our business with Al over the years grew to where he gave up supplying his craft and furniture customers. He rented a larger building, hired more employees, and focused on our business almost exclusively.

One time, in 1994, having never met Al face-to-face, I decided to pay him a visit. After landing in Phoenix, I rented a car, drove toward Apache Junction, exited the interstate, and found myself on what turned out to be a dusty dirt road. After about a half hour, I approached an old, weathered, rusty metal building surrounded by a barbed-wire fence. I was in the middle of nowhere. There were several chickens and a farm dog patrolling the front yard of the building, which was covered with mounds of what appeared to be firewood, landscape debris, and branches. As I pulled up to the front gate, my suspicions were confirmed. This was indeed McLaren's Desert Woods.

A German shepherd greeted me at the entrance along with a rather rough and well-tanned woman. I introduced myself and the woman confirmed that I was in the right place. Al was expecting me and would be there shortly. As I waited, I walked around and could see that the mounds of wood were freshly collected cholla cactus skeletons in various stages of processing. I was proud of the fact that my business with Al provided an income and a livelihood. And I was impressed with his obvious ingenuity and perseverance in being able to scrape out a decent living in the desert. I got an even better feeling about Al when I noticed a large sulcata tortoise coming toward me from around an old Softail Harley Davidson motorcycle. Two of my favorite things in the whole world.

Finally, Al came along. We hit it off right away and ended up going to a small, local Mexican restaurant for dinner where we shared stories about animals, particularly reptiles and specifically tortoises, passions of the both of us.

After I returned to Chicago, Al and I kept in touch and a few months later, I went to see him again. We enjoyed each other's company immensely. Al was a colorful guy with an easy laugh and never-ending stories of his past experiences. If he wasn't living on the open range as a sheepherder, he was studying cacti and succulents while working in a major nursery in Arizona. He was well versed in many animal husbandry matters, especially reptiles. His inquisitive nature made for broad knowledge of all sorts of different topics.

One of our discussions evolved into the lucrative potential of breeding sulcata tortoises for the pet trade. One thing led to the next and we were soon shaking hands on a 50/50 business partnership in a tortoise breeding operation.

Sulcata tortoises make exceptional pets. They recognize and enjoy interacting with their owners. They're extremely easy to care for, as long as you provide adequate space to accommodate their large growth. Back then, they were scarce and in high demand. Hatchlings retailed for as much as $200 to $250 each, wholesaling for $80 to $100. We estimated we could average between fifty to seventy hatchlings per female annually.

A key factor to the tortoise's success was the southern Arizona climate, which replicated their natural West African habitat. Al had the property and was willing to maintain the operation for his half of the partnership's responsibility. I agreed to kick-start the operation by financing the construction of the enclosures, providing all the fencing and supplies, and buying a commercial incubator. Plus, I'd fund the necessary working capital for the first year. Al felt our biggest hurdle would be acquiring the breeding stock but with my connections in the reptile community, I felt I could easily handle that.

In 1995, I formed Arizona Herpetological. I had Ken Bellah draw up a simple partnership contract. I trusted Al 100 percent, but I'd learned years earlier that in business, you have to always put it in writing if, for no other reason, to avoid any honest misunderstandings later on, whether the business is failing or prospering.

Now it was my turn to acquire our breeding stock. Years earlier, I'd done business with a well-known reptile importer named Robert Sands in Tampa, Florida. Robert dealt primarily in tortoises and iguanas. He was a hardworking guy who loved reptiles. I approached him about my new project, and he agreed to help.

Robert's connections were in Mali, Africa, and it wasn't necessarily easy for him to get what we needed. There were a lot of unscrupulous dealers in Mali and Robert had, in the past, lost a lot of money in underhanded dealings. Trust was in short supply. It took almost a full year to work out the details and logistics but we were finally successful in importing thirty-five adult sulcata tortoises. Robert kept me informed every step of the way. At the end of December 1995, we finally received word that the tortoises were being shipped, and we began preparing for their arrival. The tortoises, heavy and exceptionally large, were shipped three to a crate, each crate divided into sections so that the tortoises wouldn't harm themselves during transit. Robert picked them up in Miami and took them to his holding facility in Tampa.

I flew to Tampa to inspect and select our breeding stock, accompanied by my son James, thirteen years old. For two days, he and I carefully went through the entire shipment of tortoises, observing their behavior and examining each one for physical or behavioral abnormalities, and then separating them into groups by gender and size. After culling out the ones we weren't interested in, we separated the best of the best and started selecting our breeders. We chose one male and eight females and placed them in their own enclosure. After acclimating them in Tampa for three weeks, making sure they were eating and hydrating well, we air shipped the tortoises to Phoenix.

I flew to Phoenix to be there for their arrival. I rented a van, and after loading the crates, drove them to Apache Junction where Al and I immediately uncrated and hydrated them. Once they were all acclimated and we felt that they were adjusting well, we set them up in two different pens, rotating the new male and Al's big male, observing their daily behavior. We didn't expect any breeding or egg laying to occur during the first two years but, starting in 1999, we produced 101 hatchlings. Of the eight females, three of them weren't quite large enough to start producing for another two to three years but each year from then on, our production increased substantially until we were averaging between 250 to 320 hatchlings per year.

When we started our partnership, we were able to sell the hatchlings for $125 each but over the years, as more and more sulcatas became available from breeders in California and Arizona, the market price dropped to as low as $55. Today, they're available in quantities at $35 to $40.

Meanwhile, Al and I were still in the cholla cactus wood business. At one of the Interzoo trade shows in Germany, with some pieces of cholla wood on display, I was approached by Bonnik Hansen, owner of a company by the name of Trixie, one of the largest pet product suppliers in Germany and rapidly expanding throughout Western Europe. Bonnik was intrigued by the product, telling me there was nothing like it available anywhere in Europe. We began a long-term business and personal relationship, and, in addition to our business throughout the US, I ended up selling several full containers every year to the European market. This meant Al had to step up production again, adding a few more employees and working longer hours to fulfill our orders. He grew his business considerably.

Almost every time I visited Al, he would remind me of how tough my buyer, Pam (Johnson) Devito, was. He said she was always squeezing him for a lower price whenever she would place large orders with him. With a smile, he would tell me that he respected her immensely and that he wished he had someone like her working for him. I of course acted as though I was unaware of her dealings because the last thing I wanted Al to know was that it was me who was encouraging strong negotiations with our vendors—firm, but always fair.

Besides being regaled with his wild and crazy stories, I learned a lot from Al. He was very knowledgeable when it came to nature, wildlife, cactus propagation, sheep herding, rattlesnakes, and Gila monsters. Living out on the Western plains, ranching, and even just surviving, had turned him into a nomadic type of a person. But he did have a friend whom he admired and thought the world of. Ann Dodd was a school teacher in another town not too far away. She kept him anchored in a loving and caring way.

Al lived in a one-bedroom mobile home with our sulcata tortoise pens set up just beyond his exotic cactus and succulent garden, which contained specimens from Africa, Madagascar, Mexico, and South America, all of which he was proud of. I always slept on the kitchen/living room floor after nights of talking into the wee hours of the morning about anything and everything, but most of which was animal related. On one of my visits, I surprised Al with my beautiful Kookaburra bird. Al had always talked of owning one. He had an empty aviary, and I was pleased to make him happy. He also had a skull collection, though it didn't match mine. He always wanted a warthog skull and, without him knowing, I arranged to have one shipped to him from one of my friends in South Africa whom I did business with.

At one point, Al became ill with a mysterious infection. He was weak and tired all the time, and the doctors couldn't figure out what was wrong. Al had his own theory. He was sure his illness developed as a result of ingesting some type of bacteria or parasite from drinking water out on the range when he was sheep herding earlier in his life. Meanwhile, he kept getting weaker and soon found it very difficult to manage our tortoise breeding operation. We agreed that I would take over, hoping that over time, Al's health would return to him.

In time, I was, reluctantly, forced to consider moving the whole tortoise operation. I thought of my good friend Ty Park, down in Florida, who had his commercial reptile business, supplying PetSmart. Having visited Ty many times, I thought that maybe he'd be receptive to a 50/50 partnership for the sulcata breeding operation. I was right. Ty immediately agreed, and we designed two large outdoor pens with heated shelter houses.

Al and I kept in touch and worked out the right time to move the tortoises. In June of 2010, I flew out to Arizona with my good friend from high school, Terry Speake. In Phoenix, we rented a box van for the trip to Florida, covering the floor of it with five bales of straw, and loaded up the tortoises. Looking back, although Al seemed happy and relieved, watching his operation come to an end had to be difficult for him. After a heartfelt hug, we said our goodbyes and Terry and I pulled out of the gravel driveway and headed southeast toward Tucson. We had dinner waiting for us at the home of an old grade school friend, Marlene Devere. I opened the tailgate of the van to show her the purpose of our journey and she laughed and said, "Bob, you haven't changed a bit since our grade school days!"

The rest of the trip to Florida was uneventful and the tortoises handled it well. The only scare we had was being instructed by several armed INS border patrol officers in El Paso, Texas, to pull into the inspection station. We knew they were concerned with smuggling from Mexico, but it's never a comfortable moment to be inspected by border patrol officers. They asked what we were transporting and I politely answered, "*Tortugas para zoologico en Florida.*" Then they had me open the back doors with their rifles at the ready. When they saw our cargo they chuckled and sent us on our way.

Before stopping in Tampa to have breakfast with Robert Sands and his father the next morning, we delivered the tortoises to Ty and helped him set up and then it was back to Chicago. The tortoise operation would continue, but with a different partner. But I kept in touch with Al. Every time we talked, he seemed tired, more so than the time before. And then one day, I got a phone call from Ann Dodd. I suppose I had expected it, yet hoped it would never come. Al Lawrence, my dear friend, had passed away.

33

—•—

THOSE WONDERFUL LIGHTBULB MOMENTS

IN A WAY, BRINGING sulcata tortoises to market was just one more new product idea in a long line of them. I found new product development to be profitable, creative, and a heck of a lot of fun. New ideas seemed to come to me from out of nowhere. I'd be in a grocery store, a gift shop, a zoo, a pet store, a trade show, a county fair, or pretty much anywhere, and I'd be hit with a new concept for a product. The first chance I'd get, I'd start writing, describing the product and making numerous sketches, sometimes on envelopes or scratch paper and many times even on napkins. At the top of these new product idea pages I always drew a lightbulb. That was my way of identifying a new product idea worksheet. Over time, I had a file cabinet drawer stuffed with lightbulbs.

Most of the times, an idea would hit me as a way to fill a need. Maybe it was a solution to a problem, or a way to create enjoyment, or maybe a means by which to improve upon an existing product or system. In any case, the idea was an opportunity in waiting. Some were simple; some were very involved. One continuous source of opportunities was the chain of distribution. I noticed that a lot of manufacturers overlooked the fact that retailers and distributors had their own needs. We made sure to address those by incorporating improvements into the delivery, handling, and merchandising of our products. We did everything we could not to just fill their warehouses and shelves, but to pull the products through the supply chain all the way to the consumer.

One of my first real lightbulb moments came at the beginning of my Pets International career, about a year after I bought the company. With my retail pet store background, I recognized a void in the market regarding small animal chew products. Anyone involved with guinea pigs, rabbits, hamsters, and other rodents understood the importance of offering these small animals items to chew on, such as fibrous materials, including grains, seeds, dried grasses, hay, and even wood. The incisors on these animals continue to grow and if not kept trim, serious malformations can result.

In the 1970s, there were no products on the market that addressed this problem with the exception of a small imported package of wood chews marketed solely for hamsters. Back in the Noah's Ark days, we always encouraged our small animal customers to provide their pets with non-toxic, wood-like, fruit tree branches, explaining to them that this would minimize dental health problems. At one point, a small pet shop owner in Bridgeport, Connecticut addressed the need by producing packages of various shaped balsa wood pieces, selling them to the pet industry as hamster wood chews. But, unable to produce in volume, he ignored the rabbit and guinea pig segments.

I remembered that and, ten years later, I found myself in a position to develop and outsource a manufacturing process for several items in this category. Balsa wood model airplanes were a popular children's toy in the 1950s through the 1970s. There was an American Flyer Model Airplane plant in northwestern Indiana which sold their products to the hobby industry nationwide. I contacted them about their excess cut-offs and scraps, and learned that they had an unlimited monthly supply that they were willing to part with at near "haul-away" pricing.

Then I looked for a food-coloring source and found a wholesale bakery supply distributor right in my own neighborhood, Elk Grove Village, where we could buy food coloring concentrates in gallon jugs. Then we found a state-subsidized facility in northwest Indiana that offered work programs for disabled individuals. They had the ability to produce a finished product for us at an attractive cost per item. We found a supplier for the packaging and we were in business.

After developing an entire range of small animal chews, we instructed the manufacturing facility in the exact specifications of what we needed and before long, we had an entire range of new wood chew products, all cut into various sizes, shapes, and colors. A side benefit was seeing all the smiles on the faces of the workers, taking such pride in the jobs they were assigned to. Management told me that the disabled workers really looked forward to the pallet loads of balsa wood arriving each week.

We developed several SKUs of various sizes and shapes, creating a totally new category. Our Super Pet "Bunny Bites, Carrot Chews, Hamster Nibbles, and Chunky Chews" became instant hot sellers nationwide. Later, we followed them up with other unique chews: "Bark Bites," and Branch Bites," made from apple, willow, and birch trees. We created a brand-new category that wholesalers and retailers welcomed. Not only did we provide an additional revenue stream for the pet industry, we fulfilled a need for the pet owner and, most importantly, the pet. The category of chew toys eventually expanded to where, today, there are several companies that supply similar products. Of course, one of the problems with new products is dealing with all the copycats that emerge almost as soon as the new product hits the shelves. It didn't take me long to guard against this.

One time, while in a Hong Kong pet store, I noticed several children watching some guinea pigs and dwarf rabbits nudging and rolling a six-inch-round, wire-mesh, hamster "exercise ball" that was filled with alfalfa hay. Some ingenious employee had taken an existing product off the shelf, stuffed it with alfalfa, and turned it into a round hay feeder. The rabbits and guinea pigs were nibbling through the wire mesh and, in doing so, rolling the ball back and forth. The lightbulb turned on and I immediately envisioned a new product.

I knew that the fast and easy way of proceeding would have been to have one of our wire vendors simply duplicate the product with our label on it and package it for sale. We could have had it on the market within six months. But I knew better. Vendors have a way of talking to other customers. Secrets don't stay secrets. I had a better way. It would take longer, but we could avoid the copycats.

We took the idea to a wire fabricator that we were purchasing component items from, one with no pet industry ties. We instructed them to fabricate a perfectly sized, six-inch diameter by three-inch wide wire mesh band. They had no idea what the band's purpose was and that's the way we wanted it. Then we designed a plastic twist-on side cap, two of which, when attached, created a perfectly round sphere. After building the tooling for the side cap and applying for both design and utility patents, we designed our packaging. Soon, we began receiving shipments of the imported wire bands and started producing and assembling our new "Roll in the Hay" fun and interactive hay grazer for pet rabbits and guinea pigs. Another really cool functional product that fulfilled a need. The whole process took longer, but by doing things right—keeping the product under wraps and taking all the appropriate legal steps—we were able to discourage, or at least slow down, the inevitable knockoffs.

Many of our new product innovations weren't as involved. Something as simple as redesigning the top of a guinea pig home by cutting a hole in the top wire mesh and adding a hanging hay manger that could be serviced from the outside was a definite improvement. An interior wire shelf gave the small animal another surface and a "lookout" platform, creating an accessory for other homes. New, injection molded shelves and ramps in rabbit and guinea pig homes were welcomed by pet owners and their pets. Deeper bottom bases allowed for adequate bedding and reduced the scattering of litter outside the home.

Visiting local pet markets.

There were also many innovations that we took from other industries that were used in totally different applications. A unique butter dish with cover became the impetus for a new "corner hamster potty" and joined our small animal litter pan program.

The ideas kept coming. When a pet owner gave their rabbit a carrot to enjoy, it always ended up soiled in the litter at the bottom of the cage. Why not design a carrot holder that can hang securely on the inside of the home to allow the rabbit or guinea pig to gnaw on it at their leisure, without soiling it or taking the risk of ingesting wood shavings?

Of course the Lionel train set around the Christmas tree spawned the Hamtrac. Our Japanese partners took our Hamster Runabout Ball and made a smaller version for Japan's most popular small animal, the dwarf hamster. A year later we followed suit with our "Mini Hamster Runabout Ball" for the dwarf hamster and pet mouse market in the US. Then when Lees Pet Products introduced a giant exercise ball, we couldn't allow them to slide into our market so we responded by not only introducing our giant version, but adding a Mega Runabout Ball for guinea pigs, dwarf rabbits, and ferrets. Holding onto our market meant we always had to be a step ahead. We added a glow material to the plastic during the manufacturing process that created our glow-in-the-dark hamster runabout ball. Later we added sparkles and brought out our Mardi Gras version.

The original Chinchilla dust box was nothing more than a galvanized container filled with blue sparkle dusting material and sold into the commercial breeding industry. This worked well in that market but for a pet chinchilla in the home it was a constant mess. So we created a colorful translucent plastic-covered chinchilla dust bath house, allowing children to observe the interesting behavior of the chinchilla as he gave himself a dust bath while not creating a mess.

I loved attending various animal shows and exhibits, not only to enjoy the animals, but to be on the lookout for those little ideas that could potentially become big ideas. One day, visiting a local ferret club gathering, I discovered a fun activity. The members conducted ferret races through flexible dryer hoses laid out on the floor. This lightbulb moment had us creating special lengths of clear, flexible plastic tubes in multiple colors that, with connector rings, would allow an endless variety of lengths. We packaged them in kid-friendly packaging and branded them as Ferret Flexi-Funnels, a fun and interactive exercise toy for ferrets and their owners. Soon after, we developed rigid injection molded ferret trail funnels in straight and elbow shapes that could be attached to our new Ferretrail Homes.

Of course, establishing the right pricing for our new products was critical. The key was first determining what the ideal retail price would be and working that price backward. I needed to make sure the retailer and wholesaler could both earn a fair profit while building in enough of a margin for us to be able to discount and promote the item. Over the years, I established respectful relationships with all my suppliers and customers. Many of these relationships became solid long term friendships, and I'd like to believe that a lot of that had to do with allowing everyone to benefit financially. We all had to make a profit, everyone from the small Chinese factory owner to the retail pet store owner.

Throughout all my new product experiences, confidentiality was key. To some people, I probably appeared a little obsessed and over reactive when it came to confidentiality, but I knew it was important and I worked hard at it, often times not even disclosing what the product was or what it was to be used for, as with our "Roll in the Hay" product. Often, we would buy components from a variety of suppliers, sometimes even from different countries, and then have them assembled stateside in our facility.

I also kept confidential, detailed notes of every product meeting, making sure they were not seen by anyone. I even wrote in codes to eliminate the possibility of any of my suppliers figuring out my strategies, especially when it came to price negotiations. I never left my notes on meeting room tables when it was time for a factory tour or to break for lunch. My briefcase stayed with me at all times. I never shared the names of my suppliers with anyone. I went to extreme measures not only in keeping things private, but not even having my suppliers take me to the airport so that they wouldn't figure out my next destination.

However, in spite of all of our efforts, copycatting was inevitable. We accepted the reality, knowing that it was just the way business was no matter how hard we worked to stop it. Design patents helped, but some were either ignored or else the copycat product was slightly modified to get around the patents. We tried to protect our proprietary items by vigorously enforcing our patent protection. First, we'd send courteous letters, and then would come more forceful legal threats. We never had to litigate, nor would we have wanted to. For the majority of cases it wasn't financially feasible.

Exacerbating the problem, many Asian suppliers were also a source of copying. They would take our ideas, or actual items, and offer them to our competitors. We'd confront them, but they didn't feel they were doing anything wrong. They justified their actions, telling us, "We have to keep our machines running," or, "We have to stay alive." When I came across that mentality, I knew it was time to start phasing out that supplier and immediately begin looking elsewhere.

I was never in favor of partnering, but working with Peter Geboers in Europe allowed me to see a different way of doing business. The ideas we shared with each other offered us both valuable benefits. Then, as I began working in the Far East, I spent considerable time developing products with the Japanese, and in doing so I learned that they too practiced partnering, but in a much more concerted way. Many times they'd involve both their customers and vendors in the entire process of developing new products, even openly discussing strategies and costs. I learned that this allowed them to not only gather all the input needed to make decisions, but to save time.

Most times, it all came down to trust. If you found suppliers you could trust, or even partner with, you could take a product far. And it was always rewarding to see a new product succeed. Not just financially. It was gratifying and fun to see a product being sold by a retailer, or even used by a happy pet owner, that had, at its very beginning, been nothing more than an idea I'd been struck with. A lightbulb moment. No matter how many new products we developed, that feeling never got old.

Partnering: the collaboration of professionals in developing new products.

34

—•—

CREATING MEMORIES

WITH THE BUSINESS WE had done with custom manufacturers, we'd invested in a lot of tooling, dies, and plates. These became primary assets of ours and, while using them to fill our orders, the manufacturers were responsible for storing and maintaining them. As our business with Integrated Molding, our primary supplier in the US, rapidly grew from the development of more and more new products, I began meeting almost weekly with Larry Sternal. In fact, we became close friends.

By 1996, the volume of business had grown to where I started thinking about starting my own injection molding operation. With all our new ideas for products, the thought of being totally integrated was very appealing to me, not only as a way to lower our costs, but as a way to lessen our dependence on outside manufacturers, especially from overseas.

I talked the idea over with a few different people I knew, including Fred Wise, a large custom molder in the plastics industry; Warren Henricks and John Franz, executives of Anchor Advanced Products, a designer and molder of plastic articles for the cosmetic industry; and the group at TEC. It was pretty much unanimous that I didn't have enough volume to justify starting the new business. Nevertheless, I hired Larry Sternal to do a feasibility study to determine at what point it would make financial sense. His findings told me how many molding machines, what size presses, and what supportive machinery we would need. Larry even detailed my staffing and building requirements and gave me an estimated cost in putting it all together. The end result was that we were only about halfway to where we needed to be to justify the investment.

We went along, developing new products, and I kept the idea in the back of my mind. And then, in January of 1997, Larry confided to me that he'd become disillusioned with the future Integrated was offering him. Over a series of conversations, we revisited my idea of starting an injection molding operation, with Larry telling me that he might be able to bring in outside business to compensate for the volume we didn't have.

In February, Larry and his wife, Deborah, and Denise and I, had dinner to talk about the possibilities of our collaboration. By the end of the meal, everyone was on board. Larry and I shook hands and a new adventure was born. I gave Larry the responsibility of handling the entire process of building the new company. He gave notice to Integrated Molding and, within two weeks, he sourced used injection molding machines and all of the equipment. He designed a floor layout and put together a staff including an experienced plant manager by the name of Bob Jaynes.

We named the company Accutec Systems, and looked for a location near Pets International, finding an 11,000 square-foot building just ten minutes away. Larry had his plate full as I left for a ten-day trip to Japan where we were exhibiting some of our products at the JPPMA trade show in Yokohama. One evening at the show, I had dinner with a friend of mine, Gary Bagnall, president of ZooMed Corporation. Afterward, Gary's agent, Nobuhiko, took us to a few exotic reptile and animal stores. It was a rainy night and we were running through the busy traffic from taxis to stores, carrying umbrellas and shopping bags. At one point, in the excitement and commotion, I momentarily forgot that vehicles traveled on the left side of the street. In looking the wrong way, I was hit by a car.

Gary, who had crossed, came running back to find me lying in the street either dazed or in shock. Somehow, to his amazement and relief, I was able to pop back up, no worse for wear. Maybe it was the excitement of "turtling" in Japan, but later I thought of how close I'd come to not seeing the opening of Accutec, or the future of Pets International, or, most importantly, the way the rest of my life would have turned out.

After the trade show, I came home to find Larry moving at full speed. The equipment was being delivered and everything was being hooked up while Mark Procter was making sure we were adhering to our projected budget. By the end of March, we were performing test runs and all was coming together perfectly. Larry's reputation and expertise meant that not only could we attract key personnel, but we'd be able to attract outside business too. By April, we were in operation and within a couple of months, we had migrated most of the work for Pets International from Integrated to Accutec. Meanwhile, Larry was bringing in business from the sports trophy, roofing supply, and houseware industries.

From there, things took off. Within three years, we were operating a complete manufacturing plant with 150 employees. We ran twenty-two Van Dorn injection molding machines five days a week, twenty-four hours a day. We were now producing a variety of small animal products, everything from our runabout balls, high corner litter pans, various accessories, and cage components, to several sizes of small animal home bases. We built an assembly and packaging department where wire panels and other imported items were joined together with the components we produced and packaged into finished product. With the expertise of Eva Barriga and Carol Pseno heading our own in-house design team, we created some of the most innovative and colorful, kid-friendly packaging in the industry. As we kept refining our processes, our modern warehousing and ordering systems allowed us to turn our customers' orders in less than forty-eight hours at a 100-percent fill rate.

Manufacturing became the final piece of my business puzzle. While many of the manufacturers I dealt with knew the "hows" of producing something and were always seeking the "whats" to produce, I had gone into the manufacturing business already knowing the "whats". I had just needed to figure out the "hows". And this I had done. I was now totally integrated, from retailing to wholesaling to importing and now manufacturing.

Building a great organization.

• • • • • • • • • •

Around those years, I would find myself from time to time thinking about my father and brother. Dad had passed away at the age of only fifty-five. Tom was just fifty-four at the time of his death. I was now around those ages. I thought about that evening in Japan when I'd been hit by a car. It was hard not to have thoughts every now and again about my mortality.

But eventually, I would decide to just be thankful for what I had—my wife, my children, my health, my financial security—and go about my day.

Meanwhile, Mom wasn't getting any younger. By this time, the single most important thing in her life was my thirty-three-year-old sister, Mari-Lynn. When she'd been born while I was in the Army, she'd been the joy of my parents' lives, giving them a true reason to be happy. But Mom always had to work while Dad sat home "taking care of Mari-Lynn," as Mom would euphemistically put his drinking. It didn't come as a surprise that years later, after being in and out of different schools, Mari-Lynn got involved with drugs, resulting in failed jobs, relationships, and situations.

As the years passed, my mother, true to form, always enabled her, making excuses for why Mari-Lynn wasn't around. But behind Mom's closed office door, she'd break down in tears. I began making it a point to spend more time with Mom, going out with her to lunches and dinners, hosting birthday parties that included all her friends, and holding elaborate brunches in hotel lobbies. I made sure she had an executive private office even though she only came into the office one day a week. But that day was important for her. She'd read the paper, make some telephone calls, and always ask about the business. We'd sit down together and I would share the exciting new happenings. She'd talk about her life, too, usually her experiences at the casino or her weekly poker games with her friends. Eventually, she'd bring up the latest problems my sister had created. Finally, we'd conclude her day by going out to lunch at one of her favorite restaurants and talk about happy things.

I wanted to be more involved with my sister in the hopes that I could be a positive influence on her. I started including both Mom and Mari-Lynn on various business trips to Europe where we took the time to sightsee in Amsterdam, Munich, Paris, Venice, and Milan. I introduced them to several of my international friends, even staying as guests in their homes in the Netherlands and Italy. The three of us traveled through towns and villages in Mexico, too, and while deep sea fishing in Acapulco, I was thrilled to see the excitement on my sister's face as she landed a blue marlin. I also made it a point to plan several jaunts to my mother's most preferred place in the whole world: Caesar's Palace in Las Vegas.

My favorite trip with Mom was in early March of 1999, about a year after Denise and I got married. I was at the JPPMA pet industry trade show in Kobe, Japan. Mom and Denise flew into Osaka after the show and we spent a week going to Karaoke bars and saunas, enjoying the sightseeing of Kyoto and Nara, experiencing traditional Geisha entertainment, and indulging in the cuisine of Japan.

All this was prior to the climax of our trip, an excursion to experience the traditional Japanese relaxation of natural hot springs and baths at an Onsen Ryokan in the mountain village of Shashenzi. It was an exciting train ride up to the village, and upon checking into the inn, we could tell we were in for a really different experience. Two ladies in traditional kimonos greeted us at the entranceway and did the best they could at instructing us to slip into Zori sandals. Then we were escorted to our large shared room, spartan but comfortable, and with straw mat flooring. One wall of the room was entirely glass and it opened up into a lush, private garden with a koi pond and private sauna for two. After putting on our kimono robes, we visited the massive, outdoor, hot spring saunas. Later, sitting on plush cushions placed on tatami mats in our room, we were served dinner by women in immaculate Japanese gowns. Afterward, we turned in for the evening, the three of us lying side by side, wrapped in plush, sleeping bag type comforters on the warm tatami mat floor like children on an overnighter.

The next day, we strolled through the village and enjoyed the art and handmade giftware in the artisan boutiques where I picked up two more pieces of turtle art. One was a one-of-a-kind ceramic teapot set and the other a carved wooden turtle depicting an Asian folktale of good fortune. It was a special time for the three of us, and a memory with my mother that I will always treasure.

With Denise and Mom in Japan.

35

—•—

DREAMS

BUSINESS CONTINUED TO BOOM and we expanded rapidly, renting two
more buildings in 2000, giving us a total of four locations, one for our
general offices and primary distribution, two for overstock and direct
container orders, and one for our manufacturing, assembly, and injection
molding operations—a total of 55,000 square feet. But we had to hire
trucking companies to move product constantly from one place to another
and the logistics were becoming a nightmare. Soon, we began searching for
a new building to consolidate our operations under one roof.

I delegated the responsibility of finding Super Pet's new home to Mark
Procter who grabbed the bull by the horns and found a 130,000 square
foot building in an upscale, light industrial area of Elk Grove Village. It
had everything we needed, including high ceilings, a separated portion
that could be dedicated to our manufacturing division, five truck docks, a
ground-level door, great curb appeal, nice landscaping, and a huge parking
lot with additional acreage for possible expansion. We closed the deal in
June of 2001. I hired Mitch Tarzian, a close friend of mine from my Vistage
group who owned a design/construction company, to help design our new
offices and lay out the manufacturing, warehouse, and distribution areas.
We moved the entire company in phases, wrapping everything up by the
end of the year. Immediately we started realizing the savings.

Meanwhile, I was coming to the realization that we were maxing out our small animal accessory category, and it was becoming more and more difficult to expand via new products. Consequently, we pursued a line of small animal shampoos, coat conditioners, deodorants, cage sprays, powders, combs, brushes, and nail clippers. A couple of companies had been touching on this area but not in a complete way. A brush here, nail clippers there, maybe a shampoo. I called Tony DeVos, a friend of mine in the industry, who owned Cardinal Laboratories, and set up a meeting. It wasn't long before we introduced a Super Pet line of small animal care products, even including cage cleaners and deodorizers.

All this time, without my planning it, the success of my business was starting to afford me the opportunity to create a future private life that would bring me right back to my original passion of turtles and tortoises, but in a much more rewarding way. A dream in the making.

Back in 1997, my passion had once again been stoked by my experience breeding sulcata and leopard tortoises in Arizona with Al Lawrence. Then, while in Chicago, I had kept that torch lit, every month visiting Lee Watson's Tradewinds Reptile Swap in Bartlett, Illinois. During the next few years, I rubbed shoulders with every character you can imagine, from good old boys who sold wild-caught reptiles, to backyard breeders of anything that moved. Additionally, there were small entrepreneurs who imported or commercially bred small animals, birds, or reptiles, and catered to the vast number of hobbyists, everyone from that father and his young child looking for the ideal first pet, to the biology teachers and herpetologists, all crowding the aisles of the swap. I could relate to all of them.

Around 1999, I noticed a lot of people at the swap starting to talk about kingsnake.com, a brand-new online venue for buying and selling reptiles. Some felt the days of reptile swaps were coming to an end. What was really happening was that the reptile hobby was beginning to transition to a full blown industry. Of all the different vendors that contributed to that transition, Bob and Sherry Ashley, two young entrepreneurs from Michigan, were key. I'd see them at Lee's swap every month, and I could always depend on them to have some new and unusual turtle, or tortoise book titles, or the occasional good deal on a tortoise hatchling. In time, these two visionaries would join forces with Brian Potter, a well know reptile retailer, and create the NARBC—the North American Reptile Breeders Conference. Today, this is one of the most successful reptile expos in the country.

And so Lee's swap was a hotbed of industry activity. Of course, he and I had been friends ever since that day in the '70s when he entered my original Noah's Ark Pet Center. Whenever he saw me waiting in the long line as the doors opened to the swap, he would pull me aside, put his hand on my shoulder, and walk me to the front table to get my hand stamped. One time, being intimately aware of my interest in turtles and tortoises, he put me in touch with an individual who was willing to part with his young adult radiated tortoise, an endangered species and probably the most beautiful tortoise in the world. I had trouble taking my eyes off it as it rested in the cardboard box on the passenger seat of my car while I drove directly home, even skipping my usual Starbucks stop.

The next month at the swap, Lee told me he was about to receive a shipment of spider tortoises from Madagascar. This was an extremely rare species that I had never seen before. I was immediately intrigued. Later, I did my homework and discovered that not only were they rare and critically endangered, but it was extraordinarily difficult to breed them and produce hatchlings. Only select private individuals and a scattering of zoos were fortunate enough to be working with these tortoises, and most were unsuccessful in their breeding attempts. But I wanted to try. I knew it would be a long process, but I had the time and the patience.

When the tortoises arrived, my intention was to select four to six of them, but after helping Lee uncrate them, I was so impressed with their beauty and clean health that I ended up with sixteen Pyxis tortoises—eight species each of arachnoides and planicaudas. They immediately acclimated to the special enclosures I set up in my basement with the proper UVB lighting. I dewormed them and monitored their health daily. They were doing so well that I was kicking myself for not acquiring a few more.

Being such rare tortoises, there was little information available about their unique requirements. Looking for whatever I could find, I soon met two dedicated turtle and tortoise enthusiasts, John Grigus and Marc Papiernik, both of whom had been working with, and successfully reproduced, various species. After John shared with me some of the tricks of the trade, my excitement grew and I couldn't resist increasing my collection by acquiring two beautiful radiated tortoise hatchlings. It was as though I was trying to make up for lost time during the years of growing my business. Then I went to Marc's place and saw how he had various tortoise pens set up both in his basement and in his backyard, giving me more and more ideas. I was thrilled to learn from these two guys and developed close friendships with them.

In my quest for even more information, I flew out to California to attend a master class on keeping and breeding tortoises presented by a world famous chelonian conservationist from the UK by the name of Andy Highfield. It was there that my turtle motor kicked up a notch and I became all the more determined to get my Pyxis tortoises to successfully breed, to lay that single solitary egg and hatch out a new generation.

In 2001, I learned from Lee that the person who had imported the tortoises from Madagascar had moved to Florida and set up a reptile import business. He still had several Pyxis tortoises and I decided to fly down there with Ty Park who was also interested in acquiring some. Ty and I brought back twenty that we had hand-selected and split them fifty-fifty.

But while my original group was doing fine, the new group of ten was turning into a disaster. I struggled to acclimate them and keep them healthy. I lost four of them, saving the rest only after Marc Papiernik came to my rescue. He had developed a unique protocol for tube feeding that saved the lives of these six rare tortoises, and, eventually, I was able to add them to my breeding groups.

Pyxis became the genus I decided to work with. Over the next twenty years, I learned the intricate particulars of this species—diet, temperature adjustments, humidity, estivation, and, most importantly, egg incubation, including a process called diapause where the eggs are incubated at specific temperatures and then cooled for a period of time, a procedure you sometimes have to repeat a few times. I would produce several hatchlings of these endangered species, becoming a small part of the select zoos and private breeders who worked at establishing assurance colonies in captivity.

And there were more tortoise experiences. Back in my Noah's Ark days, we had Methuselah, of course—our giant Aldabra tortoise, one of our store mascots that people came from miles around to see. I had always wanted another Aldabra tortoise and now that I was moving beyond the days of growing my business, I felt I had the time, plus I knew I could provide an excellent environment for it. I found a tortoise enthusiast in California who had a three-year-old Aldabra to sell and in February of 2002, I bought her. I named her Tosh and was in heaven once again.

That same year I joined the New York Turtle and Tortoise Society and attended a meeting where the speakers were Dr. Peter Pritchard, my boyhood idol and the world's leading expert on turtles and tortoises; and Bronx Zoo reptile curator, conservationist John Behler. Behler spoke about Madagascar and the planicauda tortoise, which continued to fuel my enthusiasm. After Dr. Pritchard's presentation on Galapagos tortoises, I was thrilled to talk with him and discover how approachable he was. It didn't seem possible that I was actually talking to a man of such high stature. I remembered his original writings, which had become my first official education on turtles. And of course later in my life, I'd sold countless copies of his newly released *Encyclopedia of Turtles*. At the close of the conference I was honored to have him sign the personal copy I'd brought with me.

As for Super Pet, while we had already discontinued the majority of the products that were not in the small animal category, we still had a few lingering products that continued to be in demand. One of the last product lines we discontinued was our Hanging Gardens, the suction-cupped aquarium and terrarium plants. In May of 2002, Rolf C. Hagen Corporation introduced a range of terrarium plants for their Exoterra reptile product line. The plants blatantly infringed on our patent. Given that it was only a matter of time before we would discontinue these plants, rather than have our patent attorney contact him, I wrote Rolf a personal letter explaining the obvious infringement. In response, he called and asked if we could work something out.

I flew to Montreal, Rolf picked me up, and we went to one of his favorite restaurants. At least eight different people, including other guests, greeted Rolf as we entered and were led to our table. Rolf had set his stage, but I was in the driver's seat and not intimidated. Right away, he made it clear that he didn't want to discontinue his terrarium plant program. The plants were an integral part of his overall growth strategy, and he wanted to make a deal which we could both live with. Then he made me a cash offer of $10,000 to allow his company to ride on our patent.

Without hesitation, I told Rolf that I wasn't interested in his money. He adjusted his chair and moved a bit closer. Then I smiled and told him that over the years we had always had a great relationship, both when I was a customer and now as friendly competitors. I had the utmost respect for the Rolf C. Hagen Corporation and their people. For this reason, I explained, I would allow Rolf to use our patent, not for $10,000, but for a single dollar and not a penny more. Rolf grinned, and reached into his pocked for a dollar.

"No, Rolf," I said, "send me a check."

"Bob," he replied, "I know what you're up to; you just want to show everyone Rolf Hagen's 'one-dollar check'!" We both laughed, shook hands, and finished our dinner. I knew I had done the right thing in not taking payment for a product that would soon be meaningless to us. My integrity meant a hundred times more to me than the money Rolf offered.

The year 2002 saw my business remain on track, my tortoises thriving, and Denise and I looking for the new home that we'd always talked about, the one on a few acres where I could have a special room or even a little building for my tortoises, and of course a pond for native turtles like the midland painted turtles I'd loved over the years. Over the following months, Denise and I would drive around every weekend looking for our dream property.

Then, one day in the spring of 2003, I got to talking to a new member of my Vistage group by the name of Don McNeil. Don happened to be named after his grandfather, the celebrity host of the morning Breakfast Club Show, which had broadcast nationally on WGN radio. I told Don about my plans with Denise to find the right place, and he mentioned a property that his family owned. As it turned out, they'd been considering selling it. Amazingly, it was right down the street from our home. I listened intently as Don described a forty-six acre, wooded, private retreat with a seven-acre lake stocked with fish, smack dab in the middle of the forest preserves. He knew about my turtle passion and was quick to throw in the fact that the lake had many painted turtles. That did it. I had to see the property.

The next day, I drove down Penny Road, glancing at the forest preserves on both sides of the street in disbelief that there was a hidden piece of nature so close. I almost drove past the overgrown entrance to the property, which was a gravel road that led past several oak and hickory trees, and an open field to the right. Finally, I came to the end of the road where the buildings were. They were all in total disrepair—a large house with blue tarps over the roof, a garage, a few dilapidated sheds, and what appeared to be a one-bedroom cabin. But behind all that was a pristine, crystal clear lake dotted with lily pads. There was an island on one side and beyond that, I could see a few fallen trees that had become beautiful worn logs over the years, and, yes, they were covered with those shiny domed objects.

I loved the property, but I knew it was out of reach for Denise and me. The buildings all had to come down, a new home would have to be designed and constructed, and just the thought of the upkeep of forty-six wooded acres made the dream completely unrealistic. I told Don the property wasn't going to work for us, but at our next Vistage meeting, he suggested I meet with his uncle Bob. A month later, I found myself in a beat-up golf cart being driven all over the property by Bob McNeil. I was sure he could hear my heart pounding as I marveled at the environment, trying to imagine it becoming ours. Bob talked about the property, and it became apparent that the family was most interested in maintaining the legacy of the McNeil family. Rather than maximizing the appraised value of the real estate, their main objective was to sell to someone who wasn't going to cut it up and develop it.

Not long afterward, Don's father and uncle came to our house to chat with Denise and me. We told them about our lifestyle and our love for nature and explained our intentions. I felt as if we were being interviewed as they emphasized the importance to their family of the property. They asked if we would be willing to sign a restrictive covenant, ensuring that the property wouldn't be developed for a minimum of ten years. Right away we agreed.

My thinking was that we could buy the property and, over time, as we could afford it, develop it into our future home. We negotiated a mutually beneficial transaction with the McNeil family where they accepted a significant down payment and personally financed the remainder over five years. To make the deal, Denise and I liquidated our assets, including the sale of our home, and moved into a small townhouse. How we would satisfy the five year note, the monthly payments, taxes, insurance, and construction costs, I knew I'd figure out as we went along.

As we were getting our attorneys involved and getting closer to a closing date, my business kept growing and the volume of Crittertrail shipments became such that we needed more space. We rented another 118,000 square foot warehouse across the street. The timing couldn't have been better; we designed a special room in that warehouse that could temporarily house my extensive tortoise collection.

In January of 2004, we signed the papers on the McNeil property and closed the deal. I had been sharing our plans of buying the property with my very close friend and fellow Vistage member, Mitch Tarzian. Years earlier, Mitch had been involved in the designing and construction of luxury homes but had entered the commercial field when the real estate market changed. I asked him if he'd like to get involved with our property and he jumped at the chance to return to his original passion. Denise and I began designing our dream home with Mitch's expertise. We reviewed photos of European architecture from some of our travels, along with designs from magazines and literature we'd accumulated. We envisioned a traditional French country home, and Mitch, perfectionist that he was, hand-drew and redrew our plans several times.

Of course, the first phase of the design was my tortoise/turtle breeding facility. John Grigus guided me in designing a state of the art facility that put my original coal bin laboratory to shame. It included radiant heated floors with special plumbing drains, an electrical system for lighting and equipment with timers, built-in shelves and platforms to hold custom designed fiberglass enclosures, a deluxe kitchen food prep area, and an area for tortoise incubators and nursery enclosures. My future tortoise/turtle facility would have dual exit sliding doors leading to an outdoor area for future tortoise pens and plantings.

While Mitch finalized the drawings, Denise and I were invited to Punta Gorda, Florida, to stay with another close friend from my Vistage group, Nancy Cwynar and her husband Fred. We needed a break so it was a welcomed invitation. Those few days became a significant experience, opening our eyes to the beauty and lifestyle of southwest Florida. The weather, the landscape, the scenery, and the restaurants were all perfect. Nancy and Fred took us on a boat ride and surprised us by cruising to stunning and peaceful Useppa Island, a private resort where we had lunch.

Immediately after landing, Denise found a juvenile gopher tortoise among the groundcover of the walkway. That little guy was a rare find; juveniles are usually very secretive. We explored the island and for the first time in my life, I was able to observe gopher tortoises in their natural environment. They were everywhere, crossing the paths, grazing in the landscape, or just sunning themselves at the mouths of their burrows. On our flight home, Denise and I reflected on what a great time we'd had, and she mentioned that if a day ever came where we would have a vacation getaway place, it would have to be on the Gulf of Mexico in Southwest Florida.

It was another dream, something maybe way down the road, if at all. In the meantime, we had our hands full with forty-six wooded acres with a seven-acre pond, and a new French country home with a state-of-the-art tortoise/turtle breeding facility in the making. But at least that dream was getting closer.

36

SAYING GOODBYE

As THE FINISHING TOUCHES were being put on our house plans, Denise and I took a quick trip to the UK to attend a formal affair hosted by Batleys, one of our top customers. The Super Pet brand was going to be recognized as the fastest growing pet product line and we were one of the few guests of honor. The reception was held in a Medieval castle, an elegant, black tie dinner capped off with the award presentations. Denise and I kept looking at each other, wide-eyed at the beautiful venue. As the photographers snapped pictures, I felt enormous gratitude and amazement, wondering how this was all happening to me.

Once back in the US, with all of the added projects I was getting involved in with our new home, not to mention my traveling and continued management meetings, I placed an ad in the *Bulletin of the Chicago Herpetological Society*. I needed an experienced individual who would be able to care for my tortoises a few days a week, especially when I was traveling. I ended up hiring a dedicated, detail-oriented individual by the name of John Bailey who not only did an outstanding job but became a very close friend.

With that concern off my shoulders, I welcomed my new responsibilities of working side by side with Mitch as he finalized the drawings of our new home. Shortly after I approved them, we leveled all of the existing structures, broke ground, and began the construction. It was exciting to see our dream home gradually coming together but sometimes at night, lying in bed, Denise and I would wonder how we were going to make everything work financially.

Before long, not only would a solution present itself, but something would occur that would change our lives forever in the most far reaching way. Over the previous year or so, I'd been receiving inquiries about the sale of the company, including legitimate interest from investment groups and four well-known companies within the pet industry, some of which I'd had personal and business relationships with over the years.

I loved my business. I had built it from an idea, an SBA-guaranteed loan, and $15,000 in life savings. And I was proud of it. Of course, I was flattered by their interest, but could never see myself selling. Bob Berk from Vistage, however, advised me to at least keep myself open to the idea and to keep the companies interested, even consider an exit plan. Another member, Russ Graunke, agreed. "Bob," he would say, "how much steak can you eat?" Several of my other colleagues in Vistage also agreed, telling me that my business was on a steady uphill trajectory but one day would peak. None of them could understand my reluctance. Even though they all admired the passion I had for my business, they couldn't understand why I wouldn't want to cash in.

I kept going back and forth. Sell my company? It was my life. I couldn't even imagine a life beyond the pet industry. For six months, Bob Berk kept nudging me, finally convincing me by saying, "Bob, you'll become a better businessperson after learning the process of selling, and if at any time you decide not to sell, you can always back away. Meanwhile, you'll get a much better idea as to what your company is really worth."

I called Susan Pravda, a Boston-based mergers and acquisitions attorney whom I had met at a conference years earlier. I'd been impressed with her presentation and kept her business card in case I would ever decide to buy another company, never thinking I'd someday call her for the opposite reason.

That telephone call would change my life again.

After two phone conversations with Susan, we set up a meeting in Chicago to start the process. Our meeting confirmed my conviction that Susan was the exact person I needed to educate me on the processes and options of selling a business. Once I described what was going on at Pets International, and the pet industry in general, she didn't try to encourage me to go one way or the other. Instead she detailed the process of evaluating a company such as mine and enlightened me as to what my company and the Super Pet brand could really be worth.

I found myself becoming more interested in selling. In truth, I was reaching a point in my career where I found myself struggling to continue the growth I had worked so hard to achieve. More and more, selling was looking like the right thing to do. I told Susan about the companies that had expressed interest and she suggested that finding the right one was half the battle. She advised me to meet with the companies and listen to what they had to say. She emphasized the importance of making sure they knew I was not necessarily interested in selling right now. Gather information, find out what they were planning to propose, and not make any commitments.

During the following months I met with each of the companies, while Susan kept me on course, coaching me in sorting out the details. I paid heed to a statement I'd heard at my Vistage meetings over the years: "An entrepreneur sells their business only once in their lifetime and they would be remiss in not seeking all the professional experience they can get during the selling process." And so in addition to Susan's counsel I established an informal advisory board from my Vistage group consisting of Bob Berk,

Jim Mack, Nancy Cwynar, and Bill Gunlicks. Each of these people had specific strengths and each helped me immensely, allowing me to bounce "what ifs" off of them and spend time discussing strategies during what would ultimately turn out to be a fifteen-month process.

I established my own criteria. My very first priority was of course the purchase price. It had to be sufficient to create total financial security for my entire family, allowing Denise and me the freedom to do what we wanted, and financially assist my children and future grandchildren. Plus, allow us to contribute to the charities of our choosing.

My second priority was my employees' future. I wanted my employees to continue having not only job security but opportunities for growth. I also wanted to be able to bonus out a big "thank you" to my key people.

Of course I also wanted continued growth for Super Pet and as long as it remained focused on the small animal category, I wanted the company to continue supporting the independent pet industry. Lastly, I didn't really want to hang it up. I was fifty-seven years old, felt like I was still in my forties, and still had a lot to offer. I wanted to be a significant part of the continuing growth I envisioned in the pet industry that I loved so much.

The meetings with the suitors continued and as they intensified, I began meeting with the executives of the companies more than once. One of these companies was Central Garden and Pet Corporation. They were a publicly traded corporation consisting of several top notch manufacturing and distribution companies in both the pet and garden industries. And they happened to be my fourth largest customer behind PetSmart, Petco, and Batleys.

While conversations and meetings were happening with the other interested parties, the vice president of business development for Central Garden and Pet paid me a visit and asked point blank what I needed in order to make the sale happen. We talked in detail and, over the next couple of months, all the while being coached by Susan Pravda and my advisory board, I had two follow up meetings with CG&P culminating in a financial arrangement based on a formula known as EBITDA—Earnings Before Interest, Taxes, Depreciation, and Amortization. It's a measure of core profitability and, using an agreed-upon multiple, you can arrive at a company's overall value. We were getting closer.

As part of the courtship, Jim Heim, president of Central Garden Pet Division, and his wife Theresa, invited Denise and me to fly out to California to join them on a wine tasting trip to Sonoma Valley. As it happened, Jim Mack, on my Vistage team, had a winery estate in Sonoma and he and his wife Gloria invited all of us to stay with them. Over two days together, I got to know Jim Heim well. He represented his company very professionally and sold me on the fact that our principles and methods of operation were similar. He was down to earth and someone Denise and I really enjoyed being with. Most importantly, I felt that I could work well under his leadership.

After our trip, CG&P put a proposal together and I found the price acceptable. I could see that the potential for the continued growth of the Super Pet brand was strong. CG&P had no other companies in their group that competed with our product line and especially with Kaytee, the nation's largest producer of bird and small animal consumables, Super Pet was a perfect fit. I found that their employees were stable and they had an excellent corporate infrastructure. But they absolutely needed our management, which, in turn, gave our people job security. Last but not least, they needed me to continue running the company. This I was especially happy about because I wasn't quite ready to ride off into the sunset. I turned the negotiations over to Susan Pravda to cover the details, and then signed CG&P's letter of intent.

Denise was extremely supportive during the entire process, dealing with my sleepless nights and long evenings strategizing at the kitchen table. But the time had finally come to sit down with Bob Jr., who had become such a vital part of the company, wrapping himself up in it for the future he anticipated. We drove out to the McNeil property I had just purchased and sat beneath the porch of the old summer home. I explained to Bob what was happening and he did not take it well. It was like his world was collapsing around him. We sat looking out over the lake, both of us with tears in our eyes.

The closing was on June 2, 2005. I was fifty-eight years old and had all the financial security I could have ever dreamed of. I didn't feel any different; I was still that guy who loved turtles. Well, that's not completely true. I did feel a little different. Super Pet wasn't mine anymore. I was now the president of a company under the umbrella of a larger, publicly traded company. But I didn't let that change my drive and enthusiasm. I was intent on making every effort to continue the growth that I was accustomed to.

During this time, the construction of our house continued. I had previously wondered how we were going to accommodate the financial requirements, believing that somehow we would. With the windfall from the sale of the company, that was no longer a concern. We even added to the house, adding upgrades to the interior, exterior, and landscaping.

As we were happily enjoying the progress on the house, and I was adjusting to my new corporate position, I had something else to be happy about: my sister gave birth to a beautiful little girl. She named her Mary Jo, and Denise and I became godparents while my mom once again became a grandmother.

But it wasn't easy trying to rejoice in these wonderful changes. While all of this was underway, Mom's cancer had returned and another difficult time in my life was about to begin. I watched as each day, my mother, who had been with me through thick and thin, became weaker and weaker. I cherish the memory of the last game of gin rummy we played on what would become her death bed. Then as her mind went in and out, she stressed her deep concern for the welfare of my sister and Mary Jo, beckoning me to watch over them and keep them out of harm's way.

Mari-Lynn was with her at the hospital on her last day and called Denise and me to tell us that the time was near. It was early on the morning of November 15, 2005 and we rushed to the hospital to be with her as she passed.

Looking back, I was at peace knowing that I had done the very best I could for Mom, especially over the last ten years of her life. I tried to be there for her in every respect. I thought about those lunches we had, the trips to Europe, Mexico, Las Vegas and, especially, that trip to Japan. All of those times together ended up becoming my small way of saying thanks for that little green turtle she bought me almost sixty years earlier.

· · · · · • • · • · · ·

The next two years saw a lot of changes with Central Garden and Pet, one of which was the departure of the president of Kaytee. I accepted a promotion to replace him and was presented with the responsibility of bringing Super Pet and Kaytee together into one unit. This meant blending the cultures of both companies, and I spent many days in Chilton, Wisconsin, home of Kaytee, conducting meetings and working with my new staff. The person I related to the most was James Glassford, Kaytee's VP of marketing. He was a true team player. To show Jim the many as-yet-unrealized opportunities in bird and small animal consumables, I had him accompany me and Larry Sternal, my VP of operations, on a trip to Europe to visit some of the companies I'd established relationships with over the years in Holland and Germany. We came back excited and with all sorts of new ideas.

Then, in July, CG&P instituted another new initiative, monthly and quarterly call-in budget reviews. All the other company presidents and CFOs were involved in these conference calls. I was a bit out of my comfort zone, but Mark Procter and CG&P's corporate CFO, John Negovetich, guided me through the process. Without them, I don't know what I would have done.

I noticed as time went along that we began making company decisions based on the results of these monthly and quarterly revenue reviews. Shareholder value, in other words, was guiding our direction. I found myself making decisions that I would not have made in years past. And feeling the pressure. There was restructuring, and I had to say goodbye to people who had been side by side with me as we'd enjoyed the struggles of growing the company. I soon dreaded running the company and had to keep reminding myself that it wasn't mine anymore, and convincing myself that, this being a publicly traded company, there were reasons why things had to be the way they were, even if I didn't agree with them.

On June 2, 2007, two years to the day, as required if I planned to leave the company, I gave my one year notice and felt immediate relief. Two months later I was advised that my number one priority was to find my replacement. As it turned out, corporate did the job-searching but I participated in the interviews, hoping that my input might at least have some impact. Eventually, I hired a past executive of Kraft Foods, Chris Mings. I handed him my corner office, took a small side office, and planned to work with him as long as he felt necessary. Before long, I saw that it was time to get out of his way. Chris had a totally different style, and I accepted that.

As my time with CG&P was winding down, corporate advised me that we would be consolidating further departments in both sales and finance. As a result, this meant Mark Procter would be out of a job. I broke the news to him and managed to work it so his departure would be phased over a three-month period, allowing him to find an ideal position with another company.

Bob Jr. also left, finding a position in the catering business. Tina Drews moved into another industry altogether too, while I helped place Brian Kindl with Prevue Pet Products Company. I was happy to see that Larry Sternal and Jason Casto continued transitioning the marketing, manufacturing, and product development divisions where they both remain as executives to this day.

June 2, 2008 was my last day. The company hosted an employee lunch where I gave a farewell speech, thanking everyone and saying my goodbyes. Then I walked to my car and drove away, glancing in the rearview mirror at the company I had built and loved so much. I felt a lump in my throat, then decided, figuratively and literally, to focus on the road ahead. I knew I still had a lot of life to live.

37

— · —

TERRAPIN RIDGE

I FELT LOST. DENISE and I were living in our dream home and everything should have been wonderful. Even my tortoises were doing fantastic and starting to produce fertile eggs. Nevertheless, not working as an entrepreneur was a hard adjustment. It's all I'd ever done. So, when I was asked to join the advisory board of Machinery Systems Incorporated, the largest provider of Mazak machine tools and CNC machines, I jumped on it. Before long, my involvement there made me explore the possibility of either purchasing or starting another business.

Having an interest in wildlife, especially that which I encountered on a daily basis, I was always keeping my eye on the backyard and nature products industry, all the while coming up with ideas on how to improve many products that were already available for feeding, nesting, perching, and sheltering, I had several ideas for brand-new products. I soon pursued the purchase of a company that manufactured and imported feeders and accessories for wild birds, hummingbirds, and critters. Then, in the midst of putting my business plan together, it occurred to me that I could start a profitable consulting business. I had the expertise in marketing channels as well as numerous overseas contacts. I could offer a valuable service to companies that were interested in pursuing offshore manufacturing and sourcing. I established an LLC, naming it Ark Innovative Solutions.

Then, inevitably, inescapably, turtling intervened. I should have known. I never did do anything with the consulting idea, eventually dissolving the LLC.

I acquired an adult pair of radiata tortoises from John Grigus after networking with a well-known Madagascar tortoise expert, Dr. William Zovickian. Both John and Bill became valuable resources in my husbandry protocols. In addition to radiated and Pyxis tortoises from Madagascar, I built a breeding group of pancake tortoises from East Africa, which I simply loved. Denise had her South American redfoot tortoises, which began laying large clutches resulting in several hatchlings. The redfoots were more common and easier to care for, and made great gifts to people we knew who were up and coming tortoise enthusiasts. And of course Tosh, our Aldabra tortoise, became our favorite family pet.

Denise with Tosh, our Aldabra tortoise.

The hours and days I spent taking care of my tortoises seemed to fly by. I established my daily routines of cleaning, hydrating, feeding, and egg collecting, constantly improving my protocol. I documented my procedures on diets and food preparation, egg collecting, incubating, and especially diapausing. Soon, I was enjoying the fruits of my labor with the successful hatching of my Pyxis tortoises. My priorities were changing, and I discovered a new life for myself. My turtle passion was being enriched in a most rewarding way. Yes, there were disappointments in some of them not making it, but I knew that other breeders were having the same results. Indeed, it happened in nature too.

I soon discovered the Turtle Survival Alliance (TSA), a relatively new organization comprised of individuals with a passion for turtles and tortoises, all working together to develop conservation programs to save some of the most critically endangered vertebrates. In August of 2006, attending my first TSA meeting at their annual conference in St. Louis, Missouri, I was shocked. I had no idea there were so many people with a passion like mine, and from every walk of life. The members were an assortment of academics, biologists, business people, zoo professionals, and laymen. Dr. Peter Pritchard was among them, all conservationists in one form or another interested in the same goals.

Over the years, the TSA grew into one of the world's premier freshwater turtle and tortoise conservation organizations, and their work around the world taught me that chelonians everywhere were in trouble. The main causes were due to habitat loss and fragmentation, not to mention the pet trade and the international black market for food and medicine. Because of my involvement with Pyxis and radiated tortoises, I was especially concerned about what was happening in Madagascar, where they were working hard to protect these endangered species. My turtling passion was taking on a new form: conservation.

Meanwhile, there was a large demand for my Pyxis hatchlings and I had lists of serious enthusiasts waiting for offspring. I created an organization I called Ark Chelonia, and I deposited all the proceeds I received from the sale of my tortoise hatchlings into a new trust I established for charitable donations. This trust funneled annual contributions to the TSA and various other turtle and tortoise non-profit conservation organizations.

My life with my exotic tortoises was everything. But being that our home was just a few steps away from the shoreline of our own little lake, I was able to stay close with my initial passion, midland painted turtles. When the weather started to warm up that first year after retirement, I was pleased to notice their daily activities, which made it difficult for me to concentrate on my projects. I simply had to sit and observe their behavior. I loved watching the adult's movements as they swam toward each other with the males quivering their appendages to attract mates. Seeing the actual courtship and mating became extra special.

Denise and I watched as the egg-laden females traveled throughout our entire property to seek out nesting sites. We couldn't believe how many of them there were. We marveled at their perseverance. They nested in various shoreline locations around the lake but it seemed like a few of their routes took them around to the front of our house and down through our field to a sunny area on the ridge of our orchard. During these long, but rapid trips, they would survey a specific area and if they didn't find it ideal, they'd return to the water. If, on the other hand, they decided to start nesting, they would sometimes dig a test nest to see if the soil was acceptable. If not, they'd move. Other times, we'd notice them returning to the water without depositing their eggs in the open nest they left behind. When they finally found the perfect spot, they'd scan the entire area and only after feeling safe would they begin digging their nests. Once they deposited their eggs, they'd cover the nest and be on their way.

I was sure that all these behaviors were documented in published biological papers somewhere, but we wanted our personal observations to help us figure it all out on our own. Denise and I, always competitive, had a contest to see who could find the most turtles nesting throughout the season. This brought us both out during the best times to see the turtles, which were every sunny morning and late afternoon. We'd scan the areas sometimes until the sun had fully set.

Then, the following mornings, we would make some disturbing discoveries. We would see opened nests with scattered egg shells everywhere, the obvious work of a nocturnal predator. It didn't take us long to figure out it was raccoons. We cut pieces of wire mesh to put over the nests but the raccoons easily pulled them out. In addition, every once in a while we'd find turtles in the lake with damaged carapaces; some were even missing a leg. And then we'd stumble on the remains of an adult turtle on the shoreline. That year, we learned much about the trials and tribulations that turtles must endure. The midland painted turtle, being a pond turtle, continuously travels from location to location for the purposes of nesting, mating, and habitat relocation. I learned that due to their longevity, slow maturity, and extended reproductive life, adult producing females are of the utmost importance. Once removed, a population can easily crash.

Denise and I have always understood the importance of a balanced environment and how our ecosystems rely on all the inhabitants, both plant and animal. But in this day and age, humankind has provided an unnatural abundance of food via garbage cans, dumpsters, road kills, and handouts. We've created what's called "subsidized predators," which can overpopulate their habitats. Raccoons have become one of the most common subsidized predators and their overabundance is now adversely affecting the balance of the environment nationwide. The next spring we began the controversial practice of live trapping and relocating raccoons.

We were careful not to transfer our problem to someone else by choosing ideal remote areas that could support the raccoons, and far enough away so that they wouldn't be able to return. It was a much better alternative than ending their life; after all they were only trying to survive in the fragmented environment that we human beings created. There were seasons when I relocated more than thirty raccoons, but the predation of the turtle nests persisted. Eventually, we installed strong welded wire cages over the nests, zip tying them together and spiking them into the ground around the nests. That worked perfectly.

Throughout the summer, I spent hours turtling around our lake. Kayaking quietly into the coves and along the lily pad covered shorelines was one of my favorite pastimes and it never got old. Observing painted turtles from a distance is one thing but nothing compares to being up close. Sitting still, watching them swim to the surface and poke their heads out between the lily pads always put a smile on my face. My biggest challenge was locating the secretive little hatchlings. Those little guys, and the juveniles, are really special. Being so small, from one to three inches in carapace length, and beautifully camouflaged in their carefully chosen shoreline environments, they can be basking on a lily pad or a branch extending out onto the water's surface and yet be completely undetectable to the inexperienced eye. But not always. Many times I noticed them being complacent. Inexperience on their part. It can be deadly. I would see them nonchalantly swimming up onto my paddle and it was those times that I'd worry about the great blue herons and white egrets, not to mention those giant bullfrogs that were so adept at remaining perfectly still until the ambush.

One practice I developed in all my years of herping was the habit of leaving the environment the way I found it. What seems insignificant to us can be a major disruption to the micro-habitats that reptiles and amphibians call home. Returning that flat board, log, roofing tile, piece of tin, flat rock, or old tree stump to the exact position it was found is very important. One needs to respect the homes in which the reptiles, amphibians, insects, and various critters live. Even when turtling in my rowboat or kayak along the shoreline, I was always careful not to rearrange the furnishings of branches, lily pads, and aquatic vegetation.

One day, I discovered an ancient snapping turtle living in our lake. He was enormous and had to be at least fifty years old. I was keenly aware of the fact that snapping turtles contribute to the demise of the protein they come in contact with. With this guy confined to such a small environment, there was a high probability that many painted turtles were included in his diet. I set out to safely capture him so that I could relocate him into a much more desirable habitat down the road in the Fox River.

I saw him more than once basking, which snapping turtles rarely do. He was on a half-fallen willow tree that was suspended over the water in a cove on the far side of the lake. One day I spotted him again in the exact same spot. I got my long-handled net and quietly paddled my kayak in his direction while Denise followed me in hers to witness the event. The turtle must have really been into his basking for I noticed, as I approached, that his eyes were shut. As I reached the end of the submerged part of the branch he was on, I lunged with my net, but to my surprise, it bounced off his back, too small to get around him. He slid into the water and disappeared. I kept my eye open for him over the next few weeks, but he never returned to that location.

Then one day, a close turtle friend of mine, James Barzyk and his son, Harrison, were with me on the patio overlooking the lake when Denise came running back from the other side of the lake. While walking Maggie, our westie, she'd seen the snapping turtle. He was floating on the surface of decomposing leaves and vegetation along the shoreline. I grabbed the biggest fishing net I had and a large plastic trash can. Jim, Harrison, and I followed Denise, all running to the other side of the lake, hoping the turtle was still there.

He was. And this time the poor guy couldn't move fast enough. My excitement was unbearable as I twisted and wiggled the net in an attempt to get it around him, but soon I had him and we were able to drag him ashore and slide him into the trash can. I put him into my pick-up truck, took a photo of him, figuring that no one would ever believe his size, and drove him to Fox River where, hopefully, he's still happily living out his life.

To study the nesting behavior of our midland painted turtles more closely, Denise and I established zones to mark and label the nests. We then recorded hatch dates, and hatchling counts, entering the information into a database. In addition, we placed orange marking flags on each nest to avoid any accidents by our caretaker, Rodolfo, who soon became a tremendous asset. We began including him on all the steps necessary to protect our turtles. Over the years Rodolfo contributed immensely to our painted turtle conservation program. His keen eyes found many nests that Denise and I missed.

Throughout the mornings and early evenings of the nesting season in the Midwest (May 15 thru July 20), we carefully watched for the egg-laden female turtles in search of their nesting sites. We also worked hard at canvassing the areas for telltale signs of nests where eggs had already been laid. Of the sixty to eighty nests we'd find throughout the property each year, we found most in roughly the same areas. The nesting females often returned to the same spots year after year. We surmised that the incubation periods varied between 90 and 110 days, depending on weather, moisture, the amount of direct sunlight, and the type of substrate. The nests contained anywhere between a few to as many as a dozen eggs, all dependent on the age and size of the female.

Rodolfo and me opening nests, 2020.

Once hatched, the hatchlings would remain in their nest chambers as they absorbed the yolk sack on their plastrons. Then, at the right time, usually prompted by warm rains, they would collectively dig toward the surface. Many nests, however, would remain intact over the ensuing winter months with each of the little hatchlings miraculously transforming into a suspended and frozen state through winter, until prompted to come alive again by the warm rainy period of spring.

In spite of our dedication to this entire process, we were painfully aware that the majority of these little guys were never going to make it to adulthood due to various reasons, predators being the main one. Both in the late summer and the following spring we would see them beginning their life's journey after finally making it up and out of their nests to the surface. They'd sometimes have to fight their way through long distances of grass, undergrowth, twigs, and branches. If they were fortunate enough to avoid the ants, beetles, birds, and varmints, they'd finally make it to the water. But their battle wasn't over. As they attempted to establish their new homes in the secluded shorelines, their diminutive size and fragile condition made them perfect targets for bullfrogs, bass, and shorebirds.

During our third year, Denise and I decided to give them a helping hand. At the 100-day mark, we took the fully developed hatchlings out of their nests and brought them, many times by the hundreds, into our temperature-controlled turtle facility where we fed and cared for them. Our enclosures were set up to replicate their natural environment, and our goal was to allow them to acclimate and become stronger until they reached a size of two to three inches. This gave them a fighting chance at surviving through their first full season. We would then release them the following spring in the same exact three or four aquatic habitats their family groupings lived in.

As I waded into the shallow waters to release them, I'd select specific locations that provided immediate coverage and forage. I couldn't believe how quickly they accepted their new environment. Many would immediately dive or hide. Others swam on the surface, checking out the new world they were just introduced to. Then I'd watch them dive into the submerged autumn leaves and substrate, amazed to see them immediately foraging and nipping at vegetation and small aquatic invertebrates. These moments gave me chills, and I couldn't help thinking back to my many encounters with painted turtles as a young boy. To be in the water with them now as a conservationist was exhilarating. I later learned that the process Denise and I developed in helping the hatchlings is an accepted practice called "head-starting," a practice that chelonian biologists have been carrying out for years.

Wading along a shoreline releasing hatch-lings.

In time, we began working with universities and nature centers, educating school students and members of our community on the importance of turtle conservation. We've learned that conservation comes in many and various forms, everything from protecting the different environments turtles live in, along with educating the people who share those environments, to captive breeding in zoos as well as the private sector. I'm convinced that we've made a difference in helping those little guys by giving them a helping hand and making sure they received a good start in life.

During a twelve-year period, from 2011 through 2022, Denise and I went from locating eighteen nests per year to over eighty, averaging 6.7 hatchlings per nest. In that time, we successfully hatched out and released over 3,000 baby midland painted turtles, the large majority of which would otherwise have never seen the light of day. It's upsetting to think that, as a boy, I encountered many different species of turtles that today have disappeared. At the time, I'm sure I thought they'd always be around, but they and their habitats are no longer. And so it became our goal to help common turtles remain common.

Just a portion of the 3,000-plus hatchlings
we've headstarted over the past twelve years.

Proud of our accomplishments, and to create our own legacy, we eventually erected an enormous bluestone slab with gold lettering at the entranceway of our property, naming our home "Terrapin Ridge," representing the favorite nesting destination of our midland painted turtles.

38

— • —

Fazah Bae

Besides my own backyard, I observed turtles in their natural environments on many turtling trips after my retirement. One such trip was in 2007. John Grigus had introduced me to Jim Barzyk, the friend who would be with me later when I would snag that huge snapping turtle. As it turned out, Jim owned two pieces of wooded property in the county of Muskegon in Michigan, and years earlier he had discovered different habitats where he encountered eastern box turtles, North American wood turtles, Blanding's turtles, and the elusive spotted turtles. Jim and John took annual excursions together, photographing and recording data to see how stable the different turtle populations were, often encountering the same individuals every year. Rather than performing the common practice of notching the carapace for ID purposes and disfiguring such beautiful specimens, Jim photographed the plastrons, which were always patterned uniquely.

I felt privileged when John invited me in April of that year to join them on their trip to Michigan. I wasn't accustomed to turtling without my net, but John and Jim assured me it would be cumbersome and unnecessary. Instead, the absolute necessities for each of us were wading boots, gloves, a backpack, a change of warm clothes, and the ultimate sassafras or blue beech walking stick. Jim instructed us on how to find the right candidate for the stick and how best to prepare it. The best saplings made the strongest and longest-lasting walking sticks. I still have mine to this day. A good walking stick becomes your lifeline. It helps you in hiking the changing terrain from the up and downhill wooded areas, you can use it to push aside the tangled brush and branches, and it provides stability and safety in the marshes.

That first year was a hugely successful trip and began a tradition of annual excursions that would go on for the next ten years. We chalked up volumes of memorable experiences, locating and observing great numbers of four different species of turtles, each of them occupying different habitats but all within hiking distance from each other. The eastern box turtles were beautifully patterned with orange and yellow stripes and blotches, no two ever alike. We encountered them in the fields along the forest edges, and in and around the marshy areas sunning themselves as they blended into the dried grasses, branches, and leaves. A common location where we would look for them was around large rotting logs and branches. Their dappled patterns made perfect camouflage.

John Grigus and me with eastern box turtles.

The North American wood turtles all had elaborately deep-patterned carapaces, as if they were carved out of a piece of wood from a walnut tree. They were prevalent in and around the slow moving, crystal clear river that flowed through Jim's property. As we'd hike in and alongside the sandy bottom, from a small footbridge near an abandoned outhouse (a flashback to my boyhood days on Kroll's farm) into the sun-dappled forest, we would find wood turtles either in the water or sunning themselves between the marsh marigolds and ferns along the riverbank.

In early spring, the Blanding's turtles could be found in the ponds that would form throughout the open fields as a result of beaver damming. We spotted them either sunning themselves out of the water in the dry cattail and reed beds, or, on warmer days, in the water, peering out with their long yellow necks.

The spotted turtles, being the smallest species, were the most difficult to find. They were usually in the flooded fields of sedges and brush. A brisk and sunny day was ideal for finding them sunning themselves, but they were extremely elusive, dropping into the water at the slightest sound. Sometimes, I'd find them sitting in clear shallow water enjoying the warmth of the sun. Their yellow-spotted black carapaces camouflaged them perfectly against the rich dark substrate they rested on. If you were just hiking along, you could easily walk right past one, sitting precariously on a sedge overhanging the water. Midland painted and snapping turtles were also fairly common in the areas we surveyed and I found it interesting that their colorations were different from those I was accustomed to seeing in Illinois and Wisconsin, a result of diet or water condition.

The marshes were the ideal microhabitat, but were not without their hazards. The water depth was only ankle to knee deep for the most part, but there would be sudden, deep drop-offs, the result of underwater beaver tunnels. I learned quickly why, instead of my favorite turtling net, a strong walking stick was the preferred accessory. Many times we would fall into an aquatic hole, sinking immediately, with our walking sticks stopping our descent. The first time this happened to me, it readily brought to mind my boyhood experience at Camp Oconto.

Every forward movement required picking your leg up high. A few hours of walking like this felt like a full month's workout. Old dead dogwoods and other understory trees that had fallen created additional shelter and basking spots for the turtles, while adding variety to the steps of our adventure. Mounds of last year's cattails created occasional dry areas of high ground that provided temporary resting spots. Without shame, I lay in them more than once absorbing the sun's rays and warmth as I gave my legs a break.

In the early years of those trips, and with my commercial business mindset, I'd catch myself spotting a turtle and, by habit, unconsciously putting a dollar value on it. After a few years, I was able to finally stop doing that, appreciating the discovery of them and leaving them right where they belonged.

Some of the trips we were accompanied by Jim's son Harrison, who was a real asset. His speed and stamina helped us locate and retrieve several specimens. My son James also came along on several trips, not only locating many turtles but taking hundreds of photographs as reference data in the wildlife artwork he was always engaged in.

I learned many things from these trips, but a major lesson came from John Grigus: the importance of silence and patience. On many excursions through the marshes, Jim Barzyk and I would be in constant pursuit, silently moving from one low area of the marsh to another, canvassing every possible micro habitat. John, on the other hand, would stay back, frozen like a statue, waiting and watching. One time, I noticed a basking spotted turtle in a flooded area along the road as we drove by. We immediately pulled over and got out of the car, stealthily returning to the spot, this time with nets in hand, but the little escape artist dove into the duckweed-covered water. Jim and I started canvassing the entire area, while John patiently sat. A half hour later, as Jim and I were packing our nets and boots into the car, we could still see John in the distance, frozen like a dead tree at the side of the water. The next thing I knew, he was running back to us with two things: a big smile on his face and the spotted turtle. We took photos and measurements, and had a good laugh as we let that little guy return to his home.

I also learned caution and some humility. Once, I was with Jim and my son James in waist-deep water noodling with my stick and boots for Blanding's turtles when I hit gold. I hollered out, "Got one!" and reached down with both hands to grab the turtle that was leaning up against my boot. I ended up with a mouthful of marsh water as I submerged low enough to grasp with both hands what I was certain was a Blanding's. But when I brought him to the surface and held him up for everyone to applaud, I noticed the Blanding's turtle was actually a very unhappy snapping turtle, its neck craned toward my face and its mouth gaping open, ready to take a chunk. I yelled and tossed the turtle back into the water, listening as my anticipated applause turned instead to laughter.

On one trip, my close friend, turtle biologist George Heinrich, flew up from his warm home in Florida to accompany us on a very cold April trip. We were all wearing heavy coats, winter hats, and gloves, and not really thinking we were going to locate many turtles. George had his crosshairs focused on locating a Blanding's turtle in its natural environment. I felt bad that our chances of accomplishing that seemed unlikely. As the sun came out, we were eventually successful at locating a few eastern box turtles seeking the warmth of the sun's rays, but I could see the disappointment in George's cold, reddened face. Then, when we were about to abandon the area, George wandered off and, just a few yards away, there it was, sunning itself in the piles of dead cattails, looking like an old army helmet. George was the only one to find a Blanding's that trip and I'm sure he talks about it to this day.

I continued looking for more opportunities to observe turtles in their natural environments and one day happened to catch an advertisement for a ten-day eco trip to Madagascar's southwest spiny forests, sponsored by Bill Love's Blue Chameleon Tours and accompanied by none other than Dr. Peter Pritchard. Madagascar, a third-world island country that split from the Indian peninsula millions of years ago, offers numerous species of fauna and flora that can't be found anywhere else in the world. And being the habitat of the radiated and spider tortoises that I was passionately involved with, it seemed as if this tour was designed especially for me. Plus, what would be my chances of ever traveling and spending ten days with an icon such as Dr. Peter Pritchard? I spoke with Denise about the trip and, as usual, she was supportive and understanding. She would always encourage me to follow my passion in all my ventures. I could never have done so without her.

I told John Bailey about the trip and he immediately agreed to go along with me. Sadly, however, the tour ended up being canceled due to lack of participation. Well, the excitement of going was too much for John and me, so we decided to travel there by ourselves. We learned that the best time to go was during the rainy season, November through March. This was their springtime, when the weather was bearable and animals were out seeking food and procreation. After seeking advice from Rick Hudson, president of TSA, we found a guide, a Dutch national by the name of Klaus Pederson who years earlier had married a Malagasy woman, started a tour business, and settled in the town of Antsirabe, right in the heart of Madagascar. And so we traveled there in January of 2009 and met Klaus.

The first order of business when we arrived was for Klaus to inform us that the plans had changed slightly. A pilot strike meant that we wouldn't be able to fly to Toliara, the main town bordering the remote south portions of Madagascar. We needed to go to Plan B, renting an off-road vehicle and driving there.

There were five of us in an old Mitsubishi Pajero: Klaus, a guide trainee who was a young Malagasy woman, the driver, and John and me. It took us three days of intense driving to get where we wanted to go, the first two of which had me questioning my sanity for even taking such a trip through such a God-forsaken rough and remote country. Ninety-five-plus degrees with humidity to match was the order for each and every day. And this was the cooler time of year!

Then things got worse. I picked up some type of bacteria that took two painful days to get out of my system. I lived in the back seat of the Pajero, drinking orange Fanta pop and eating John's entire cache of Pop Tarts. Nothing else would stay down. I wanted to go home. Meanwhile, as we passed through the small villages the distances between them became greater and the conveniences offered to travelers became fewer. When I finally started feeling better, we were a day out of the remote Spiny Forest. Then, over the following two days, we drove into the wilds, heading south using maps that described our route as dirt roads. This was an overstatement. Our backs ached from gripping the chicken bar for hours on end. The roads were rocky, then sandy, then made of red dirt, and then replete with huge boulders. We experienced holes big enough to lose a truck in (or at least a Mitsubishi Pajero), flooded sinkholes, raging river crossings, and rocky cliffs. Once we had to be pulled out of a fast-moving river by a passing beer truck while we sat in knee deep water inside the vehicle. We were pushed out of several sink holes by young boys from the villages who seemed to come out of nowhere. I learned that they sit in the shade waiting for travelers like us to come along and get stuck, collecting the money that people are more than grateful to pay for their help.

After the fourth day, we started adjusting to the temperature, food, and of course, the water we brought with us to drink, which had become quite warm. I wasted no time learning how to say *mangou tika bae*, which means, "Make sure it's very cold," a phrase I repeated every time we entered a little village with a storefront, typically a wooden shack. We could spot these places by the ubiquitous "THB" signs that hung outside advertising Three Horse Beer, the only brand available in the country. Turns out, the THB brewery was owned by the family of the president of Madagascar, thus explaining the absence of competing brands.

Every evening, we'd stop at some village, and of course, we always stood out to the villagers. Children would run over to us and yell out a Malagasy greeting, "*Fazah Bae! Fazah Bea!*" I had brought a big bag of small pieces of wrapped candy to hand out to the Malagasy children, a practice that had served me well in my world travels, and it served me well in Madagascar too.

We overnighted in old wooden shacks that were rented out as "motels," primarily for truck drivers. They had old, worn bedding but they were more or less clean. There was no plumbing or electricity. Candles and matches were always waiting on a table. One place even provided a complimentary condom, carefully placed in an ashtray. When, in rare circumstances, we would find a place with electricity (usually from generators), it was typically on only until around 10:30 p.m. Fortunately, our passion—the tortoises, and seeing them in their natural habitat—kept us on the straight and narrow. Otherwise, there were several times we would have turned back.

About a third of the way through our trip, Klaus began not feeling well. One morning, his assistant told us that Klaus needed sleep and she would take us to our destination, Villages De Tortuga, outside of Toliara. The place was a famous tortoise conservation facility where northern Madagascar spider tortoises were bred, and radiated tortoises that had been confiscated from illegal traffickers were kept until they could be returned to the wild. We had previously agreed to bring temperature and humidity loggers with us to bury in the tortoise pens so they could be picked up and monitored by TSA turtle biologists a year later.

We were pleased to be able to keep our promise that day, and then we returned to our seaside bungalows where Klaus was doing worse. As it happened, he had contracted malaria years earlier and was getting another bad reaction. We drove into town and picked up some medication for him, but during the next day's leg of our journey, he kept passing out in the back of our vehicle. The assistant guide contacted Klaus's wife and we arranged to meet her and her son, but we were two days away from there and there were no hospitals or medical facilities anywhere near us. We feared for Klaus's life, but he made it to the meeting spot. His wife drove him back to Antsirabe where there was a hospital and Klaus was able to recover.

In the meantime, we were now in the hands of the assistant guide, who did a fine job in completing our expedition. After dropping off Klaus, we made it to the Mozambique Channel on the coastline of the Indian Ocean, and the scenery was breathtaking. Our guide had never seen the ocean before and it was fun to see her reaction. John and I went in for a swim at the beach, and were soon encircled once again by children greeting us with, "*Fazah Bae! Fazah Bea!*"

From that day forward, we encountered a myriad of wildlife—chameleons, tortoises, snakes and lizards, different species of lemurs, birds, bats, and butterflies. To see lemurs everywhere, running and skipping without fear across the roads was amazing, something I'd only ever expect to see on a National Geographic special.

To stumble upon our first spider tortoise chomping down on guavas that had fallen from a tree was indescribable. Spider tortoises are a critically endangered species. We also saw Madagascan boa constrictors slithering across the dirt roads after a light rainfall, necessitating abrupt stops so we could pick them up and photograph them. The occasional giant chameleon, which we allowed to climb on us, reminded us of the exotic environment we were so privileged to be in.

Me and John Bailey with Pyxis arachnoides.

Then, the long-anticipated day came when we spotted our first radiated tortoise. I'm sure our screams of excitement were heard for miles. There it was on the side of a dirt road. We must have spent half an hour taking photos and admiring it in its natural environment. Ten minutes down the road, we came across another one. Soon we saw more and more of them. We took detailed pictures until there were just too many to stop and photograph. In all, we recorded 179 radiated tortoises in a six day period, marking each one's GPS coordinates. I was in my glory. And happy to be a part, however small it might have been, of a worldwide conservation effort to save these animals. The troubling situation in Madagascar continues. Trafficking in these beautiful tortoises for consumption and smuggling for the pet trade continue to be rampant problems.

The flora was also exotic and unique, indigenous to Madagascar only. We encountered several of the iconic and sacred Baobab trees, and learned that this signature tree of Madagascar was the true symbol of Malagasy life and hope, able to thrive in such a desolate landscape. Cacti and succulents were scattered among the rocky slopes and ledges, while the fields and rolling hillsides were dotted with beautiful Blue Fan Bismarck palm trees.

I found that the rural Malagasy possessed a wonderful culture, and in spite of the fact that their country was one of the poorest, everyone seemed happy. I saw lots of smiling people, dressed, mostly, in their native dress—long colorful wraps to shade them from the penetrating sun. Sometimes, we saw children wearing nothing more than old, dirty t-shirts, the more fortunate ones with shorts. They loved having their pictures taken by us, especially when we showed them what they looked like on our digital cameras. In one little village I taught the children how to sing "Old Mcdonald," and they simply loved the "E-I-E-I-O" part.

Our travels were truly in the bush. We broke down a few times, got stuck in the middle of a rushing river as we attempted to cross, and once became submerged in a sinkhole. Our driver was a godsend. He was driver, mechanic, and interpreter, and it didn't take but a few evenings before he became proficient at gin rummy as well, a result of our insistence that he join us in our nightly games.

During the days, we would drive for hours and see no civilization whatsoever. Then we'd encounter little villages with the people running out to the road to greet us. The people of these villages might have a few chickens and a couple of zebu cattle. They harvested rice, their daily staple. It didn't appear to me as if the men did much beyond sleeping and having sex. The average family unit consisted of five to six children per wife, and some men had two or three wives. The women would collect water from holes in the ground that you wouldn't consider washing your dog in. They carried firewood and everything else imaginable on their heads. Along with rice, the people of the villages would harvest mango, papaya, Opuntia cactus fruit, bananas, and other seasonal fruits and vegetables and sell them on the roadsides with their local staples, cassava and sweet potatoes.

Women did the cooking and washed clothes in rivers. We would watch them along the rocky shores beating the clothes. Then, after a final rinse, they'd lay them out to dry. Entire hillsides became rainbows of color, covered with hundreds of pieces of clothing. There was no schooling for the children in these remote villages. They would learn everything they needed to know from their elders. Older children would take care of younger children. Girls would learn to cook, and collect water and firewood. The boys would learn to herd goats and cattle.

At one point, I insisted we go into a family village to see if we could go into their homes to learn how the people lived. We drove along a dirt road to a typical family spread. There were seven or eight, ten-foot by ten-foot, wood and grass huts spread out fifty or so feet apart. Some looked newer than others but most were dilapidated and simple. Some had a cloth hanging in the doorway while others had a wooden door of sorts. We learned that as the children reached the age of marriage—fifteen for girls and eighteen for boys—the boy chooses a girl from another family village. After marriage, she moves into his family village where a new home is built.

When our guide explained to the people that we wanted to learn about their lives, they welcomed us graciously. We again took pictures and showed them their photos on my digital camera. Their smiles and laughter brought tears to my eyes. As we entered one home, we startled a young couple lying on the bamboo matted floor. Our guide introduced us as they brushed themselves off and immediately brought out a couple small benches for us to sit on. We exchanged courtesies and inquired about their lives and family. He was twenty-nine and she was nineteen. Their two children were three years, and ten months. We sat and talked while the mother nursed her baby. In the corner was a tiny wooden table and above it was a shelf that held their treasured possessions, including an old, worn family photo. In the other corner hung what few clothes they had.

Outside the hut was their kitchen. They cooked on a charcoal burner, and they stored their rice, grains, and other dried foods in old pottery. Of course, there was no electricity, no plumbing, no conveniences whatsoever, and one common latrine out back. Fresh protein was running around outside in the form of underfed chickens, a couple of ducks, and a turkey, skinny and malnourished, but a turkey nonetheless. The turkey, we learned, was only for special occasions. Perhaps the most amazing thing was how happy they appeared. They had nothing but the necessities. I couldn't help but wonder if there was a lesson there.

The trip was a life-changing experience for me. I succeeded at accomplishing my original goal, which was to pursue my passion and see first-hand my beloved tortoises in their natural environments. I went to Madagascar to learn as much as I could about the habits and behavior of both the radiated and spider tortoises, but I returned with so much more. The Malagasy people made the difference. They have so little, but in another sense, they have so much. I came away with a profound appreciation for the simple things in life.

Oh, and I learned one more thing, this as the trip came to a close. Our guide finally explained what "*fazah bae*" meant. It referred to our light skin color and literally translated to "strange one." We laughed, but in the end, had to agree with the assessment, even beyond the skin color. Certainly from the point of view of the Malagasy, we must have been strange sights to behold indeed.

39

—•—

More Adventures in Turtling

My turtle adventuring was never-ending. In 2009, Ty Park accompanied me on an eight-day "turtle tour" throughout the state of Florida, hosted by the Florida Turtle Conservation Trust and sponsored by the New York Turtle and Tortoise Society. We met other turtle enthusiasts, including the leader of the tour, turtle biologist and conservationist, George Heinrich. It was a fascinating and memorable eight days driving around the state to the carefully planned habitats, trying our darndest, for my benefit, to occasionally reroute through a town that had a Starbucks. Our days were full of hiking, kayaking, and snorkeling. We found and photographed Florida box turtles and gopher tortoises on Egmont Key, and Gulf Coast box turtles in Tallahassee. We kayaked through rivers and springs encountering Florida cooters, sliders, Florida soft-shelled, loggerhead musk, and Barbour's Map turtles.

Snorkeling in crystal clear springs gave me a whole new perspective on the movements of turtles underwater, something you could otherwise see only in a nature documentary. Being mesmerized by quietly snorkeling alongside numerous Florida cooters made me recall the exhilaration I felt the first time I had a similar experience with midland painted turtles several years before.

Two of the most memorable parts of the trip had nothing to do with turtles. One was observing the ballet movements of one of the members of our group, Kathy Rumpler, who demonstrated the expertise she learned while performing years earlier in the Joffrey Ballet. The other was just before the trip was over. We stopped in Perry, Florida where George introduced us to Deal's Famous Oyster House and I somehow put down forty-eight raw oysters in one sitting, a very happy way to conclude our journey.

In 2010, I joined the Turtle and Tortoise Propagation Group (TTPG), a non-profit organization founded by Russ Gurley and a few turtle enthusiasts I had met at a TSA conference. The mission of the TTPG was to emphasize the importance of captive breeding as a vital cog in the wheel of conservation. Russ had invited me to join the association and attend the November conference in Mesa, Arizona. The plan was for me to fly in a day early so Russ and the gang could take me to see the operations of two local tortoise breeders.

The morning after my arrival, I was greeted out in front of the hotel by a large, black SUV and three rough-looking guys with tattoos, long beards, piercings, and shaved heads. Tucked between them was a clean-cut guy who, for all I knew, could have been their hostage, and Russ was squeezed in next to him. We took off and I tried to make sense of the circumstances I found myself in. As the driver took off and we proceeded toward the highway, the men began conversing with one another with the subject quickly turning to the loose Arizona state laws regarding the possession of firearms, along with the necessity of owning one. Someone wondered aloud what the best course of action would be if one were stopped for a traffic infraction. At that point, the driver reached into the glove box and pulled out a handgun, slamming it down onto the dash. "This is all you have to do," he offered. "Never keep it concealed." My life seemed to be passing in front of my eyes. All I'd wanted was to see some tortoises and maybe learn some new techniques about their care. *What did I get myself into?*

Eventually, we arrived at the driver's home and I soon saw a completely different side of Drew Rheinhart, Kurt Edwards, Barry Downer, and, the clean-cut guy, James Badman. They turned out to be great guys with the same kind of chelonian passion as me. I would learn a lot from each of them. We visited the homes of both Drew Rheinhart and James Badman. Both had extensive outdoor chelonian set-ups that were unbelievably impressive.

Over the next few years, we stayed in touch and met again at various turtle and tortoise conferences. And the TTPG would grow into one of the world's most beneficial resources for captive breeding of turtles and tortoises. The presentations at the conferences were informative, and the dialogue and discussions before and after the formal agendas were even more valuable. The knowledge and expertise shared was something you could never get just from reading. Turtle experts from around the world have turned the TTPG's annual November conferences into the single biggest resource of its kind.

From 2010 through 2018 I traveled to Florida two or three times a month, staying with Ty, helping with the sulcata tortoises. My friendship with Ty developed into a strong bond as we spent a lot time traveling together visiting other reptile breeders, trade shows, conferences, and expos. Some of the most rewarding times were the evenings when we would sit and talk about anything and everything—new ideas, business, different concepts—always thinking out of the box to come up with ways to do things better.

With our sulcata breeding operation, things started changing. We weren't able to successfully produce the quantities of hatchlings I had become accustomed to due to the fact that the climate conditions in Florida were less than ideal. The Southwestern US climate better replicated the native climate of the sulcatas, and the many breeders in that area were able to produce thousands of hatchlings every year. As a result, the value began to drop and the popularity of the tortoises increased. As years passed, another problem rose its head. While doing fine in the backyard settings of homes in the southern states, the sulcatas struggled up north. The sulcatas grew very large, and people had no way of properly maintaining them indoors. Ultimately, the profitability of our tortoise breeding operation in Florida came to an end.

While my concentration was on tortoises, Ty began to concentrate his efforts on breeding rare and endangered iguana species, amassing a collection that even the best zoos envied. He soon phased out of the commercial aspect of his career, which was providing reptiles to PetSmart, and his interest in iguanas grew to the point where he became the world's largest producer of Cycluras (island rock iguanas), concentrating on rhinoceros iguanas and Cuban hybrid blue iguanas. Ty became well known within the reptile community worldwide as a result of his accomplishments, as well as his generosity to those who were less fortunate.

Never one to forego a trip to an exotic place, I accompanied Ty to Huatulco, Mexico where he was invited to speak at the International Iguana Foundation conference. Huatulco was a quaint little fishing village on the southern Pacific coastline in the state of Oaxaca. Ty wanted to visit a few private iguana breeders and larger iguana farms. Not being fluent in Spanish, he asked if I could help him line up an interpreter. Who else besides my good friend Antonio Estrada, the Mexican biologist I had become close friends with years earlier? Antonio was happy to oblige. Besides the conference and the visits to the breeders, we also managed to meet with a few local conservationists who took us to a beach one evening to witness the release of several sea turtle hatchlings. Another item on my bucket list was checked off.

Back in Punta Gorda, Ty really put me to work. He wanted to hold a fundraising event for iguana conservation, calling it Iguanafest. He picked a date and started promoting it every twenty-seven minutes on Facebook. Then he handed the reins over to me. My son James and I devised a plan, laid out a strategy, and created a list of tasks that needed to be addressed along with a timeline for accomplishing them. We worked on everything from finding tents, tables, and chairs, to lining up vendors and sponsors and signing up volunteers. Ty spared nothing in putting together what turned out to be a very impressive event that raised over $60,000 that was funneled to various conservation programs for rare iguanas.

During one of our evening conversations, I happened to talk to Ty about the time Denise and I visited Nancy and Fred Cwynar in Punta Gorda. We'd had such a great time enjoying the southwest Florida lifestyle that we felt the area could someday offer us a second home destination. One thing led to the next and before I got up to make that second cup of coffee, Ty was online finding a couple of listings in an exclusive beachfront community called Manasota Key in Englewood. The next day, Ty and I canvassed Manasota Key Road where we found a vacant piece of beachfront property with a "For Sale" sign on it. The following week Denise and I checked it out and bought it. Not long after that, we were building another dream home, this one right on the beach.

Meanwhile, I kept traveling but now I was intent on involving my children more. Andrew and I went on a ten-day wildlife adventure aboard a small yacht through the Galapagos Islands. It was a small and intimate wildlife tour, specially tailored by fellow TTPG member and tour leader Professor Fredrick Caporaso. We observed orcas gliding alongside our yacht and manta rays as big as tables. We hiked through different coastal terrains and encountered sea lions on beaches and rocky cliffs. We saw different types of shorebirds, including pelicans, blue footed boobies, massive albatrosses, and exquisite cormorants with bright red, inflated throats. We observed colonies of tiny Galapagos penguins diving in and out of the water from the rocky shoreline. We ascended into more desolate habitats of the volcanic terrain, too, coming across rust-colored Galapagos land iguanas, some of them huge, standing in stark contrast to the agile, black, miniature, dinosaur-looking marine iguanas that covered the rocky shorelines.

Andrew and I spent a considerable amount of time on the island of Santa Cruz, observing the tortoises as they slowly moved about, grazing on the vegetation. We witnessed marine turtles breeding in the natural and hidden estuaries, as well as dolphins swimming past us as we snorkeled. We also observed the gentle Darwin finches with their various beak shapes. For the most part, the wildlife was approachable from a reasonable distance. The animals seemed to have no fear of us.

We also spent a half day visiting the Charles Darwin Research Station, home of the conservation icon, Lonesome George. He was the last known of the species of Pinta Island Galapagos tortoise. I was sorry to learn that he passed away a mere five months later. Thus the extinction of a species.

In January of 2013, my son James and I went on a seven-day Peruvian tour down the Amazon on a riverboat. What made it particularly special was that our tour leaders were two famous herpetologists, Bill Lamar and Dante Fenolio who guided us and our other reptile "passionates," Kim Anderson, Bob and Sherry Ashley, Mark and Kim Bell, Ken Foose, Tell and Eileen Hicks, and John and Sara Mack. As we headed downstream, we almost immediately began encountering different types of birds and animals, from green iguanas in the trees to macaws overhead. Over the following week, we were able to interact with local Indian communities as we explored various areas in search of reptiles. We observed monkeys, anacondas, Podoc river turtles, and a Mata Mata turtle. We could see three-toed sloths high in the trees of the tropical forest. At night we searched for black caiman using smaller boats, encountering several species of treefrogs in the floating islands of vegetation.

One afternoon, we anchored in a quiet cove to fish for piranhas. As we began catching one after the other, Ken Foose, always the unpredictable one, jumped off the upper deck right into a massive school just to prove his point that they were not the man-eaters we see on TV. Instead, they made for tasting eating themselves, as we learned after roasting them on an open fire.

We concluded our Amazon riverboat excursion and James and I extended our trip by three days to join Tell and Eileen Hicks and Kim Anderson on a visit to the lost city of Machu Picchu, an impressive archaeological site built by the Incas and rediscovered in 1911—just one more wonderful adventure brought to me courtesy of my never-ending turtling passion.

40

—•—

Heinz 57 and Other Adventures

Back in the early 1970s, when eastern indigo snakes were available in the pet trade, I purchased two from a reptile dealer in Florida. They had calm dispositions and were the most beautiful snakes I'd ever owned. And they were perfect as display animals at Noah's Ark Pet Center. The memory of those snakes stuck with me over the years and I always thought that someday, when I could devote the time, I might like to own one again.

Today, the eastern indigo snake is a protected species due to its rarity. In the past, collection for the pet trade likely had the most negative impact on the population of indigos, but since 1978, when they became listed as a threatened species under the Endangered Species Act, the primary culprit has been habitat destruction and fragmentation.

Thankfully, this species is now being monitored by various conservation organizations, and public awareness of this animal's difficult situation has gone mainstream, especially within the southeastern US. The news media, zoos, nature centers, parks, and eco-friendly programs have all contributed, resulting in protected habitats throughout the snakes' former and existing ranges in Florida, Georgia, and Alabama. Captive breeding programs are now in place for repatriation and for providing display animals to licensed facilities for educational purposes.

In 2014, I decided I wanted to try my hand at raising an unrelated pair of indigos with the goal of getting them to reproduce. I felt it was a way to give back, to help, in my small way, to overcome the threats to their existence. Curt Harbsmeier, a well-known wildlife attorney and avid reptile herpetoculturist and conservationist (especially with crocodilians) presented me with two neonates, an unrelated pair of captive-hatched, gorgeous, solid blue/black pieces of gold, each in their own cottage-cheese-sized plastic containers. In between his full time law practice and serving on the board of Tampa's Lowry Park Zoo, Curt had also been working with eastern indigos since the early 1990s, successfully producing offspring.

After setting the snakes up in separate enclosures, my quest to raise them to adult breeding age and getting them to reproduce began. Over the following three years, I kept detailed records of each step along the way, every feeding, every shed, and every notable occurrence. I weighed and measured them regularly. They soon grew to an impressive size, the male being heavier and just over six feet long. He was my favorite show animal, extremely popular with young and old alike, and he took on the role of ambassador for my conservation efforts as I displayed him at various educational reptile venues in the Chicago area.

I finally witnessed several successful breedings in November of 2016. After providing the female with a plastic nesting container filled with slightly dampened sphagnum moss, Denise and I patiently waited. Eventually, in April of 2017, the female laid eight large, beautiful eggs that all turned out to be fertile. I transferred the nest container into an incubator and they all hatched around a hundred days later. I made arrangements to place all eight neonates with recognized nature centers and experienced captive breeders in our area while requesting donations to the Orianne Society in Florida, the Gladys Porter Zoo in Brownsville, Texas, and the

Chicago Herpetological Society, all in the name of our eastern indigo snake program. Then I proudly checked off yet another item on my bucket list.

While this was all happening, I was also toying with the idea of a return trip to Madagascar. A few friends of mine in the reptile community had expressed an interest in going and asked if I'd be willing to put together an itinerary. I'd always wanted to return to Madagascar. For one thing, on my first trip there, I was unable to see the Pyxis planicauda tortoises due to the fact that they could only be found in a remote habitat of the Kirindy Forest, an additional two-day drive that our tight schedule didn't allow for. The second thing was that I never forgot the images of all the children in those extremely poor villages of the deep south. In spite of the smiles on their faces, the sight of them in nothing more than soiled and torn t-shirts and tattered shorts really affected me. I always knew that if I went back, I'd take some children's clothes with me.

I put together a three-week itinerary that included two days in the Kirindy Forest for nine people including me, Bob and Sherry Ashley, Ken Foose, Kim Anderson, Tell and Eileen Hicks, and Mark and Kim Bell. Hoping that my old tour guide was still alive and in good health, I searched for him but without success. Ultimately, I found another tour guide by the name of Jean Claude.

Everybody on the tour appreciated my desire to help the children and by the time of departure, we had collected hundreds of articles of clothing. Though he didn't initially have much wildlife experience, Jean Claude turned out to be a great guide, even being willing to hold a large Madagascan boa constrictor we found crawling across a dirt road. We encountered wildlife of all sorts including a variety of songbirds, birds of prey, flamingos, and different species of lemurs, some of which were so accustomed to people that they didn't hesitate to approach us.

Return to Madagascar, 2015.

One day we hiked in a dense forested area and encountered hundreds of giant fruit bats, many hanging high in the canopy while others soared from branch to branch. There were giant hissing cockroaches, and iridescent, emerald green day geckos hanging out by the outdoor patios we stopped and had lunch at.

In the Kirindy Forest, we spent two days turtling under the sun-dappled forest canopy, home of the rare Pyxis planicauda tortoise. Besides being a diminutive foraging species, planicaudas are only active a few months of the year, during the rainy season, spending the remaining months aestivating beneath the leaf-litter substrate in the sandy soil. After the first couple of hours of our first day's exploration, we were starting to wonder if we'd even encounter one, but we continued on and, sure enough, I spotted one with its head fully extended, resting motionless under the leaning branches of a small sapling. After I announced my find, we spent several minutes taking photos, after which we picked the tortoise up and examined it. It was an alert, beady-eyed, gorgeous female in perfect condition. The smiles on everyone's faces as a result of that first discovery are still deeply embedded in my mind. After returning her to the exact same place we found her, we continued our search, soon encountering more, some of which were very young adults displaying clean and striking beige, white, black, and caramel colored markings on their carapaces. What an exhilarating experience.

Two days later, entering the desolate Spiny Forest, we encountered numerous radiated and Pyxis arachnoides tortoises. I could see how vulnerable and fragile they were even in their native habitat, something the majority of chelonian enthusiasts might not be able to grasp without seeing for themselves.

One day we entered a village and Jean Claude explained to them that we had gifts for about fifty children. Before long, smiling kids were everywhere, putting on their new clothes. We too had smiles on our faces, but ours were accompanied by a few tears. On every level, this trip to Madagascar was a huge success.

Madagascar children.

Back home, my son James was well on his way to being recognized as an up-and-coming, world class wildlife artist. His herpetology artwork was being exhibited in a dedicated wing of the Peggy Notebart Nature Museum in Chicago. Our whole family shared in the pride I felt for him for this accomplishment.

Then, at the August 2016 TSA symposium in New Orleans, he exhibited his artwork to chelonian professionals from around the world, and it was there that I noticed Dr. Peter Pritchard hanging out at James's display, clearly impressed with his South American redfoot tortoise painting. At the symposium, Dr. Pritchard and his wife Sybille asked James and me to join them at their table during the TSA's special honorary luncheon, dedicated to Dr. Pritchard and his lifelong contributions to chelonian conservation.

Later that year, the Pritchards invited us to visit their home in Oviedo, Florida, and to take a personal tour of the Pritchard's Chelonian Research Institute across the street from their home. We were accompanied by chelonian conservationists George Heinrich and Chuck Schaffer. When we entered their home, James presented Peter with the redfoot tortoise painting that Peter had admired at the TSA symposium. Sybille prepared an outstanding lunch, after which we all spent a couple of hours enjoying one-on-one personal time "turtling" in the Pritchard's library as we looked at old photos and talked turtles. At the Chelonian Research Institute, we got a glimpse of Peter's world travels, checking out his artwork, preserved specimens, and turtle shells and skulls. Outside, we took several photos of his Galapagos tortoises, admired his Rolls Royce, and bid my lifelong hero farewell.

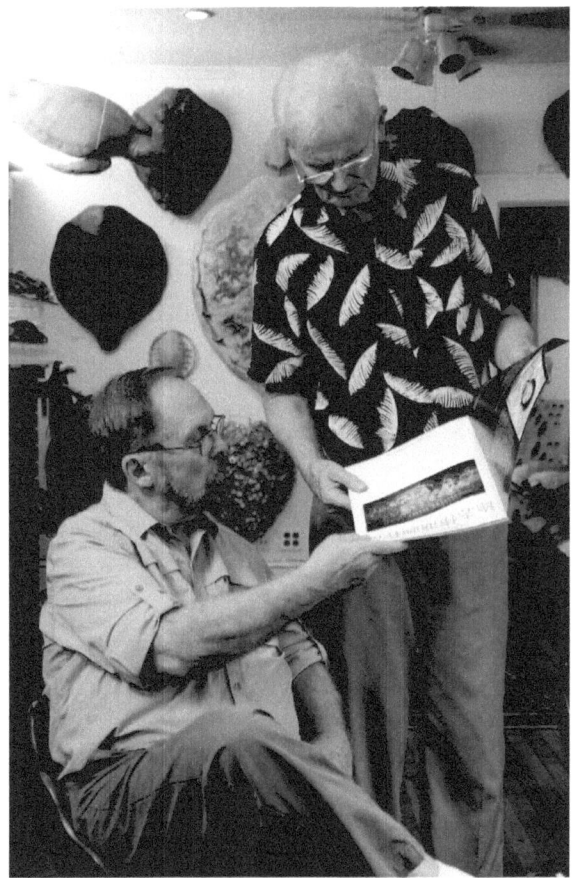

With Dr. Peter Pritchard.

Just a few years later, on September 26, 2020, Peter passed away. He had left his mark on me as well as so many people around the world. As Chris Leone, a well-known turtle conservationist, put it: *"Dr. Peter Pritchard was by far the world's most famous turtle biologist. He was an incredible man and the things that he has done for turtles as well as the knowledge he shared with us let alone the knowledge we gained because of him, is a true treasure to anyone into chelonians as well as wildlife in general."*

· · · · · ● · ● · · ·

As much traveling as I was doing, George Heinrich and fellow biologist Tim Walsh came up with an idea that even I could not have dreamed up—touring the country for a year in an attempt to find as many of the nation's fifty-nine species of turtles as they could. It was one heck of a challenge. They shared their plan with other turtle biologists, conservationists, and enthusiasts, and soon "the Big Turtle Year" became a much-discussed event. What a great way to draw attention to the plight that chelonians faced throughout the country—the dwindling habitats and the threats of extinction.

My son James, James Barzyk, me, George Heinrich.

Sponsored by the Florida Turtle Conservation Trust, George and Tim set out on January 1, 2017. They mapped out a plan with several itineraries, meeting up with local turtle experts in numerous locations around the country. Turtle enthusiasts from all corners jumped in and volunteered their expertise. I was happy to be one of the sponsors who helped offset the expenses, but, more importantly, I was proud to be one of the partners who were selected for two of the study sites that George and Tim were headed for. In May, James and I joined James Barzyk in guiding George Heinrich to the first site—the secret habitats in Michigan of spotted turtles, Blanding's turtles, wood turtles, and eastern box turtles. Then a few days later, we took George to the second site, a protected grassland habitat in the Great Plains of Illinois on the Iowa border where we successfully located another rare find: the ornate box turtle.

As the year unfolded, the Big Turtle Year website was updated to document all the successes George and Tim were having as they traveled across the country. In mid-December, I got a phone call from George. The tour was winding down and he had already accepted the fact that he and Tim were not going to hit the fifty-nine number. They still had four species left to locate and the chances of doing so were slim. Two of the remaining species were impossible to find due to weather conditions, but George felt they had a chance with the other two—the hawksbill sea turtle and the chicken turtle.

"Bob," George said, "I'm planning on going to the Keys in a week or so. I've got to find a hawksbill turtle. Can you join me?"

As it happened, we were now firmly in the Christmas season. Denise and I had plans to welcome twenty-two people for Christmas dinner. How could I break away? But Denise overheard the conversation and said, "Go for it, Bob." It was just like Denise, the most supportive wife a guy could ever imagine.

The day after Christmas, I flew to Tampa where I met George, and then we stopped off on our way down south to pick up James Barzyk and his son, Harrison. In the Keys, we took a rickety little boat to a reef where we were assured we'd have the best chance of finding a hawksbill. I stayed aboard as the other three dove into the water to snorkel around in what turned out to be pretty rough waves. I kept my eyes on them, becoming worried now and again whenever I'd lose sight of one or two of them beneath the surface. Eventually, George broke through, shouting, "Wahoo!" He'd found a hawksbill turtle below. As he came aboard the boat, I just had to take a picture of his big grinning face, and I couldn't help but laugh when he turned to me and said, "I like turtles."

We telephoned Tim Walsh who was up in Massachusetts to tell him we'd found Number 56. His response? "Go find 57!"

James and Harrison left the next day, but with Tim's directive on our minds, George and I headed through the Everglades to Big Cypress to find the chicken turtle. We got little help from local conservationists and the day came and went without a sighting. The next day would be our last. We spent the morning searching through what we believed were ideal habitats, but came up empty. After lunch, we hiked through Fakahatchee Strand State Park, but as the afternoon started coming to a close, we agreed that finding Number 56 was no small thing and that we should be grateful we at least did that.

With the sun setting, we took one last ride along a narrow, secluded, tree-canopied dirt road. As we approached the end of it, both of us realized without saying it aloud that our quest for the chicken turtle was over. After struggling to make a U-turn, we slowly started heading back, and suddenly George cried out, "Turtle!" I spun around and looked where George was pointing. With a sliver of remaining sunlight bouncing off its hard shell, it was posing on a log with neck stretched. George took out his binoculars and made an even more excited cry. "*Chicken* turtle!" Then he dropped his binoculars, threw his arms around me, and planted a kiss on my left cheek. Neither one of us could stop laughing. The turtle was apparently just as happy as he stuck around and posed long enough for George to take some photos, before sliding off into the water. Number 57, appropriately named "Heinz," was found. And I was honored to be there.

41

—.—

THE BEAT GOES ON

WHERE HAS THE TIME gone? It seemed like just yesterday that I sold my business and became fearful of not being able to reasonably justify my worth any longer. But then over the ensuing years of turtling, it became clear that my worthiness was revalidated by becoming friends with so many turtle and reptile enthusiasts who shared in the same passion.

My close friendship with a very successful tortoise breeder by the name of Ralph Till is a prime example. Ralph patiently built a captive-raised breeding group of Pyxis tortoises, adding them to his unique and successful protocols that he had developed in breeding endangered Egyptian tortoises. Then there was Michael Ogle, curator of reptiles at the Knoxville Zoo, and biology professor Chris Manis of Dalton State University in Ooltewah, Tennessee, just two more friends who years earlier had visited my Pyxis breeding operation in Illinois, and later purchased some of James's artwork.

One time, Michael invited James and me to take a behind the scenes tour of the Knoxville Zoo's reptile department. Besides being able to spend a day with Michael and learn a few new techniques in chelonian husbandry, the main highlight was a visit we took with both Michael and Chris to a well-kept secret environment of the nation's smallest turtle, the critically endangered bog turtle. This site was part of a conservation program the zoo had initiated years earlier, now in the hands of Michael. Over the years, his department had been nurturing these turtles and doing population assessments. James took several photos of the turtles and their habitat for a painting he had planned, as I enjoyed, in awe, the unique environment, unlike anything I'd experienced before. The home of these turtles was a wetland meadow that was fed by groundwater, thus creating a bog. It was interspersed with hidden streams covered by ferns and sedges. The clumps of moss that were everywhere made you feel miniaturized, like a mythological gnome from a subterranean world.

Chris Manis, James Krause, Michael Ogle in
Tennessee bog turtle habitat.

Guided by Michael and Chris, we carefully treaded throughout the bog and were thrilled to locate and photograph five bog turtles that afternoon. Given that adult bog turtles are typically between three to four inches long, it's fair to assume we missed several others. I've since learned that much of their fragmented habitats throughout their native ranges have either been developed or drained, underscoring how delicate their survival status is.

And then there's Marc Cantos, another person I've reaped the rewards of developing a friendship with, a person with the same turtle passion and one of the most knowledgeable experts in chelonian husbandry I know. He took his passion and built a company called The Turtle Source, one of the nation's most successful commercial turtle breeding operations, providing turtles to enthusiasts worldwide. Another turtle expert with whom I became close friends was John Richards, one of the most interesting people I know, a visionary who took his passion and love for turtles and, over several years, rescued giant alligator snapping turtles from Louisiana and Arkansas that were destined for the soup pot. To see the elaborate breeding operation in the ponds he set up in Missouri, eventually producing thousands of hatchlings each year, was inspiring.

Once, my son James and I took a trip not only in pursuit of our dome shaped, shiny objects, but for the legless reptiles that so many people unnecessarily fear: snakes. In 2017, John Archer and Michael Dloogatch of the Chicago Herpetological Association invited us on their annual fall excursion to Snake Road in southern Illinois during the annual fall migration of thousands of snakes to their choice winter hibernaculum in the nearby cliffs. The road runs through Shawnee National Forest and is actually closed to vehicles during the migration seasons. James and I joined a small group for two full days in the field. As we drove into the forest, our first encounter was not a snake, but a beautifully marked young male eastern box turtle sitting in the middle of the asphalt road. We pulled over and admired him before placing him to the side of the road in the direction he was heading. Soon, we were hiking down Snake Road and coming across many more reptiles, some crossing the trail, some in the adjoining brush and wetlands, and some moving along the rock walls of the cliffs. We encountered several species of snakes including common water, ribbon, rough green, red bellied, garter, and ringneck, in addition to three venomous species—water moccasin, copperhead, and timber rattlesnake. I was amazed at how many eastern box turtles we came across, all sharing the sun- dappled woodlands with various amphibians including leopard frogs, gray and green treefrogs, eastern spotted newts, as well as marble, tiger, spotted, and cave salamanders. It was a fascinating trip and I was happy to see the work being done to conserve these beautiful creatures.

In November of that year, at the TTPG conference in Arizona, I met another inspiring individual who also had a lifelong passion for turtles: Greg Wittstock, the founder of Aquascapes, the nation's largest creator and builder of ponds and water features. Coincidentally, it turned out I'd done business with him eleven years earlier. Denise and I had hired his company to design and install an elaborate koi pond and waterfall on our property. Greg and I stayed in touch after the conference, and in August of 2018, he asked if he could film a video for his YouTube channel describing my painted turtle conservation program. Over the next couple of years, Greg produced three videos, one of which was during an Eastern Illinois University biology study conducted by Dr. Beth Reinke and several of her students. I had volunteered our site for this interesting painted turtle project, and assisted in collecting data relating to the function and variance of plastron colorations of midland painted turtles.

Greg and I would get together from time to time, and at one point I gave him several hatchlings for his educational displays at his retail facility. Then in October of 2019, he asked if I would like to join him and his longtime key executive, Ed Beaulieu, on a trip to Georgia to join turtle conservation-ist Greg Brashear for an evening expedition in search of alligator snapping turtles. He didn't have to ask me twice. After my afternoon flight down to Atlanta, with only water shoes, gloves, and my safari vest, I found myself in an ankle- to knee-deep water hiking over slippery boulders and rocks through the center of a swiftly moving, tributary of a crystal clear river. Fortunately, there were several sandy bottom areas that made navigation easier at times. That evening, we encountered several different species of turtles, including an eastern river cooter, a loggerhead musk, an eastern painted, and a beautiful, young alligator snapping turtle. Another highly successful trip.

Soon, the Covid years were upon us and during that time, Denise and I began planning for the future. We loved the lifestyle our new home in Florida offered, and decided to downsize by (sadly) selling our home and wildlife sanctuary in Illinois and purchasing a much smaller home with the intention of splitting our time between Illinois and Florida.

At the same time, I was helping Ty with a project of his. He was planning to open a reptile zoo called Iguanaland and I was happy to offer what I could by the way of my strengths in strategizing, planning, designing, and organizing. And since I was so busy with our houses, I knew, for the time being, that I couldn't properly continue with our breeding program, so I placed my valued chelonians with other facilities. In addition to donating several to Iguanaland, my beloved Aldabra tortoise, Tosh, went to my good friend Debra Sydney in Austin, Texas, while the majority of my breeding operation went to Ryan Stewart, an up-and-coming tortoise breeder in Florida. My plan was to resume again once we got all settled in, but with another species or two.

Reptile conservationists at Iguanaland.

In the meantime, Denise and I were loving our time in Florida. She became involved with collecting fossilized shark teeth, I was able to keep turtling in various habitats, and we were both happy to see all of the loggerhead sea turtles that were nesting on our beach, along with all the gopher tortoises that were calling our sand dunes home. I began networking with our new friends on Manasota Key, developing a program to bring awareness to the gopher tortoises and the occasional mishaps I'd encounter on the road. I designed and manufactured an attractive "Gopher Tortoise Crossing" sign, and installed several of them throughout the Key. I figured it was the least I could do for my new chelonian friends.

I was beginning to see that our time in Florida was offering so many more new and exciting turtling opportunities, especially with half of the fifty-nine turtle species in the United States calling Florida their home. I couldn't wait to get started.

Turtling in Florida.

Every little effort helps!

Then, before I knew it, I found myself savoring the moment while in the middle of a cypress swamp less than an hour from our new Florida home. It was a warm, sunny January afternoon and we slowly waded in and out of ankle-deep water doing a population assessment of Florida box turtles, which had been prevalent just a few years earlier. I was again with my good friend James Barzyk who had years earlier relocated his family to Florida. As we wandered farther apart, I approached an opening in the tropical tree line where the sunlight revealed a waist-deep pond filled with aquatic plants. I carefully entered the pond, watching as an ibis took flight from the suspended horizontal perch of a fallen tree.

Gopher tortoise living on our sand dune.

I stood motionless, observing the surroundings. In a few minutes, I noticed sporadic movement among the floating greenery about fifty feet in front of me. There was a splash and then a fluttering in the water, then a dark movement, then nothing. Soon, the movement and splashing began again, and then abruptly stopped. This continued on and off for a while. I imagined maybe it was an alligator feeding on a school of fish, and I cautiously moved a bit closer to make a proper identification. I motioned to James who had already started wading toward me. He then suggested that it might be an otter.

I kept moving closer, slowly placing one foot in front of the other, taking my cell phone out of my pocket as the water got deeper. Then, twenty feet in front of me, I saw it. It was neither gator nor otter, but a beautiful, young adult Florida snapping turtle. Apparently, it had just resurfaced among the dense vegetation, and as it extended its neck, I could see its black, beady little eyes peering right at me. Again I stood motionless, wondering why it hadn't immediately submerged to safety. Finally, it lowered its head into the water and I made my move, grabbing it by the back end. I lifted it up and was stunned to see that I'd actually lifted up two, connected together. I had interrupted the lovemaking of a pair of my most revered beings. Immediately, I returned the young couple to their original position and all was good. I smiled with contentment.

We moved on, continuing our search that day. This fragmented swamp was full of cypress trees with extravagant root structures, draped with mosses, and surrounded by ferns, palms, native tillandsias, even a few native encyclia butterfly orchids, all of which typified what was once a vast tropical environment. Various aquatic and marsh plants were all around us. Thousands of gambusia were hitting the water's surface, and little anole lizards were scampering about, seeking safety as we approached them.

At one point I stopped, just to look around and soak in the serenity of this untroubled mini environment. And I thought about how many environments I had been in, how many habitats I had hiked or waded through in my years of turtling. I thought back to Camp Oconto when I was just a boy, rowing a boat toward those shiny, domed objects I saw dotting the logs at the far end of a cove. It had been almost a lifetime since then, a lifetime of following my passion, through ponds, lakes, swamps, and on into the business world where my passion would carry me around the world. I thought about all the trips I had taken since retirement, all the turtles and tortoises I had seen in far flung places like Madagascar and the Galapagos, places I couldn't have even dreamed of that day at the Woolworth's pet department when I brought home that little green turtle, the day my love affair started. I smiled to myself, thinking of how blessed I'd been. Even though I'd never put much value in the concept of luck, I had to be the luckiest guy in the world.

Then I noticed James was getting ahead of me and I shook myself out of my reverie and waded on. There were more turtles to find. I just knew that there would always be more turtles to find.

Epilogue

As I explained in the introduction to this book, turtling to me means entering a turtle or tortoise's environment to photograph or catch them, or sometimes to just quietly observe. But it also means enjoying the camaraderie of other turtle enthusiasts, sharing information and swapping stories. But these are the broad brushstrokes of what I have come to think of as turtling. In more specific terms, turtling has, in my life, also come to include those mornings on our patio when Denise and I watched the painted turtles climb one by one onto their basking logs, or the time I felt the exhilaration of seeing a bog turtle in the Tennessee wetland, or even the feeling of relief I had knowing that Pyxis planicaudas still existed in the remote Kirindy forest of Madagascar.

Then there were the times I'd holler, "Just a few more minutes!" when Denise would call out that lunch was ready while I was downstairs in my specially designed facility working with my turtles and tortoises. Or walking up and down the aisles of all of the reptile expos seeing what's new, or picking up a newly published book on turtles, or a captive-raised hatchling I just had to have. Sometimes it was flipping through the pages of a good turtle book, like *The Year of the Turtle,* by David Carrol, and not being able to put it down. Of course there were the many times I was with my fellow enthusiasts at the TSA and TTPG conferences, trying to fulfill that insatiable desire to learn new techniques in turtle and tortoise conservation or husbandry. Naturally, turtling has to include my travels to exotic destinations like the Galapagos Islands and Madagascar, or even that time in Japan when I stumbled upon an aquarium filled with hatchling fly river turtles. Most importantly for me, turtling must include the days of observing my midland painted turtles, and providing the special care of headstarting and rewilding thousands of them.

All of that constitutes turtling, and I have been fortunate to have done all of it in my lifetime, driven by a passion that carried me far beyond anything I could have imagined as a boy, affecting and enhancing my life both professionally and personally.

In the course of writing this book, I've had the chance to think a lot about the circumstances of my life. I said earlier that I've never put too much value on the concept of luck. Certainly, however, there are uncontrollable factors that come into play in anyone's life. Factors like who your parents were, your time and place of birth, as well as your gender, race, and upbringing. All of these have an undeniable influence on a person. Each becomes raw material that a person has to work with. Once that stage is set, however, and a person moves on in life and reaches a point where they are able to start making their own decisions and choices, I'm convinced that the role of random luck lessens considerably. At that point, I believe we start making our own luck and a lot of success is now the result of hard work and developed skills combined with smart decisions.

I was once told that you should picture yourself on the shoreline of a rapidly flowing river. The river represents the movement of time in your life, and on its surface are several different objects floating by. These are the choices and decisions you have to make throughout your life, some small, some large, and many of them disguised and difficult to recognize. Which ones are for you and which ones are not? Which are good choices and which are bad? Importantly, where are the opportunities? Do you take a risk and grab one before it is swept downstream?

Looking back, I believe that the majority of the decisions I've made were predetermined and inevitable. My "momentous" choices linked me to future experiences and opportunities, therefore becoming my destiny. This is what I mean by making your own luck. I call it "unintentional momentousness." Yes, we're all subject to chance, but we can tilt the balance of luck in our favor. I have learned in my life the truth of Roman philosopher Seneca's words: *luck is where preparation meets opportunity.* In my life, I have tried to be prepared and I have looked for opportunity.

It has taken me a long way.

Ah, but I have farther to go and much more to do. And, of course, my future will be guided by my passion. Today, my primary turtling interest is conservation. Denise and I have been protecting the breeding populations of wild midland painted turtles and their nests for the past twelve years. In addition to protecting the nests from predation, we headstarted the hatchlings and juveniles and then reintroduced them back into their natural habitats once they were a bit larger and stronger and more capable of defending themselves from the many different predators and hazards, including the encroaching presence of humans. To date, we have released over 3,000 juvenile turtles into safe habitats.

And now my passion for turtles has somehow brought me to Manasota Key in Englewood Florida, one of the most productive loggerhead sea turtle nesting sites in the state. The frosting on the cake is that the protected gopher tortoise is also commonly found living on and near the dunes throughout the key. We even have a few active burrows on our property where I'm beginning to propagate various indigenous plants that are commonly consumed by the gopher tortoises.

In addition to habitat loss, turtles are threatened by an insurmountable number of predators, many of which are subsidized by human presence. Today, many of us are living in environments that have been disturbed and re-disturbed many times. In doing so, mankind has indirectly introduced or encouraged the existence of many turtle predators, including raccoons, skunks, coyotes, bullfrogs, herons, egrets, ravens, and crows. Programs aimed at securing the future of turtles and tortoises everywhere are more important than ever.

I support the following non-profit organizations, whose turtle biologists, educators, and breeders are steadily making progress in the protection of threatened and endangered turtles and tortoises around the world:

The Florida Turtle Conservation Trust (FTCT): A focused, hardworking chelonian conservation organization focused on educating the public on the plight of turtles and tortoises in Florida. .

The Turtle Conservancy (TC): A well-structured turtle conservation organization dedicated to protecting threatened turtles and tortoises and their habitats worldwide, and to promoting their appreciation by people everywhere. .

The Turtle Room (TR): Primarily an education-based conservation organization with a mission to advance survival of the world's turtles and tortoises through education, conservation, and research programs. .

The Turtle Survival Alliance (TSA): The world's largest non-profit organization with a mission to protect and restore wild populations of tortoises and freshwater turtles through science-based conservation, global leadership, and local stewardship. .

The Turtle and Tortoise Preservation Group (TTPG): A one-of-a-kind organization devoted to providing education and information to all turtle keepers, from beginners to advanced, young reptile enthusiasts, and anyone interested in the conservation of turtles and tortoises. These folks work to develop captive breeding programs to not only take the pressures off wild chelonians collected for the food and pet trade, but if and when the day comes where populations cannot succeed in the wild, as is already the case with certain species, these captive assurance colonies will ensure their future survival. .

The United States Association of Reptile Keepers (USARK): A well-structured and focused organization concentrating on education and information for both the ever-growing reptile segment, and government lawmakers at the state and federal levels, providing reasonable guidelines for animal care, transporting, and ownership. .

Each of these organizations consists of hardworking, dedicated people just like you and me. Their efforts in one way or another in putting people and resources on the ground to protect the earth's 360 turtle and tortoise species are working. If you love turtles, please consider visiting these organizations and giving them your support.

And let us all *keep on turtling!*

ACKNOWLEDGMENTS

Throughout my entire life I have been so fortunate to meet and interact with the most inspiring people. My passion for turtles has led me into many endearing friendships, from schoolmates and business professionals to dedicated employees, reptile enthusiasts, as well as chelonian conservationists.

In distant foreign lands, as well as my travels in the United States, and especially with my friends at home in Illinois and Florida, my passion for turtles has had a significant impact in bringing us all close together.

This passion enabled me to travel the world where these relationships got their start. These were friendships I made while riding my Harley throughout the Americas, to driving a Mercedes throughout Europe, as well as the friendships made while cruising down the Amazon in a riverboat, or lying in a field of grass observing tortoises in the Galapagos Islands. Then there were the turtling experiences through the various wetlands, fields, and forests of America, and all the way to the spiny forests of southern Madagascar. And how can I not include the peddling of a bicycle on that dirt footpath between the rice paddies in Malaysia, to being driven in an open air rickshaw in China or Bangladesh, not to mention those crazy, hazardous rides in the tuk tuks of Thailand and the Philippines? These were all the journeys I chose. The enlightenments I received from each and every one of those hands-on experiences cannot even begin to be measured. I owe so much to the people that allowed those experiences to happen.

MY FAMILY
My wife, Denise: How could I ever begin to thank you for being there every step of the way. You've become the single most important person in my life. You not only accepted but you embraced all of my initiatives and various interests from that day I cut the tail off of that roadkill raccoon to the many days we worked with those hatchling painted turtles, or the times you helped me carry all of my tortoises inside before the sun set. Most importantly, you helped me become a better person to my family and friends. Thank you so much. **My children, Bob Jr., Lisa, James, and Andrew:** I value our relationships more than you realize, each and every one of you are different in so many wonderful ways. I thank you for your encouragement while at the same time I'm gratified in seeing each of you having the determination to discover your own individual passions and to follow your dreams. Each of you makes me so proud. **Bob Jr.:** You've become the most successful entrepreneur and are now teaching all of us how to work smart. You and Jill are just beginning your journey together. Sit tight,

put on your seat belt, and get ready for the ride of your life. I wish you only the best. Our experience together at that seventh game of the 2016 World Series in Cleveland will live on forever. **Lisa:** You've shown me another perfect example of focus and following one's dreams. I'm so proud of how you've turned those dreams into reality. You and Mark have so much ahead of you and I'm so happy to be a part of it. You are most definitely a wonderful product of both your mother and father's fabric. **James:** You've taught me patience and balance. Determination and creativity have become your middle name. It's so comforting to see how you and Angie have come together as one and I just love to see how you're both moving forward in your lives uncovering the opportunities that lie ahead. I absolutely loved all the times we spent together turtling. **Andrew:** You are the planner. You've demonstrated what it takes to be a success in business. I admire how you and Crystal encourage each other in everything you both pursue, especially in being such devoted and caring parents. I wish I could have been more like you. **To my grandchildren, Striker and Athena Krause, as well as Jakob:** I wish you all of the above successes in your lives. Discover your own passions and follow your dreams. **My mother, Mary Krause, and my father, Albert Krause:** I thank you both as well as my other long-lost family members who supported the idiosyncrasies of a young boy collecting snakes, bugs, and turtles. I thank my father for encouraging me to pursue a career in data processing along with pushing me in so many different ways, many of which I could never understand until looking back later in life. In particular, and most importantly, I thank my mother who allowed me to have that very first little green turtle. And then throughout my entire life she was always there helping me "make things happen." She was the rock of our family. **My brother, Tom:** Oh, how I wish you were still here. The things we'd be reminiscing about, the successes in our lives and seeing our children following their passions, and even though there were those times when we were younger and you'd start World War III by blowing on the dining room table while I was meticulously mounting my butterflies, I really miss you. **My sister, Mari-Lynn:** I love and thank you. We've been through much together and you have taught me a lot not only in dealing with the various challenges of life but in raising the most wonderful child that anyone could dream of. Denise and I are so happy to be the godparents of **Mary Jo:** A young woman on her way of becoming more successful than she already is. We love being a part of your journey even though I miss those "mummy tuck days." **Gramma Krause:** I don't know what would have happened if you weren't there to open your home to me and nurture those first few grade school years. You taught me so much about life and doing what is right. I learned what determination means as you eked out a living in every way you knew how. I thank you, Gram, for all those memories. **Grandpa Cascio:** I thank you for being there for me and always setting the example for our family in doing the right thing. **Marie Alfonso:** I thank you, my high school sweetheart whom I married the day I turned of legal age, and as brief as our lives together were, you helped me every day, especially giving me a son that I watched grow into the wonderful and successful man he is. I know you're looking down with a smile on your face. **Joe Krause:** My special nephew. I want to thank you as well for staying close and I assure you that your father is looking down as proud as can be watching you become the epitome of a family passion. Your love for animals and especially reptiles had to come from somewhere. **The Razaitis Family:** Thank you for all that you do, Doris and Larry Adams, Deb Razaitis, Dawn, Nicole, Joe and Jennifer, and especially A. J. and Austyn, my little "turtlers." I also want to thank my young uncle, **Dr. Samuel Cascio:** who seventy years ago, while in his mid-twenties, stopped over at our house on his way home from golfing. He was intent on dropping off what turned out to be my very first midland painted turtle; the one which was crossing the fairway and interrupting his concentration while attempting to tee off. **Linda (Scoville/Moore) Krause:** We had great times together and brought three wonderful children into this world. They became a part of our legacies in the experiences we provided, which allowed each of them to choose the successful paths of life they're now on. I'm confident that you're as proud as I am.

PERSONAL LIFELONG FRIENDS

A special thanks to my **Wednesday "31" card game buddies: Steve Biondo, Bill Kiesler, Tim Randazzo, Terry Speake, and Tom Willis:** You guys kept my interests and pastimes varied and gave me that diversion I needed. We sure looked forward to our Wednesdays, even though Steve always kicked our butts.

And thank you for that big smile on my face as I reminisce about all of our **Ballbuster motorcycle trips: Rick Augustniak, Dennis Benton, Steve Biondo, Don Carino, Jay Cwynar, Fred Cwynar, Milan Fridl, Mike Hoffer, Andy Kovari, James Krause, Jerry Padulo, Dennis Peterson, Lance Ranier, Larry Sternal, Tom Willis, and Fred Wise:** We sure had some great rides together, from that very first ride in Arizona when in forty degree rainy weather, Jay blew out a tire and had to ride as my bitch for the next seventy miles down to Tucson. I want to thank each of you for all the great times we had together on those rides throughout the Midwest, as well as into Mexico, Canada, Sturgis, Daytona, The Tail of the Dragon, the Blue Ridge Mountains, and even Puerto Rico. And your patience on those rides every time we had to pull our Harleys over for me to get a turtle off of the road was sincerely appreciated. I also want to thank you for that out of the way "side trip" to Turtletown, Tennessee, even though I couldn't find a store with a Turtletown t- shirt.

To my friends in the **U.S. Army and Navy: David Sabarese, Samuel Singer, Frank Cerillo, and Tony Banzuello:** Those were the days, and some of the most tumultuous days in our country's history. We worked at the Pentagon together not fully understanding the level of our importance back then, all the while trying to make something of our young married personal lives. I also have to thank each of you for tolerating my box turtle collecting from Herndon Virginia.

To my school, boyhood, and personal friends: Steve and Vicki Biondo: We've become very close in the recent phases and had some great times together; thanks for the memories. **Ann and Bob Boch. Laurel Jashob Carlson:** My first real love at twelve years old, and a special thanks for helping me carry that bag of Great Plaines garter snakes. **Brian and Stephanie Cecola. Bill and Barbara Chew:** I'll never know how in the world you guys put up with me over all those years filling those pizza boxes with my hatchling sulcata tortoises to my leopard tortoises I set up in your backyard, disturbing you with their breeding grunts. **Bill and Paula Demlow. Bobby Detlaff:** Thanks for my very first hatchling snapping turtle. **Marlene Jerling Devere**: thanks for your understanding as I pulled into your driveway with a van full of tortoises. **Nick and Becky Diacou. Ray Dreifuss:** Wherever you are, I still hold strong feelings for the relationship we had together from our high school days in biology class to our California trip and then our brief journey going into business together. We were both young and seeking direction. I'm contented to know that you accomplished your journey as well. **Bill Dulski:** I'm sorry again about the gravestone. **Skip and Tomisita Dusik. Norris Graser**: You were there from the beginning of the Noah's days as you transitioned from one of my best turtle customers to one of my best turtling friends as we traveled back and forth to those Wisconsin lakes. To this day, I smile every time I enjoy a Payday. **Mike Green. Don Guanci. Kameron Helmick:** The young man with a great positive attitude for life and the determination to go with it. You're an inspiration. **Terry Hlavac:** Those two summers turtling at Camp Oconto will be engraved in my good-times memory bank forever. **Dr. Babette Horn. Sue and Guenter Kempf. Bill and Tanaya Kiesler:** Bill you witnessed the many transitions in my life from the grade school turtling days up at your family's cottage through my Noah's Ark career era and now into my turtle conservation days. You've seen it all. **The Kroll family:** Wherever you may be, thank you so much for allowing the Krause family with their two young children become a part of yours. The memories created and the lessons learned during those summers on the farm gave that youngest child a foundation to build upon, and that, he did. **Rodolfo Lopez:** You were much more than my caretaker; you became one of my best turtlers, assisting with our painted turtle conservation program. "Couldn't have succeeded without you." **Rich and Paula Lundgren. Tom and Kindra Lutz. Rita Maiss. Orlando Martinez:** I'm sure you're somewhere in Florida making big business deals. A struggling Cuban migrant back in the 1960s who had the perseverance to make a better life for him and his young family. That was you, Orlando. Then when you had the foresight to attend a computer programming school while learning the English language, no one knew back then that you'd talk your way into a computer operator's job while constantly searching for an entrepreneurial future.

Orlando, during those long evenings at the IBM 360 running programs, you taught me much, not only in how to put together a formal loan request to the bank but in never giving up. *Saluda con un saludo, mi amigo.* **Bill and Sue Mazurek:** I appreciate you being there during those initial stages of my turtle passion. I'm still convinced that on that day, Bill was the one who took Oscar, my box turtle. Luv yah, Sue. **Bonnie Horton Niedert:** You will always be that most successful ironing board model who never failed to put a smile on my face. **Ed Pawelko:** You are indeed the one who livens a party and, to me, the one who reinforced the importance of "Focus." **Dr. Russell Pearl:** You were a great friend demonstrating patience and precision in all that you pursued. **Gordon Pieske. Tim and Ann Randazzo:** I'm still convinced it was the wrong sized shoes you got Mazurek. **Dr. Eugene Ray:** My high school biology professor, I thank you for validating my unusual passions while so many others thought it peculiar. **Ron and Kerri Resech. Mel and Fran Rozanski. Tony, Wally, and Eddie Sekut:** You three brothers made an impact on me which I could have never imagined and even today while shopping or at home in our pantry, I still find myself making sure the canned goods are straight and facing forward. **Ed Smith. Dr. Steven and Lisa Smith:** You both will be there during the next chapter, for sure. One of our goals will be to make Manasota Key Road safer for our gopher tortoises. **Terry Speak:** We sure had some great times traveling together throughout Asia, Europe, and our best one of all, moving my sulcatas from Arizona to Florida. **Dr. Lauren Stewart**: Your patience and love for your clients, both two legged and four, have been an inspiration to both Denise and me. We're so happy to see that you are now living your life at your own pace; good luck to you. **Christine Kerwin Stone. Jimmy Swatalla:** I lost track of you and your brother Raymond who opened that initial door during my grade school years when I was introduced to the world of nature. All the inhabitants of that abandoned golf course, especially the basking turtles on the adjoining Chicago River shoreline gave me my first taste of turtles in a natural environment. It was then that I learned the basics of herpetology, entomology, and animal husbandry, all contributing immensely to my future direction in life. I'll never forget the day we rolled over that old rotting log in the Cumberland Forest Preserves and for the record, I'm sorry for trumping your "Dibbies" when we captured that milk snake. **Jim and Barb Tipman. Don and Susan Wetherald:** You were there during the early days, the great times we had together along with the challenges we overcame will never be forgotten. **James Wilde. Tom Willis**: You and Steve were the few I trusted riding side by side on our many Harley excursions. **Fred Wise:** A great businessman who helped me get started in injection molding. Thanks Fred and, by the way, you and Cindy have become turtlers and you're doing great with those red foot tortoises. **David and Kerri Witters. Joe and Kelly Yario.**

MY SPECIAL TURTLER FRIENDS

My heartfelt admiration and respect to my fellow passionate turtlers. You are the ones who have and are continuing to improve the lives of chelonians throughout the world. Your efforts and successes are making a huge difference in spite of the threats of habitat loss and fragmentation which we are now experiencing worldwide. We all know that chelonian conservation comes in many forms, from protecting the environments they live in and educating the people who share that environment, to what I embrace the most—captive breeding in both zoos and the private sector. Each of the following people have contributed in one form or another, allowing me to learn volumes from the conferences I've attended to the firsthand experiences both near and far. Thank you for allowing me to be a part of such a dedicated group: **Eric Abaka. Jason Abels. Carl Ackerbauer. Collette Adams:** Your contributions to the turtle community go back years. Where in the world do you get your energy? **Will Ahrens. Ben Anders:** You have to agree it's a small world. Enjoyed that dinner together in Kowloon. **Kim Anderson:** I knew right then and there when you beat me out on that beetle as we walked down the street in Peru, that you were my kind of girl. **John Archer:** A great leader who has done so much for the Chicago Herpetological Society. Thanks John. **Bob and Sheri Ashley:** You both have demonstrated that along with a lot of hard work you can be successful by following one's passion. You can be proud of the fact that you have introduced the world of reptiles to literally thousands of young minds, many of whom will someday be involved in turtle conservation. **Ray Ashton. Dr. Ben Atkinson:** "A hero who conquers the hurdles… for the conservation of turtles. **James Badman:** Thank you for your untiring accomplishments in bringing those young hungry minds into the world of herpetology. **Gary Bagnall:** My real passion being turtles has over the years caused many people to ask me, "Why haven't you gotten involved with developing products for reptiles instead of hamsters, rabbits, and ferrets?" My answer was only two words: "Gary Bagnall." Tough to compete with the best! I miss those strategic conversations we had. **John Bailey:** You put me to shame as it relates to being detail oriented. Thanks John for helping me along the way in looking after my tortoises. That trip to Madagascar was indeed the best. Your Pop Tarts saved my life. **Scott Ballard DVM. Michael Bargeron. Michael Barrera. Jeff Barringer. Bret Bartek. Dr. Stephen Barten:** Thank you for your years of service and your contributions to the reptile community. My Aldabra tortoises thank you as well, in spite of what they may have left you on the floor of your clinic. **James Barzyk:** It's impossible to put into a few words how you have impacted my life. In all of the field studies we performed, you taught me so much about evaluating turtle habitats for the health of their distribution status and natural history. All of those excursions are emblazoned in my mind forever. **Tim Beard. Ed Beaulieu:** Thanks Ed for your enthusiasm and professionalism. Keep drinking the Kool Aid. **John Behler:** You were there in the beginning helping create the path that we're all on today. I recalled your words as I explored the Kirindy forest in Madagascar. Your memory will live on forever. **Mark and Kim Bell:** Where has the time gone? You have accomplished so much for the reptile community not to mention your generosity for turtle conservation. **Bob Blome:** Our passions run deep even to the point of questioning our sanity. **Savannah Boan**: A bubbling, tireless, positive influencer to the reptile community who contributes so much in the most entertaining way. **Danny Bowlin. Greg Brashear:** Thanks for what you do in educating the public about turtle conservation. That evening turtling with you will never be forgotten. **Tyler Brooks. John Cann:** The icon of Australian chelonian conservation. Thanks John for your leadership. **Marcos Cantos:** You are responsible for introducing so many young children into the world of turtles. Keep the passion, Marc; you're my good friend. **Fred Caporaso**: The best Galapagos guide/friend in the world. **Rob Carmichael:** Thanks for bringing your students out for a hands-on experience with our midland painted turtle conservation program. They are our future. **Archie Carr**: The grandfather of turtle biologists. I must have read your books till they fell apart. **David Carroll:** And speaking of books, I treasure every one of yours. I reread them whenever I want to dream. **Keith Chitwood. John Coakley:** Thanks John for setting Ralph Till on the right track. **Tim Cole:** A great experience you gave me on my first rattlesnake encounter in Texas; and thanks for the brownies. Miss you. **Vanessa Costanzo:** I get tired just watching you. Thank you for being the most dedicated and hard-working number one ambassador of TTPG and USARK. **Richard Crowley. Tom Crutchfield:** Thanks for the years of doing business together, Tom. You've seen every side of the reptile community from commercial to now conservation, and I agree with you that we will never succeed without a balance. **Andy Danault. Mark DaSilva:** Funny how life is like a full circle; I wish I knew you back when you worked for my company. I really like what I see. **Bernard Devaux. Tomas Diagne:** You indeed have earned that title: "The Peter Pritchard of Africa". **Amy Diaz:** A turtle girl for sure and always with that beautiful smile. **Douglas Dix:** A good friend and animal husbandry extraordinaire, someone I respect for his unfaltering support of his family. **Mike Dloogatch:** Without whom, there would be no CHS. **Sean Doody. Barry Downer. Amanda Ebenhack:** Thank you for your *Tortoise Health and Care* book; it's one of my favorite reference books. **Devin Edmonds. Kurt Edwards:** You have so much to offer as it relates to chelonian husbandry. Start writing, Kurt. **Steve Enders**: You've made "ROOM" for turtles in many people's lives. **William Espenshade. Stephan Ettmar. David Fabius. Dante Fenolio:** Thanks again for your expertise during our Amazon riverboat journey; biodiversity has become your middle name. **Jerry Fife:** You've shown us your passion as you continuously shared your knowledge on how to remain a responsible community of reptile enthusiasts. **Richard Fife**: I've learned a lot from just listening and observing. You and your brother are heroes to all of us. **Ken Foose:** There's no way to describe your contributions to chelonians over the years; many good times together. **Carl James Franklin:** I just love your demeanor and enthusiasm. You've added so much enjoyment to the conferences you presented at. The work you're doing is being watched by all of us. Thank you.

Jay Frewer. Eric Goode: Thank you for your untiring dedication. I've watched you from the sidelines for several years and you are indeed the prime example of "walking the talk." Many people questioned your initial direction but in a short period of time you have achieved a lifetime of accomplishments as it relates to turtle conservation. Your business expertise has allowed you to model an epic organization). **Todd Goodman:** Silent in so many ways as it relates to your monumental support of the reptile community all the while adding so much fun to our get-togethers both in serious and amusing dialogue. Love being with you. **Phil Goss:** The epitome of passion for sure, as it's impossible to repay you for all that you have done and are doing for reptile enthusiasts everywhere. **Jordan Gray:** You have indeed earned the title of the "VOICE," as it relates to worldwide turtle and tortoise conservation. You help make the TSA what it is today. **John Greene:** Your love for turtles can only compare to the friendship you've made with all of us. **John Grigus:** Our relationship means the world to me. Ever since that first day of turtling with you at your home and the natural environment you created, I saw that you were someone very special. Your generosity in helping Denise and I transform our property into the wildlife utopia it is, cannot be measured. Then, the volumes I learned from you while guiding me in my pursuit of breeding endangered tortoises to the many field trips we took together observing turtles in their natural habitats; you were a great teacher whom I chose to follow in so many ways. **Russ Gurley:** Your mission of captive breeding has become one of the most important messages to the entire world of chelonian conservation. We're all there behind you. **Chris Hagen. Jutta Hammer:** Our brief encounters at the TSA conferences showed me what a committed conservationist should be. **Christopher Hansen. Curt Harbsmeier:** You are one heck of a professional who understands the importance of balance as it relates to protecting endangered species. The bonus is that you are indeed a good friend. **James Harding:** If there was one person who portrays "speak silently but carry a big stick" it's you, Jim. Your contributions to the reptile community are endless all delivered with an insatiable love for turtles. **Kenan Harkin:** You have become a top influencer in the most responsible and entertaining way. Never lose your passion and stay focused the way you are right now. Don't worry about becoming a great leader; you already are. **Brian Hauge. John Heidecker:** I've learned a lot from you, John. Not only are you a dedicated breeder of rare reptiles but you're an excellent visionary. **George Heinrich:** You are a walking encyclopedia of turtles, George. You have shown me so much all the while explaining what it all means and where we all fit into the big picture. You make learning so interesting. You are a man of unfaltering dedication to turtle conservation with a rare sense of humor intertwined with the reality of what is happening to the world we live in. I can still eat you under the table with oysters. I value our continued friendship. **Sarai Helstrom:** Sarai, I've met many energetic young ladies in my life but not too many can hold a candle to you, and the kicker is that you always have that smile on your face. **Andrew and Juline Hermes:**

You can never be separated as a result of what you both together have been able to create and contribute to the chelonian community. **Manny Hernandez:** Ever since that first day I met you at our first Iguanafest, there was something about you that I really liked, but it wasn't until I saw your compassion and dedication to the environment while eking out a means of supporting the family you love so dear, that I saw what it was. You are indeed my friend. **Tell and Eileen Hicks:** Tell, your artwork will live on forever but could never match the friendship I have for both you and Eileen. Maybe it was that day in Madagascar when, tired and overheated, we all sat to take a break with a cold beer and you broke out your harmonica and joined that small local band. I'm really not sure; perhaps it was our guinea pig dinner in Cusco, Peru. **Andy Highfield:** During your master class I attended, I picked up on your common sense approach to chelonian husbandry, which helped pave my way into captive breeding. **Wayne Hill:** You were way ahead of your time with the first international reptile expo. Thanks for being that visionary and in looking back you should be proud of what you started. **Bill Holmstrom:** As you were moving on in life, I was just beginning my chelonian conservation direction. The brief encounter we had on that bus ride made me wish we could have moved the hands of the clock back a few years. **Jason Hood. Brian Horne. Rick Hudson:** Rick, your demeanor is absolutely spot on as it relates to being the face and leader of the world's most important turtle and tortoise conservation organization. Your consistent hard work is appreciated by all of us. Thank you for your untiring dedication to those shiny domed shaped objects we all love. Looking forward to our next meal at the Crab Shack in Punta Gorda. **Curtis Ippolito. John Iverson:** I admire your passion and the studies you performed on painted turtles. **Pete Jansema:** The man responsible for providing a much improved captive environment for turtles. We all thank you, Pete. **Kelly Jeanne**: I wish I could have met you earlier in my journey. **Jill Jolay:** I only wish your passion for iguanas could have been channeled towards turtles and tortoises. We could have enjoyed many excursions together. **Cristina Jones:** Such an enjoyable, intelligent young woman with a dedication to conservation that is incomparable. **Mike Joseph. Mark Kirchner. Pete Koplos. Deb Krohn:** Someone who has dedicated her life to educating children and families about the attributes of reptiles, in addition to being an excellent "herper," putting even the most experienced to shame in locating box turtles. **Gerald Kuchling:** I'm not sure if it's me being hard of hearing or you whispering when you speak, but you are indeed the silent giant of chelonian conservation. **Bill Lamar:** Thanks Bill for a great Amazon riverboat experience. **Cameron Lamb. Rob Lawracy:** A resourceful and hard-working friend always there to help out, and where he comes up with so many out-of-the-box ideas, nobody dare attempt to discover. **Dwight Lawson. Shawn Learmont. Chris Lechowicz:** A leader and strong advocate of captive breeding as a conservation tool. The respect I have for you can only compare to our mutual friendship. **Chris Leone:** Your accomplishments in turtle conservation are inspiring. Congratulations to both you and your wife,

Casey. **Thomas Leurteritz**: Thank you for your insight and guidance regarding radiated tortoises. **Andrew Lewis. Richard Lewis:** Thank you for sharing your Madagascar experiences and guiding us on our maiden journey. **Mallory Lindsay**: You must return to your wonderful educational postings. I'm sure you will when the time is right. You're an amazing young lady. I knew that the first day I observed you taking photos of rhinos. **Rodolfo Lopez:** You are a fast learner and have contributed so much to turtle conservation while at the same time becoming a teacher yourself; I've learned from you as well. **Bill and Kathy Love:** The journeys throughout your reptile passions have taken you in so many different directions. The publications, photographs, and experiences you've given all of us will live on forever. **John Lucas. John Mack:** Your consistent hard work for the betterment of the pet industry is admirable but could never compare to the friendship we've developed together. **Douglas Mader, DVM:** A chelonian doctor extraordinaire; I wish our paths would have crossed years earlier. **Linda and Andy Malawy:** Your devotion to the CHS brought us together into that valued friendship we have today. **Chris Manis:** I loved spending time with this focused chelonian conservationist and field herper. **Lonnie McCaskill**: The adventurer extraordinaire who ends up educating all of us from the most exotic places in the world. **Bill McCord, DVM:** The man who has accomplished so much as it relates to chelonian captive breeding. We're following your footsteps, Bill. **Erica Meade McVeigh:** I knew you were a keeper ever since that first day when you took on the temporary responsibility of caring for my indigo snakes. **Ryan McVeigh:** "Hard Working" and "Dedicated" are your middle names and now that I see your focus is on new and innovative reptile care products. I can't wait to see where this will lead you. **Don and Betsy Meeker:** A most compassionate couple who are giving so much to us, not only in the knowledge of animal husbandry but in what it takes to be better human beings in helping the less fortunate of the world. **David Mifsud:** Environmentalist extraordinaire; keep the passion, Dave. **Russ Mittermeier:** The world famous conservationist who made me feel terrible when I outbid him for that rare crocodilian skull at the TSA auction. The reason it ended up with him was because I knew it had a better place to be displayed under his watch. **Charlie Moorcraft. Theresa Moran. Vic Morgan:** The Manouria father—our hatchlings that came from you back in the 90s are now back in Florida at Ty Park's Iguanaland getting ready to reproduce. **Bill Mullen:** A hard-working family man/wildlife conservationist with principles. **Eric Munscher. Michael Joseph Nesbit:** You can join me again at my next painted turtle hatchling release. **Bill Nineslling:** Another old timer who has been there from the beginning of our turtle conservation journey; thanks Bill. **Cord Offermann, DVM:** Your reputation in chelonian husbandry precedes you, and I know firsthand that the people and turtles you've helped appreciate that expertise. **Mike Ogle**: A true friend who shares in the same corners of our pyxis passion. Thanks Michael for welcoming my son James and me, and graciously allowing us to do a field study with you in that bog turtle habitat. **Lance Paden. Marc**

Papiernik: That day we sat there and you secured one of my planicauda between your legs and showed me how to tube feed a tortoise was the day I knew we'd be friends forever. I will continue to be there for you till the last day. **Ty Park:** Going back to 1997 during your Mid America Reptile days, we sure have been through a lot. I'm very fortunate to have been a part of your dream come true with Iguanaland and only hope that I've helped you as much as you've helped me. Our journeys together contributing to the importance of conservation will continue till that last soccer ball puts you under. Thank you Ty for your valued friendship; you are like a brother to me as well. **Matt Patterson:** A valued conservationist who captures the moment in his the most amazing chelonian artwork. You've inspired so many, including myself. Never put that brush down. **Dan Pearson:** Our silent and modest planicauda expert who has shared his experiences and knowledge for the betterment of the species. **Anthony Pierlioni:** A focused turtle conservationist who is raising the bar of captive breeding as he works with some of the most critically endangered species. **Hans-Dieter Philippen:** You have left your mark on so many. Your passion and friendships with all of us will live on forever. **Richard Porter. Brian Potter:** You are the face and voice of the NARBC. We all look forward to your continued leadership. **Peter Praschag. Dr. Peter Pritchard:** Peter, before we even met you inspired me and helped channel my direction in life, as I'm sure you've done for so many. Our relationship was very special from the very first day I met you when you signed my *Encyclopedia of Turtles* book to the days of emailing each other regarding the arribadas, which were being affected by local turtle egg collectors in Costa Rica. Then the several conferences we met at, to the day we spent together with you and Sibille at your home and the Chelonian Research Institute. You left a wonderful mark on the entire world turtle community. Thank you. **Sibille Pritchard:** Such a powerful woman. I immediately saw that from the day we met. It would be fair to say that you have been the backbone of an amazing person all the while being an amazing person in your own right. Thank you, Sibille. By the way, you prepare one heck of a chicken Kiev. **Hugh Quinn. Jean Claude Ralainiaina:** You are a determined and successful person. I thank you for guiding our group through the wilds of Madagascar and allowing us to share our tortoise passion with you. **Michael Rapley. Dr. Beth Reinke:** Thank you for your kind words but it was you who was an inspiration to me in seeing your passion and skills of teaching your class while being involved in our midland painted turtle hatching season. **Drew Rheinhardt:** A true friend and a man of many faces but the one I like most is his hard work and dedication to his family not to mention the way he enjoys life. I like pickup trucks too. **Anders Rhodin:** Someone I admired from afar and learned a lot from, especially with his Chelonian Conservation and Biology Publications. **John Richards:** Not only my alligator snapping turtle guru, but an expert in the culinary arts of fine food especially on Bourbon Street, and, oh yeah, thanks for removing that tick. **Maurice Rodrigues. Kingsley Rodriguz. Christine Roscher. Dan Roselli. Evan Rosenoff. Kathy Rumpler:** A passionate turtle lover for sure. I'll never forget your ballet demonstration in the Florida wilderness. **Eric Russell:** Always there both representing a great company and supporting the reptile community in every respect. **Robert Sands:** Talk about being a visionary and a focused one at that. An outstanding example of a family man who loved his father and loves his family, supporting them in every way possible. Thanks for all you've done regarding our tortoises; couldn't have done it without you. **Sam Scalz. Chuck Schaffer:** I first met you Chuck while climbing that volcano in the Galapagos, never knowing that you and I would become close friends in the chelonian world. I miss you. **Darrell Senneke, Ken Siffert, Steve Sifuente. Phil Simpson. Andy Snider. Craig Stanford. Ryan Stewart:** A determined tortoise guy who I believe in and is going places for sure. **Zdena Straka:** Caring and loving of turtles in so many ways. You have something that can never be replaced. I enjoyed our times together. **Deb Sydney:** The times we spent in the TTPG conferences learning more and more about chelonian husbandry brought us together. That shared passion allowed me to see that you were the right person in caring for my beloved Aldabra tortoise, Tosh. **Chris Tabaka, DVM. Nancy Jane Tetzlaff:** Thank you to a good friend; you have not only inspired me but your accomplishments as a conservationist and founder of the Naples Zoo, Florida are remarkable. **Michael Thathuvaswamy. Jeremy Thompson. Ralph Till:** Great times together, Ralph. You've got so much to offer to tortoise husbandry. Not only have you become a valued friend but I'm also glad I have you in my side pocket when I'm ready to jump back in. **Tom Trout. Dennis Uhrig. Peter Paul Van Dijk. Paul Vander Schouw. Bradley Waffa, DVM. Tim Walsh:** Another hardworking turtle conservationist whom I admire and, by the way, thanks for helping me keep George on the straight and narrow. **Joe Waslewski:** Thanks Joe for all you do educating young and old about the reptiles we care so much about. In seeing what you've accomplished over the years, I compare you to Marlin Perkins even though there's a slight age difference. **Lee Watson:** What an impact you made on my life going back to my Noah's days, with those special events and petting zoos, the promotions with Roger the mountain lion and the Mastercard elephant TV commercial. Then there were all those days at the reptile swap talking turtles and ultimately turning me on to pyxis tortoises. Thanks, Lee. **Romulus Whitaker:** I knew from that first day I met you at the TTPG dinner that you were someone special, never knowing that Ty Park and I would soon be joining you and biologist Joe Wasilewski on that Burmese python hunt in the Florida Everglades. **Dylan Whitehill. Mark Wilson:** You've accomplished so much regarding chelonian husbandry protocols. We've learned a lot as a result of your research in chelonian incubation and husbandry. **Greg Wittstock:** With the energy of an entire platoon. I get tired just watching you. You're an amazing person with so many great ideas and your business expertise is right on. You are the single best team builder I know. I'm happy our paths finally crossed, and to think your direction in life, like mine, was initiated by a turtle. You have inspired me in many ways. Thanks, Greg.

Dr. William Zovickian: Thanks Bill for all your guidance back in the days before diapause. You were way ahead of your time.

NOAH'S ARK / NAPCO / NAPCO INTERNATIONAL (1971 thru 1984)

From the very beginning of my entrepreneurial days, as a naïve but determined twenty-five-year old, to the following years wholesaling, importing, designing, and manufacturing pet products, it became the most exciting thirty-five-year journey that anyone could have imagined. All of the fantastic, loyal employees I had over the years at Noah's Ark Pet Center and NAPCO, many of which remained in the pet or animal related fields, are the ones who deserve the credit for our accomplishments. Thanks to each and every one of you. Your dedication and hard work allowed our companies to make a positive difference in thousands of people's lives. I attempted to include all of you, but I'm sure I missed a few and for that I apologize: **Pat Adamik:** Your contributions behind the scenes as our graphic artist were appreciated. **Debbie Adkins. Lisa Atansio. Judi Bade:** Such a conscientious manager contributing so much to the growth of Noah's through new store acquisitions as well as your expertise in our puppy department. **Jim Bailey. Eva Barriga:** From that first day I met you while you were working for my brother Tom, I somehow knew we would do great things together. **Brian Bartlow:** Harlem/Irving was a great store offering excellent care and advice; thanks, Brian. **Mary Bastek:** You led a great team as Norridge store manager. **Vicki Beauchamp:** You were appreciated in so many ways, especially how well you treated our customers. **Joe Biezlack. Paul Birkenbach. Ralph Bormann:** Our Harlem/Irving star store manager. You ran a great store. **Scott Bowman. Phyliss Bradbury:** Another loyal employee from the early days helping to build an outstanding company as you took on the responsibility of managing the Naperville location. **Ted Breden. Charles Breiter:** You've become the epitome of following your passion from the days of wiping algae off of those twenty high aquariums when you were a high school student working part time, and then into store management and, eventually, becoming our central district manager to the ichthyologist you are today. A journey to be proud of. **Linda Brizzi. Debra Brose. Dennis Brown. Bob Brown:** You became the anchor of our entire retail operation. When you joined Noah's Ark in 1979 you went from store manager to district manager and then in 1981, when we acquired twelve Pet World stores, you gave stability and direction every step of the way as you partnered with my brother Tom in bringing those stores on board. Thank you so much. Your leadership and guidance allowed us to attract and keep the most professional management team throughout the entire company as you achieved one of the highest positions in our company. **Marie Cerny. David John Chelberg:** One of our top producers in our Matteson store location. You contributed to the overall success of the company in so many different ways, including the acquisition of new stores. Thanks, Dave. **Dawn Chelmecki:** You earned the Crystal Point store manager position as a result of your hard work and team leadership. We thank you for your dedication. **Heddy Chendler. Sandy Christensen. Dottie Clark Elliott:** I can still see you running from one responsibility to the other. You never sat still and in doing so set a prime example of an excellent manager. **Ed Colgan. Ron Comer:** Soft-spoken puppy professional providing expert puppy care to our customers. You were indeed a professional. Thanks, Ron. **Lauren Cooke. Dean Cooper:** A bird department specialist who serviced our customers with avian expertise. **Ron Davis:** One of our best Elk Grove Village fish department sales professionals. **Al De Jesus:** Thanks for your animal expertise and your constant push on educating all of us on proper animal husbandry. **Diane Devine. Ralph Diaz:** We had some great times together, Ralph. Our early days creating a wholesale company; our open house, the Bookmobile, Pets and Pots, Oak Park Pet Shop, Pet Ranch, Grand Aquarium, our expansions breaking through another concrete block wall, the meetings with Migatz and Finucane—those were the days. Wish you were still with us; thanks for all you did. **Sonja Didrickson. Mitch Drain:** You were a valued contributor of all of our advertising artwork as you worked hard in our Noah's art department. Thanks Mitch. **Randy Drain:** Your job of keeping the stores stocked with all of our bulk merchandise was one of the most important positions in the distribution center and you did it so well. Thanks, Randy, **Donna Drake:** First of all, thanks for your compassion and care you gave to our puppies, along with running a successful store location. **Al and Tina Drews:** We had many, many employees fall in love, marry, and follow their dreams together but if I didn't say it then, shame on me. You were the most important couple of my entire professional career. Each of you was always there, working hard at all hours, evenings, weekends, trade shows, and even leaving your family behind as you traveled overseas while putting your all into your careers. Thank you, thank you. **Terri DuBiel. Robin Dugan:** Thanks for your leadership and hard work through our rapid growth period. You were a valued manager. **Mark Durband:** Thanks for your dedication to the Noah's Ark mission of being that professional retail pet center it was. You were a great leader as a store manager and then as district manager of several stores. You set the example. **Lori Eckhart Norkey:** Your expertise in fish care raised the bar for our employees to follow as it helped so many hobbyists expand in the tropical fish hobby. **Lynn Eckhardt:** You were such a team player in all that you did, especially as our Randhurst store manager, not to mention your expertise at our Stratford location. **Lauren Elliott:** Thanks, Lauren, for all you did in becoming an award-winning store manager at our Orland Square location. You built a dedicated crew and in doing so, achieved top notch customer service and record sales. **Kip Ellis:** Worked at Hawthorn and Deerbrook, and your hard work and loyalty earned you the position of Crystal Lake store manager. Great job, Kip. **John Farris:** You went from store manager to downstate district manager in charge of four store locations and eventually became our quality bird and animal buyer. Thanks for handling those important responsibilities without getting frazzled. Your rare calm demeanor gave us all stability. **Debbie Finucane. Corie Fissinger. Tom Foley:**

Thank you for running an excellent Noah's Ark as our Lakehurst store manager. **Erin Foy. Carol Frazetto:** Thanks for the support and guidance you provided in managing the finances as our controller. **Steve Freed:** Another store manager who represented our company philosophy perfectly in both our Hillside and Randhurst store locations. Thanks, Steve. **Ruth Frigo. Denise Fugelseth:** You ran an excellent store and made us so proud of our Deerbrook Noah's; thanks, Denise. **Nancy Gabel. Kim Gamberale. Julie Garrett:** Such a great team player; you not only did a great job at our Normal location but you were an outstanding manager of the year at our Davenport, Iowa location with the best attitude all the time; thanks, Julie. **Kristen Gassman:** You were an immediate asset to the Randhurst Noah's and I personally respected your concerns about the environment. **Dale Gaston:** You were always there behind the scenes making sure our prices were kept current and our catalog was updated. Dealing with all of the manufacturers and related inventory control issues was always a major responsibility, which you accomplished so well. I can still see you behind that desk sorting out your daily responsibilities; thanks Dale. **Chris Gibbons. Bobby Goodin:** Back in the early days you were Sandy McLain's right hand and shadow. I can still hear your and Sandy's voice in the backroom processing dry goods orders. **Andrea Gorecki Puetz:** Your hard work and sincere love for your job shown throughout your entire career as it took you from Noah's to Pets International (Super Pet) to Central Garden and Pet (Kaytee). Thanks Andrea. **Chris Gutmann. Connie Haberkorn. Donna Hall. Connie Hartgenbush:** Your signature was on so many pieces of printed material as you performed your artistic talents for Noah's. **Sue Liegel Heather:** You were the absolute perfect choice as the first "Manager of the Year." Your professionalism was always shown throughout your entire tenure with Noah's. You've become a close friend as well and I'll always be there for you. **Kim Hedland. Lanny Helford:** You believed in Noah's Ark and our mission of being that professional retail pet center chain. Your contributions in developing merchandising and training manuals, and helping refine policies along with the classes you conducted for our employees contributed immensely to our success. You were a team player who made a difference. **Lovi Helton. Teresa Higgens:** You were one of our best store managers and always with the best attitude. We were happy to see you following your passion by opening up your own retail pet center. **Lynn Hoff. Chris Hoppe:** One of my very first direct report employees who became a huge asset in our bird department. You were a conscientious young woman with hustle. Those were the days, Chris. **Geri Ramano Hoppe. Dr. Susan Horton:** Sue, it's no surprise to me that after all those years of caring for our puppies, that may have had some impact on your career path decision to become the top-notch veterinarian you are today. Another wonderful journey. **Alan Jacobe:** The term "jack of all trades" was your label. Your commitment to the various tasks you were assigned over several years allowed you to master the supply chain management of our company from stocking the shelves and merchandising displays as well as becoming our first rack job salesman when you serviced a pet department within a chain of drug stores. One of the most dedicated and loyal employees ever. **Mike Jacobi. Donna Jennison. Gary Jester:** Thanks Gary for all of your efforts in managing the world's largest pet center with twenty-two employees. You were a great leader and set the example on how to motivate employees and give all of them encouragement in reaching their goals. I am happy to feel that those experiences helped you take the plunge in opening your own retail store. **Ken Jordan:** Your tropical fish expertise and leadership made you a great member of our management team, **Ken Kaminski:** You got your start at Noah's and you performed the jobs we gave you so well. I'm sure that all of that turned out to be the foundation you built on and eventually put you into the important management position you hold today at APET Corporation. I'm proud to have been a part of your career. **John Kasprzyk:** You had your hands full managing two departments in our Elk Grove Village store; we were fortunate to have you. Thanks, John. **Eva Kedziora:** We saw that you had what it took to be an excellent store manager at our Harlem Irving location. You built and led a great group of people; thank you. **Bill Kelsey. Ellen Kilbridge. Kristin Kindl. Denise King:** What can I say? You've always meant the world to me. Who would have known that day back in the 1970s when that shy school girl applying for a cashier position at Noah's Ark Pet Center would follow her passion and contribute so much to not only Noah's Ark, but the pet industry all the while living her life surrounded by dogs, horses, and the people she loves. **Dan Koruna:** Thanks, Dan, for always knowing what needed to be done. You managed your responsibilities as if you owned Noah's Ark. You set an example for all to follow; thanks, Dan. **Dee Dee Macin Krampert**: Thank you Dee Dee for being a conscientious store manager as well as a team player. Your steady sales increases represented a well-run store. **Debbie Krumm:** Your love for the animals along with your leadership allowed you to excel as our River Oaks store manager. **Phyllis Kunz:** You started at our Crystal Lake location and became an excellent addition to our team. Not only was it your management skills, but your flexibility and willingness to take on additional challenges made you a sincere asset to our organization; thanks, Phyllis. **Randi Kurka:** A long time employee of Noah's and a well-deserved store manager at our Lakehurst location; thanks, Randi. **Steve Kurka:** you did an outstanding job in the Elk Grove bird department providing excellent customer service while managing the department. **Connie Lally:** Yes, you were behind the scenes at Noah's but your artwork shown through to all of us; thank you. **Judy Lambert. Joe Leonard:** You were one of my first mentors and for sure the first one to see the future of Noah's Ark Pet Center. You taught me much and for that I thank you. **Jerry Lindquist. Terri Locke Wegner:** It's easy to see where your love for tropical fish came from but where in the world your uncontrollable energy came from nobody knows. I thank you for your expertise and passion along with bringing me your parents, Dick and Rose, who became my valued friends. **Kim Lopez. Bette Louiselle:** Back in Noah's inception, you were such a great contributor in our puppy department; then you moved on, got your advanced degree as a biologist, and the last I heard from you was when I sent you several woven bird nests for your South American field studies. I hope you are doing well. **Tom Lowden:** You added such expertise to our small animal and reptile departments and for that I owe you immensely. You definitely contributed in putting Noah's on the map as being the source for quality reptiles. **Bill Lucey:** Your expertise and love for the business allowed you to take that big jump and land you on a successful career path. Thanks for your contributions, Bill. **Jerry Machmer:** From store manager to the internal administrative support you provided, you were always there. **Jennie Macino. Julie Madson. Kevin Mazikowski:** Your passion for tropical fish was demonstrated in so many ways from taking care of that beginning to the more advanceed hobbyist all the way in eventually opening up your own store. Thanks Kevin. **Clara McCall:** We immediately saw that our Noah's in Quincy, Illinois was in excellent hands with our bird lady of Quincy. Your dedicated leadership made our job simple in awarding you our second "Manager of the Year" award. What an outstanding person. **Helen McCullom:** Don't think that we didn't appreciate the excellent customer service you provided along with the TLC you gave our avian inventory; thanks. **Michelle McDonnell:** A dedicated professional store manager who ran our Matteson store location with expertise, earning her a "Manager of the Year" nominee position. **Faith McHenry**: Our valued Peoria store manager; thanks, Faith. **Dave McKelvy:** Wherever you are now, Dave, I'm sure you're continuing to deliver that avian knowledge you have ingrained within you. You left a permanent mark on so many people's lives. Thank you. **Don McLain:** You were the tropical fish expert teaching all of us about every facet of the tropical fish hobby, especially filtration requirements. **Sandy Mclain:** You had the absolute best attitude and work ethic. I thank you for your loyalty and that every day smile. **Jeff McNamara:** Your love for birds really showed in all you did for Elk Grove Village's bird department. Great job, Jeff. **Kelly McWilliams:** A leader extraordinaire who practiced the importance of building and appreciating a great team in the bird department. **Barb Mendoza:** Our most dependable Galesburg location store manager setting records for outstanding customer service resulting in increased sales. **Denise Metcalf. Don Metcalf:** Thanks, Don, for your many years of providing top-notch customer service at Noah's Ark. **Joe Mickus**: Our Fox Valley store manager. **Kathy Miller**: Thank you for the times we had together. **Rich Molhman. David Moody:** You ran a tight ship in Galesburg, Dave. Thanks for your dedication. **Randall Moody:** You were there from the very beginning and became a strong asset to the reptile and small animal department. I still have that framed cartoon drawing you did of my brother Tom and me. Thanks, Randy. **Holly Morgan. Cindy Moriarity. Gail Mueller. Gary Murphy:** You were the lifesaver I needed just weeks before I began my entrepreneurial career. **Dennis Norkey:** You were a very creative product designer at Noah's Ark, not only in your package designs for all of our

Noah's brand bulk foods and bedding, but in our thousands upon thousands of take-home tropical fish bags. In addition, you handled so many different responsibilities in upgrading our stores when you and Lanny Helford spearheaded our remerchandising programs. You did them all so well, but the one item I admire the most today is the three-foot by four-foot poster I have hanging in my office, the one you designed depicting the Noah's Ark logo with all of the animals around it. **Tom Nuenkirchen:** Tom, you were not only one of our bird experts but you were an excellent leader who set an example to all of our Fox Valley store employees. **Marilyn O'Dea:** We couldn't have succeeded in getting our Fox Valley Noah's off the ground if it hadn't have been for your and Sharon's hard work and dedication. **Liz O' Hare. Monica Olson. Tom Openshaw:** An excellent asset to our Woodfield Noah's, you excelled in both management and sales. **Chris Orban:** Our loyal, hard-working River Oaks store manager. Thanks for your dedication, Chris. **Laura Orozco. Dave Ortman. Sharon Otto:** Thanks, Sharon, for taking on so many different responsibilities throughout your career with Noah's. You were "Ms. Dependable" for sure. **Helen Papadapoulos. Beth Parlier. Gloria Pederson. Bert Pineda. Mike Pittman:** You managed a great team as our Galesburg manager. **Barb Pollock:** Your contribution as a great store manager as well as a valued addition to Pets International were a credit to your true caring and practical sense. Thanks, Barb. **Lynn Pressley. Rhonda Prosser. Pat Ramig. Randy Rasmussen:** Your hard work paid off as our Hawthorn store manager. Thanks, Randy. **John Real and Stephanie Mayhak Real:** As our top-notch store manager of the Woodfield location, Stephanie, you found a second love which transitioned into another success story where two dedicated hard working individuals met, fell in love, and moved on together, following their passions for the love of their pets and birds. We were always happy to see our dedicated employees move on in their lives, especially when they continued their animal passions. **Leslie Redlin:** Thanks, Les, for keeping everyone in line back in the distribution center, and with a smile to boot. **Barb Rendack. Robin Reeser. Dean Riggins:** Your organizational skills were exceptional. You were a great manager, allowing your detail oriented way to add an immense amount of professionalism to our organization including running the largest pet center in the world. I also thank you for selling me your '56 Chevy. **Michelle Rita:** You left your positive mark on our Lincoln Mall, River Oaks, and Hillside store locations. Thanks, Michelle. **Cindi Roeder. Steve Rook:** You represented Noah's in the most professional manner in everything you did, in each of the locations you worked in; you left your mark in so many ways, allowing us to constantly raise the bar. Thanks, Steve. **Laura Roth:** A loyal store manager at both our Yorktown and Randhurst locations who took charge while promoting sales. **Peter Ruffolo:** Pete, you were a joy to have as an employee who loved our bird department; it must have been part of your genetics. **Laura Sandri. Laura Schiller:** Your passion for animals, especially reptiles and small animals, became apparent as you took on your responsibilities in the Elk Grove

Village small animal/reptile department. **Dorothy Short**: It's not always easy becoming an employee when you were once the owner and sole decision maker. Your transition was a positive sign of your positive outlook on accepting change. **Karen Schmidt:** Thanks, Karen, for supporting Tom in everything you did. You both were a great team. **Marilynn Schmidt:** Great memories. **Stacey Shoemaker. Sue Schreiber. Gayle Schroeder. Todd Schuldt. Brenda Schur:** you deservedly earned the title of our Lakehurst Noah's Ark manager; thanks so much for your contributions. **Mark Schuster:** You started out at the age of sixteen and with your tenure and dedicated hard work, became a great store manager at our Lakehurst Noah's. **Lee Scoville:** We've been through so much together. I would have a tough time knowing where to begin but it's got to be when you started part time bagging goldfish and over the years becoming a huge asset to both Noah's Ark as well as NAPCO. I am gratified to see where all of that took you to becoming your own very successful entrepreneur. **David Silvestri:** You were one of our top salespeople in the Elk Grove Puppy department. That title was a result of not only your hard work, but your ability and desire to provide excellent customer service. **Gail Stilke. Bill Stinson:** With always a great attitude and a smile, you jumped right into it and made things happen. You were a prime example of a great leader. **Cher Stram. Dr. Gregory Stram:** Why do I smile when I think of those beginning days at Noah's when I would always see you working like crazy, hauling those 100-pound bags of gravel and sacks of bird and small animal food and operating our packaging equipment transforming them into smaller resalable sizes? It shouldn't have surprised me to see you becoming a successful veterinarian after recalling all of those times you gravitated into the puppy department to help out. **Sharon Strickland. Kim Sudatas:** Your love for her job allowed you to become a bird expert overnight. **Paula Szewculak. Renee Tater:** A great leader who set the pace in allowing our Yorktown Noah's Ark to excel in puppy sales; thanks, Renee. **Liz Timpe:** You were a dedicated and hard-working Quincy store manager, earning a Manager of the Year nominee position. **Danice Turner. Lori Turner. Kathy Unger:** Our loyal store manager of Galesburg; thanks, Kathy. **Nancy Utter**: Tinley Park Noah's Ark was your store and you ran it like you owned it. Thanks, Nancy. **Sue Walker. Deanna Waltrip:** You ran a tight ship as our Lakehurst store manager. **Al West:** You were an outstanding asset to Noah's whom we continuously relied on. Thanks for your loyalty and hard work as well as the friendship we had. **Patricia Westerfield. Don Wetherald:** During the brief time you worked at Noah's, you added a direly needed level of professionalism and calm. Your relaxed demeanor expressed confidence and integrity to our customers. **Bill Williams:** Your deep passion for reptiles got its start at Noah's and brought you to the respected expert you are today; thanks, Bill for all you did for Noah's. **Lori Lee Williams. Laura Wisnieski. Mike Yehl**: Your passion for reptiles and small animals was apparent and it allowed you to eventually become the department manager. Thanks, Mike, for all your dedication. We along with all of our customers recognized that. **Regina Yurkonis:** A store manager who left your positive mark on our Fox Valley, Normal, and Woodfield store locations, thanks, Regina. **Randi Zagorski:** Thanks Randi for your many years of loyalty and dedication to Noah's Ark, especially your management responsibilities at our Hawthorn location. **Wes Szymborski:** Thanks for your hard work and management skills during Noah's rapid growth and acquisition period. **Karen Zwicker.**

WACKY WARNINGS (1983-1984)

Jerry Padulo: That day when you walked into Noah's with those crazy little signs, how were we to know that our long and successful journey together was just about to begin? That little company of ours accomplished so much and received the support of just about every pet store in the United States. And I still see you lying flat on your Suzuki's gas tank whizzing by all of us on our Harleys like we were standing still.

PETS INTERNATIONAL (SUPER PET) (1985 – 2005) (ACCUTEC)

Eva Barriga: How can I even begin to thank you? Back in the beginning you were my entire product development department. I miss those days when we sat on the floor cutting out cardboard mock-up ideas of different products. Then the day came when you persuaded me to purchase our first Mac system for product design and then after creating an entire department, you shot us out of a cannon in new packaging designs, sales, and marketing material, as well as our beautiful full-color catalogs each year. And I didn't steal you from my brother; it was all part of the grand plan. Miss those days too, Eva. **Doug Blanchard. Jeff Boeing. Jennifer Bondelli:** You took your job seriously and excelled in all you worked on. Those were great days in the history of Pets International and you contributed immensely; thanks, Jen. **Matt Bourseau:** You were one of the best at building relationships with our customers. Your customers always raved about your honest, sincere, and friendly manner. Thanks, Matt. **Shirley Campana**: You held it together. In the first couple of years of my Pets International days, I can still see you walking into my office every Friday afternoon when we'd play the lottery to see who was getting paid that week. **Mike Capace:** You were able to develop your own rapport with your customers and they all believed in you, trusted, and loved you for who you were. **Terry Coleman:** You were right Terry, we finally discontinued those commodities, and talk about someone who their customers loved. At trade shows I was repeatedly told how our customers looked forward to your visits. **Beverly Carino:** Mark couldn't have done it without you. I always said to keep an eye on our cookie jar, and that you did so well. You also added so much to our entire office environment. Those were great days. **Jason Casto:** You followed your passion from pet shop employee to a marketing degree and into the major leagues of the pet industry. I absolutely knew from that day I was involved in interviewing you that you were a keeper. I saw in you back then, the great things that you would achieve, and that you are consistently doing to this day. **Don Dahlstrom:** Thanks, Don, for believing in my vision for Pets International and the Super Pet brand. What you accomplished in your pet industry career is much too long to list here, but I would never have accomplished as much as I did without your guidance from day one. You showed me the way and I thank you. **Mike Dibas**: You were one of our most conscientious team members, always fulfilling those special customer requests; no one behind the scenes meant more to the company. **Pam Johnson Divito:** You and I worked side by side as we established a protocol in reordering and purchasing, and before I knew it, you took charge and handled the department 100 percent, doing an impeccable job. Your consistent dedication and organizational skills kept my out-of-stocks to a minimum and my vendors on their toes. Thanks, Pam. **Tina Drews:** Always there for me and reminding me of the details I overlooked. As many of our overseas clients asked, you were indeed "my traveling wife." Thanks for all of your dedication and hard work. I still hear your voice whenever I'm briskly walking through an airport: "Slow down, Bob." **James Frascone:** Jim, thanks for your organizational skills and the leadership you always showed in everything you pursued. You added so much to our production department. I want you to know that everyone loved you and your daily presence; you were known as the teddy bear of the company but most importantly, you were and still are a good friend. **Lucretia Hackman:** You were the one who originally opened the West Coast market for us as we were just beginning to grow. You represented our company so well. **David Hitsman:** It's almost impossible to describe all of the positive impacts you made on Pets International. You were a great leader and always set an example for many to follow. Your intuitive nature and love for the pet industry allowed you to excel in creating new products for the Super Pet brand. Thank you for your commitment to our vision of becoming the number one source for small animal products that enhanced the lives of the pet and pet owner. I wish you the best, Dave. **Kim Hirshfield:** We always prided ourselves on having experienced and professional women within our company and you were most definitely a leader in that area. **Joe Hodel. Bob Jaynes**: Thanks for your patience and stick-to-it attitude. You were the hands of our entire manufacturing operation and you did it so well. Always remember the Golden Rule, Bob. **Brian Kindl:** We had many good years together Brian, going back to Fox Valley Noah's Ark and into a management position, then when you joined the sales department of Pets International. Thanks, Brian, for being that honest straight-shooter you were to our customers at all times. Your integrity did the selling for you while the credibility you established represented the company so perfectly. **Bob Krause Jr.:** I can't believe how you jumped right in and took charge, recognizing sales opportunities at every turn. Then when you created new programs that catapulted our revenues, it was simply unprecedented. I know that your presence was one of the main reasons for our growth and ultimate success. Thanks, Bob. **James Krause:** While you were going to school for that art degree, and then after graduation, you made such an impact on not only the graphic arts department but the entire company. Your out-of-the-box thinking allowed you to create new ideas in packaging as well as the products themselves. Crittertrail X was yours from day one; thanks, James. **Judy Krause**: Followed me from my Noah's days all the way to becoming one of those professional women who laid the groundwork in our company's history. Thanks, Judy. **Tony March:** Thanks, Tony, for all of your creativity and for leading a great department. Those new product displays were the best. **Debbie Masters:** Your presence and never-ending cooperation added so much to our office environment. And you always helped to keep Chris in line. What a great team. **Jane McDonald:** Always so cooperative and consistent in your job. I loved the smile you always had on your face. **Denise Mensik:** I always considered you to be one of the most professional people in our administrative office, all the while being so dependable and cooperative; thank you. **Douglas McLennan:** I can still hear your voice as if it were yesterday. Your salesmanship was spot on as you always had a story that put smiles on people's faces. Even the story about mockingbirds flying around inside your car as you drove from client to client. **Carlos Padillo:** Everyone loved you, especially me. You made things achievable by being there for every conceivable need. If we needed it right away, you was there to get it. **Diane Woltz Pawelko:** If there was one person in the company who always brought in the sunshine, it was you. You contributed so much to our marketing and new product development departments. Your hard work became the norm in all that you did as you always had us laughing. By the way, Eva reminded me to thank you for that red sweater that I squeezed into on that cold morning. **Mark Procter:** I always considered you and me as "We." There wasn't one major decision I made at Pets International without first checking with you. I thank you for saving my company on your first day when the bank was going to pull our loan. Then as we began making the turn, I thank you for always guiding my financial decisions as well as believing in me every step of the way. We did it together, from getting out of trouble with patent infringements, to investing in new tooling as well as new companies and real estate. The vision proved solid and you helped me see the horizon. Where has the time gone? **Carol Pseno:** Your creativity is memorialized in all of our brochures, catalogs, and marketing material, and always with a smile on your face. **Andrea Gorecki Puetz:** You always made your customers believers in Super Pet. A most genuine, dedicated professional who represented the company as if it were her own; thank you. **Angie Reeder:** Angie, your energy and enthusiasm always made everyone around you appear to be in slow motion. Your friendly and outgoing personality made you that tremendous sales manager and eventual loving daughter-in law. **Patti Rehm:** You made the difference in making sure things got done in our administrative department. **Sandy Rosenholz:** I'll never forget that sales meeting when we were all discussing different ways of getting rid of discontinued product where you said enough is enough and went to the phone and sold all of our closeouts. A determined and confident man. **Allyson Schmidt**: I just had to pop into the room while you were being interviewed. Your retail pet shop experience was what I wanted to hear about but your enthusiasm and obvious positive attitude was what sold me on you and told me we had to hire this young woman. Snap my fingers and the next thing I knew, you were accompanying me on product development trips to Asia. You sure left your mark and contributed so much to our overall success. *Danke schön*, Allyson. **Larry Sternal:** It's amazing how someone's life can be affected just by one person, and that is exactly what happened to me as a result of you coming into it. As my vice president of operations you became the entire company's "go to" person, solving problems and implementing new and innovative procedures. Somehow or another, you would have a solution to any mechanical or operational challenge both in our manufacturing facility as well as in our partners facilities overseas. As a result, you became one of our most valued people and if I were to do it all over again, I wouldn't do it without you. **Bill Snodgrass. Chris Somen:** Chris, you added so much enthusiasm and enjoyment into our entire office. I miss your contagious smile. **Bill Stinson:** Thanks for your overall cooperation and that constant "get it done" attitude. Your dependability was something we appreciated. **Tara Oconner Tonti:** I can't begin to tell you how much I appreciated the consistent work you did for Pets International. You always had a great attitude and with that glowing smile to boot; thanks, Tara. **Ann Urycki:** How you jumped into your new position, created systems and showed us how to run an absolute efficient department single handedly was amazing. You impressed all of us with your consistent hard work. I'll always use you as an example of someone with a great attitude and an outstanding personality. **Steve Urycki:** You added so much stability to your department setting, a perfect example of reliability, and we all thank you for all of those zebra finches you provided.

ARIZONA HERPETOLOGICAL
Al Lawrence: You became my source of common sense and practicality, all encapsulated with interesting and entertaining experiences which you never hesitated in sharing. Our vision of breeding sulcata tortoises came together as a result of good planning. During our years together, my life was enriched by our valued friendship, never being adversely affected even by having to sleep on the floor of your kitchen during every visit to Florence, Arizona.

CENTRAL GARDEN and PET / KAYTEE (2005 – 2008)
Dr. Susan Clubb: Susan, over the years your outstanding reputation preceded you throughout the entire bird community and being that you were a valued advisor to Kaytee Products, it gave me the opportunity of working with you and getting to know the human side of such a wonderful person. Thank you for your expertise. **Kevin Fick. Jim Glassford:** You believed in me and I saw that. You taught me so much about mass marketing and I was always amazed at how you

were so adept at maneuvering through the various markets we were in. If I had to do it all over again, I'd want you back to lead the posse. **Jim Heim:** Hard to summarize how much I respect you Jim. From the very beginning of our relationship, I knew we'd do well together. You were a great leader and an example for many to follow. **Curt Hyzy:** There was something there that made us click together, Curt. I loved your positive, "get it done" attitude all the time. Miss you. **John Negovetich:** You gave me comfort in knowing that we were always on the right track. You had confidence in us even when our monthly numbers weren't where they needed to be. A true professional at your job. **Glen Novotny:** How you kept the balance in running the organization was a complete mystery to me. **Andy Rich:** You were the one with all the wisdom which you expressed from that very first day I met you at that CG and P function. I loved spending time with you. **Reggie Vandenbosch:** Your experience along with your outgoing personality was what brought you to me. You were my wild bird guru whom I had great plans for.

MY TEC (VISTAGE) FRIENDS (1990 – 2008)

Bob Berk: How in the world does one thank a man like you, Bob? You were my guiding light for several years as well as being that taskmaster that I always needed. You seemed to always have the right answers as well as knowing what questions to always ask. A great man. Thanks, Bob. **Jim Belmonti:** Jim, you were one of the most important people in my life, who always gave me encouragement and reassurance whenever I was in doubt. Thanks, Jim. **Nancy Cwynar:** You were the one that kept our entire group in line, making sure that those dollar figures we discussed were accurate. Had some great times together as well. **Rich Frain. Julio Gesklin. Russ Graunke:** You were like my big brother, always there for me and then the day finally came when you kept reminding me that there was more to life than my business and you always asked me that same question: "How much steak can you eat?" **Bill Gunlicks:** Bill, you turned it up a notch and always inserted the importance of the financial end; the EBITA was the goal you always set. **Craig Hanson:** Craig, you demonstrated the importance you placed on family relationships and for that we all learned the important lesson of balancing your personal life with your business life. You did that so well. **Jim Mack:** The number one lesson in marketing that I learned from you and I always refer to it is that people always want to hear the story. The product or service could in fact be the best, but it's the story people want to hear. Thanks for helping me in every way, Jim. **Ron Mager:** Thanks, Ron, for allowing me to be a part of your advisory board. You are an excellent leader. **Don McNeil:** I can't thank you enough for that lunch we had together when you encouraged me to just "go and take a look" at your family's "wildlife" property that featured a lake full of turtles. **Rosemary Mitchell. Dennis Passis. Steve Pinsler. Darryl Rosser:** To me you were the soft spoken wise "gun for hire" and you demonstrated in so many ways how to work on your business rather than in it; a true Blue Ocean Strategy. **Fred Stowell:**

I'll always think of you when the words patience and balance are mentioned. You were the perfect example of them. **Mitch Tarzian:** Our close friendship was something that meant the world to me. Thank you for your guidance and expertise in remodeling our corporate headquarters as well as our home design and construction. I sure miss those good times in Cancun, Mexico. **Jim Tesch:** Jim you were the first one who showed me how to take my hobby and love for turtles and turn it into a successful business. I owe you a world of gratitude. I miss those one on ones.

DOMESTIC BUSINESS FRIENDS (1971 – 2008)

(Colleagues, vendors, customers, competitors). Each of the following people have made an impact on my thirty-seven-year business career. Thank you for your guidance as I learned by watching and listening to all of you. **Deb Armstrong:** As a top officer of our bank in the early days, whenever you paid us a visit, I knew you were just checking up on us, making sure we were still solvent. Those were the days when I would put on those dog and pony shows, showing you the next big deals we were embarking upon. Then when Mark joined the company I noticed how you started believing me. What a pony ride that was. **Muhammad Ali:** I know that you were the world's greatest but you were quite the showman as well. I'll always remember your words that day I told you that you overpaid me: "I was just testing you." **Pam Askew. Barry Askinas. Evelyn Axelrod. Herbert Axelrod. Patty Backer**: my biggest international fan. **Tommy Barren. Susan Barry. Richard Bebe. Eric Bergson. Bobby Blood. Don and Jack Boeing. Jim Boelke. Brittany Bossard. Alan Botterman. Phil Brasie. Gary Bagnall:** My real passion being turtles has over the years caused many people to ask me "Why haven't you gotten involved with developing products for reptiles instead of hamsters, rabbits, and ferrets?" My answer was only two words: "Gary Bagnall." Tough to compete with the best! I miss those strategic conversations we had. **Ken Bellah:** We go back a long ways together, Ken. You've kept me out of trouble many times as we continued expanding and starting new companies. You are family. Glad you're still around, as I'm not quite finished yet. Maybe a rendezvous out at the ranch in Sanderson, Texas. **Joe Calascibetta. Alex Canales. Michelle Carlson. Les Charm. Dick Clarkson. Phil Cowen. Joe Curran. Larry Cobb:** Your impeccable reputation as a manufacturer's rep can't hold a candle to your kind and generous personality. We need to continue those conversations. **Phil Cooper:** Here's the most rounded and experienced expert in the pet industry worldwide. Phil, you are what is so direly needed in every facet of the industry, from retail to wholesale to manufacturing. You've helped so many. I'm glad you're still so passionate about the pet industry. **Brian Devine:** You were ahead of your time and it must be gratifying to see your vision still lives on with Petco. **Tony DeVoss. Rick and Kevin Diaz:** Our business relationship was definitely a two-way street. You constantly expressed your appreciation for us selling you the Super Pet line but you penetrated the Midwest market for us back when we were just beginning; thanks to you both. **Milton Docktor:** Thanks for being that visionary that allowed me to see the light in designing and opening Noah's Ark Pet Center. **Jim Dougherty:** How can it be that our journeys crossed when they did? Our passions were so similar and yet we both succeeded while taking different paths within the pet industry. Carry on, Jim. **Walt and Vi Ebers. Jim Elesh. Harvey Feinberg:** Thanks for the times we had together overseas, as well as your input on your experiences in the pet industry. **Chuck Finucane:** Back in the early days, you were my lighthouse, keeping me on course as I phased into wholesaling and then into importing. Thanks for being there for me. We need to take another taxi ride in D.C. **Don Fleming. Carol Frank. John Franz. Bob Frey:** I will always look up to you as the number one pet supply wholesaler who really knew how to promote; you were the marketing expert. I miss those earlier days as much as you do, I'm sure. **Bill Gamble:** You were the one who believed in our dream and gave me that very first break in my life. You saw something in two young undercapitalized twenty-plus-year-olds wanting to open the world's largest pet center that not many others did. Thank You. **Rick Goldman. Terry Goldman. Rosanne Gulisano:** Thank you for teeing me up and showing me the direction in writing a memoir. You've inspired so many. **Rolf C. Hagen:** You did so much for the pet industry. You were an exemplary leader and we all followed. **Rolf Hagen Jr. Ed Hartman:** One of the most professional sales executives in the pet industry; you were there for us when we just started wholesaling back in the Lambert Kaye days. I always looked forward to your visits. **Istvan Heim:** At one time you were our primary mold builder and now I miss those days haggling with you in my office as we embarked on new projects. **Warren Henricks:** Thank you for the encouragement you showed me when I was starting out in designing my own injection molded products. **Gary Hirshberg:** In the beginning you were a very important vendor but after I acquired Pets International you became a competitor. Then, shortly after when I changed my marketing direction, our competitiveness slowly diminished and my job became so much easier and rewarding. I have to say that through all of our dealings, you were always professional and a friend. **Mark Hirshberg:** You saw the light and chose your own direction, resulting in the most successful dog toy and accessory company in the pet industry. I sincerely compliment you. **Mike Hoffer:** A great retail pet store operator who was the most sincere and honest businessman I knew. You not only loved the pet industry but loved riding "tailgunner" on all of our Ballbuster Harley rides. Miss you, Mike. **Bernie Hoffman:** A man who did so much for the betterment of the retail pet industry; a man of extreme charm knowing how to promote and get things done. **Sandy and Bob Hoffman:** A great team in continuing the Animal Kingdom concept of professionalism. **Art Hopkins:** I recall the days we sat and talked turtles in my office when you were supposed to be working with our buyers. We both knew back then where our priorities were. **Rob Johannigman:** You were always complimentary in our efforts and appreciated what we were trying to accomplish in the small animal category. I sincerely recognized that. **Cathy Kane. Steve King. Erling Kjelland:** Your love for birds opened up a whole new experience for me back in the days when I was seeking direction. I learned so much from you as it related to cage birds both common and rare. You introduced me to so many different species and taught me how to care for them and in turn I saw all of the enjoyment they offered. That foundation allowed me to incorporate all of the positives about pet and aviary birds into Noah's Ark Pet Center. **Len Kaplinski. George Kroesen. Ed Kunselman. Bob Klekauskas:** Ever since that first day I walked into your office, I knew there was something I liked about you. I immediately learned that you too were always thinking out of the box. New product development was our ambition and inevitable destination; that was fun. **Dr. Theodore Lafebre:** Ted, you were way ahead of your time. I miss the times we spent together just talking caged birds and how we could improve their lives. **Lou Lauch:** A man who knew how to enjoy his life. Lou, you were also a risk taker but your passion was business and profitability, no matter what kind. You behaved like you were always on your way to the golf course with a nonchalant way about you, even when they found the only spoon (a child's Mickey Mouse spoon) in that Chinese village so you could enjoy your meal without the inconvenience of chopsticks. **Bill Lechter. Dick and Rose Locke:** Parents of Terri, one of our fish department employees back in the early days. You bred and supplied us with Discus and became an important bird supplier after you opened your quarantine station. My two dearest friends from the early days of Noah's Ark through my entire career. **Joe Locke. Steve Lundblad. Dr. Bern Levine:** You taught me a lot without realizing it. Initially you were one of my most valued live animal and bird suppliers who I could always depend on for quality. But you took it to much higher levels with your Parrot Jungle and subsequent Animal Island entertainment venue in Miami, Florida. Above all of that, you became my very good friend. **Alan Levy:** Our industry leader who understood the big picture: "Nothing happens until the pet is sold." **Steve Maciontek:** Animal Kingdom wouldn't have been what it was without you. **Richard Majeska:** a great customer and an outstanding friend. **Robby and Isis Majeska:** you became two very successful pet retailers by concentrating in a niche market and being the best at it. Thank you for not only being a great customer but very valued friends. Congrats to you. **Mary Ellen Majeska Wertanen:** Why do I see you dancing on the table at the mention of your name? **Lisa Marshall:** Way ahead of your time; you were the force of your family. Look where the alfalfa business is today. **Barry Meyers:** You were another person who changed my life by picking up the phone and asking me if I was interested in taking over your chain of Pet World stores. I'm sure it was a win/win for both of us. **Sid Meyers:** Even though you played hardball with me all the time, I saw a very gentle side of you during our five-week-long Asian trip. You'd be proud to see how far Super Pet went. **Marshall Meyers:** If I had to single out the most important person in the pet industry, it was you. Thanks, Marshall, for all those tireless hours you put in protecting the rights of pet owners for the betterment of the industry we loved so dear. **Bob Migatz. Frank Miser. Geri Mitchell. Tony Neff. Mike Neylon. Greg Nobis. Jerry Payne:** You're an amazing person, Jerry. You have a vast knowledge of the world around you and how you express yourself has impressed me so many times over. Thank you for bringing me to that next level in writing and getting me to the finish line. **Susan Pravda:** You have enabled me to live my dream. Without your expertise I would never have been able to create financial independence for my entire family. If I had to do it all over again, I wouldn't even attempt it without you. **Peter Reid:** Thank you; you were first an excellent provider of pet ferrets and then, as we both transitioned into other companies, you became an excellent competitor, but most importantly you were a good friend. **Craig Rexford. Jerry Rosen. Italo Rufolo:** I will always admire your love for your family. You were more than my barber for twenty-plus years; you supplied me with beautiful singing canaries and tame baby cockatiels, but most importantly you gave me your friendship. **Sherry Salamone. Jason Savitt. Carl Schmidt. Ken Scott. Bob Seaman. Rick Segerstrom. Elwyn Segrest. Jim Seidewand. Bob Sherman. Joe Shilkus. Mark Shilkus. Allen Simon. Bud Snyder:** You had an outstanding career in the pet industry and over the years, you and I interacted in so many different ways. I learned a lot in just watching you, Bud; you were one of my mentors without even knowing it. Thanks. **Mark Stern. Jim Stout. Tony Suk. Richard Savitt:** From that day when you had difficulty with your gym shorts at Great America Amusement Park to the many good times we had together around the world (including the chicken head incident), and the many Hong Kong dollar flips that followed, you've always been one I could depend on. An incomparable friendship to this very day. **Ray Schwenkel:** A packaging expert who understood the importance of delivering a product to the consumer in the best way possible. **Dennis Stahl:** Thank you for encouraging me to remain focused. You always saw the big picture and contributed so much to the pet industry. **Dennis Thompson:** We've been friends for many years, and to watch you follow your dream has without you knowing it inspired me by reconfirming my direction in life. Your accomplishments in creating the Gypsi Vanner Horse back in 1996 all the way to your education and cultural center in Ocala, Florida are remarkable. Another fine example of following one's passion. **Jacob Tepper. Gerry Tomas. Mark Trittschuh, David and Michael Twain, Ray Ungemach, Bob Vetere, Tim Volkes:** Sincerity and Integrity are your middle names. Many have learned from you. **Susan Wallace, Steve Ware. Sheri Warsh. Brent Weinmann:** Another pet industry professional who understands the critical importance of caged birds, small animals, and other non-traditional pets. **Paul Wentland. Jon Willinger:** One of the most creative guys in the pet industry. I admired your innovations and creative packaging. You unknowingly helped me stay focused in the small animal category when, after seeing your introduction, I filed away the several bird toy concepts we already had on the drawing boards. **Bill Wilson:** I remember back before Noah's days when you taught me the proper way of trimming parrots' flight feathers; thanks, Bill. **Jim Wilson:** You were always in my crosshairs and when the day came that your company finally made that commitment to support the Super Pet line, our company celebrated. You helped me raise the bar. **Jim Wingate. Jonathan Zelinger:** A mountain of respect you earned that evening in Kowloon when you resisted the Cantonese cuisines.

FOREIGN BUSINESS FRIENDS (1984 – 2008)

To all of my overseas and foreign business colleagues, vendors, customers, and competitors; you have impacted me in a most positive way; I thank each and every one of you. **Kuhral Alam (Bangladesh):** Your kindness and sincere hospitality as you gave me the experiences of Bangaladesh opened my eyes to the real priorities in life. You gave me much more than you can imagine. **Shafique Alam (Bangladesh). Akira Arai (Japan/Thailand). David and Joy Batsford (U.K.). Cisco and Flori Bertoldo (Italy):** I could never thank you enough for all the times we enjoyed your assistance and friendship during our travels through Italy. We want to welcome you again to the USA as soon as possible. **Frank Brandis (South Africa). Gerd Blaschke (Germany):** You're the most amazing marketer in the European pet industry; we've done a lot together in Europe and Asia; thanks, Gerd. **Tom Cellucci (Australia). Ronnie Chew (Malaysia). Jin Soo Cho (Korea):** Cho, you were one of my best pet industry agents and partners in Asia and you taught me so much. You will always be my friend. **Johan Deckx (Belgium):** A true international pet professional, hard-working and extremely resourceful. **Luc Deckx (Belgium). Pascal Defesch (Belgium):** Young and full of energy with a thousand questions and, by the way, thanks for helping me clean all those prototype small animal cages full of mice on my kitchen counters. **Antonio Estrada (Mexico):** A true and sincere friend for life. Ever since that first day I met you, I knew we'd be spending much time together. **Alfredo Garcia (Mexico):** Our business relationship was the best but not even close to the friendship we created in traveling the world together. **Peter Geboers (Netherlands):** Peter, what can I say? We not only did a great job developing new pet products together as we traveled through Europe over the years but we became the closest of friends. Many great experiences. **Robin Grant (U.K.):** Such an energetic fast learner who was a most professional sales representative in the U.K. "Robin, thanks for helping us get to New York." **Takeshi Gomi (Japan). Bonnik Hanson (Germany). Mathieu Haurit (France). Istvan Heim (Hungary). Fumi Hill (Japan/France). Van Sorrel Kung (Taiwan). Terrence Lam (Hong Kong). Philip Lau (Hong Kong). Per Lausen (Denmark). Yi Li (China). Samson Lau (Hong Kong):** Someone who not only learned the manufacturing and export process, but someone who took it to the next level by providing the best service; thank you, Samson. **Nico Marchioro (Italy):** We came together and developed several new pet products. We had many good times, Nico; thank you. **Yuzo Migata (Japan). Georgia Rabito (Italy):** Thanks for the pasta sauce recipes and now you know the American way of knowing when your pasta is cooked properly. **Sergio Rabito (Italy). Bruno Sabadini (Italy):** A true gentleman who believed in my vision and welcomed us working together in developing a premier range of bird cages for the US market. **Giovanni Sabadini (Italy):** You've seen it all, Giovanni, not only participating as our European trade show interpreter but in so many other different ways. You've contributed to our success and I thank you not only for that but for the lifelong friendship we now have. **Sanko Mik san (Japan). Bryan Sharples (U.K.):** From that very first day I spoke to you from my office while you were driving on the A1, I somehow knew we'd come together and do great things. With your expertise, we penetrated the U.K. market with new and innovative small animal products in an unprecedented way. Good times we sure had, thanks. **Alan and Kimmy Shi (Hong Kong):** The premier packaging experts of China who grew their company into a world class organization; you are true friends. **Miss Evelyn Sim (Malaysia):** Miss Sim, wherever you are, you were one of my best agents working diligently in putting me together with the best manufactures in Malaysia; thank you for all you did. **Rosalia Amparo Simon (Mexico):** One of the most determined and focused business professionals in Mexico who showed me the Hispanic way. **Katsuhiko Sudo (Japan). Heidinori Sugimoto (Japan):** Little did I know back in 1985 the impact you would make on my business career. You were indeed the perfect connection to so many manufactures, product designers, packaging experts, and logistic companies in Asia. We accomplished so much together and as a result became lifelong friends. **Katsutoshi Tominaga (Japan/China):** I cannot begin to say how much you mean to me. You taught me so much regarding the manufacturing process as well as the ins and outs of life in Japan as well as China. Although our cultures were completely different, you and I came together like brothers and shared the most inspiring experiences throughout our many years of association, and remember; "Makio Shimi." **Prasert Theerakulchai (Thailand). Sandro Terrenziani (Italy):** I miss those days in Italy when we would be bending and cutting wire mesh panels and creating new rabbit cages. We had many good times together. Thanks, Sandro. **Alphonse Vanderbroeck (Belgium). Emmanuel Van Heygen (Belgium). Pakdi Viraphongchai (Thailand):** A true hard-working Thai businessman who earned our trust and business together becoming a real friend. I always admired your tenacity. **Johnson Wai (Hong Kong). Alan Whelpton (Australia):** One of the most respected gentlemen in the entire pet industry. Not only were you an outstanding customer but you were like a brother to me. Thank you for your guidance and encouragement along the way. **Emelius Wong (Hong Kong). Wayne Wooten (New Zealand). Nobuhiko Yokoyama (Japan).**